DON'T HESITATE:

Knowing Allen Ginsberg

Letters & Recollections

by Marc Olmsted

Published by Beatdom Books

Published by Beatdom Books

View the publisher's website:
www.books.beatdom.com

Printed in the United Kingdom
Third Edition, Revised

Contents

Part 5 - Back Again
More anecdotes
p. 86

Part 6 - The Job
Performing with Allen and my New Wave band, The Job.
Letters 1980-1983
p.92

Part 7 - Sober To L.A.
Part of Best Minds: a Tribute to Allen Ginsberg on his 60th Birthday, edited by Bill Morgan and Bob Rosenthal.
p.121

Part 8 - KDK
Living in the Tibetan meditation center Kagyu Droden Kunchab, San Francisco, where Allen visits.
Letters 1989
p.133

Part 9 - Drubdra
3-year-retreat under Lama Tharchin in "Drubdra"
Letters 1993-1994
p.156

Part 10 - Last Days
His last note 1996
p.175

Appendix
p.182

For those who have trouble reading Allen Ginsberg's handwritten letters, they are also typed and arranged by chapter in the Appendix, beginning on p. 181.

Introduction

"Candor ends paranoia" was a longtime slogan of Allen Ginsberg's and something that was nurtured by his love for Walt Whitman. I believe that Allen meant that honesty and a straightforward discussion of things close to his heart through an openness of expression would dispel the fears of others. Not many people are able to be as candid in their lives as Ginsberg and Whitman were, but Marc Olmsted is that rare individual who can turn the motto inward upon himself without pretense or reserve. Like Ginsberg, Olmsted writes poetry anchored in his own life, showing warts and all, without guile or pose.

In 1967, when he first encountered the name of the poet Allen Ginsberg, Marc Olmsted was barely a teenager. Ginsberg's celebrity during the 1950s and 60s had already made him one of the most famous poets in America and that enabled him to reach millions of younger readers. Reporters at the time were more interested in the poet's outrageous behavior than they were in his prophetic poetry, but they had helped to spread the word nonetheless. Some members of that younger generation were attracted to the form and content of Ginsberg's poetry as displayed in masterworks like *Howl* and *Kaddish*. Marc Olmsted was one of those who wanted to know more about Ginsberg's thoughts and beliefs than the popular press revealed. Olmsted picked up on Ginsberg's poetry, digested it, and dreamed of meeting the bard some day. Five years later he made an attempt to track him down and received a cordial postcard in reply, but it wasn't until Marc was twenty, that the two finally met face to face. They continued to correspond and see each other until Ginsberg's death in 1997. *Don't Hesitate* is nothing if not a candid look at the intersection of the lives of these two writers.

Allen Ginsberg's relationships with men were always complicated and Olmsted's book is the first publication that tells the true story of what it was like to adore and be adored by Allen first hand. Their friendship was based in a mutual love of literature. It was tinged with sexuality and matured via a common interest in Buddhist meditation. During the course of their relationship, months and months might pass without contact, but their friendship was always quickly rekindled. At times Allen's attentions could be a bit overwhelming, but the two poets met each other on increasingly equal terms.

By the time he met Olmsted, Ginsberg had worked out his own unique personal philosophy for older-younger relationships. Allen generally found himself attracted to straight men who would make a special effort to accommodate him sexually. For the most part Allen initiated the idea of sex, but upon occasion young fans would make a pilgrimage to meet him solely to have sex with him. Ginsberg grew to consider it an even trade. He felt that he brought maturity, intellect, experience, fame, and even financial success to the relationship while and the youth contributed sexuality, energy, and creativity.

No better example exists than Olmsted, now a successful and widely published poet in his own right. This important memoir of his life with Ginsberg is remarkable for its honest look at a complex relationship. As a refreshing innovation, he has turned his memoir into a scrapbook, reproducing the actual letters, photographs, and poems that were sent back and forth between the two men. Through this device he manages to capture the immediacy of the correspondence and ties the poetry in with the lives of the poets. Fittingly, we learn as much about Olmsted through the pages of this book as we do about Ginsberg and we watch him grow as a poet and mature as a person, questioning his own beliefs and style, absorbing all that Ginsberg has to teach him, and teaching Allen something along the way.

Don't Hesitate is a masterpiece of candor. It is beautifully written and designed, making it a pleasure to read and re-read. One would like to pigeon-hole the book and say that it is a collection of poems; a collection of letters; a memoir; a love story; a character study; a coming of age story; a guide to meditation and enlightenment; but it is not just one of these things -- it is all of them.

-Bill Morgan, March, 2014

Part 1 – Starting Out

…where dried weeds had whispered under electric towers when I was a boy…

Title card: Los Angeles, 1967 - I first became aware of Allen Ginsberg when new friend Richard Modiano had a copy of the salacious and forbidden L.A. Free Press. I was 13. He pointed out an interview with Allen, which had some swirling graphics and big buzz words like ACID and ECOLOGY. He told me this is where it was at. Around this time, Richard also laid Alan Watts on me. Richard was two years older than me and made my parents nervous.

Not long after, I came through my parents' room and my mother was in bed watching some talk show – probably Merv Griffin. There was Allen, earnestly explaining to the other guests that "we are not our meat." I was impressed. Made sense to me. My mother, on the other hand, sneered behind a serious vodka buzz: "Ginsberg and his ringlets." It was the only time I ever heard her say anything that suggested anti-Semitism.

And so I began to read him. A poem I had admired that my brother's friend had written - a poem about New York City – was surprisingly very much in Ginsberg's style. I was already writing poetry myself, encouraged to write by my intellectual Dad since I was 7. My exposure had been to Edgar Allan Poe and Ray Bradbury, so Ginsberg's surreal wordplay seemed a logical extension of metaphor and direct presentation of image.

Immediately after high school, I even tried to track him down when I passed through Berkeley in 1971 on my first road trip. A rumor had me knocking on a door Allen hadn't lived at for 2 years.

As a freshman in college at the University of California Santa Cruz and living in a garage, I tried again with a letter to his publisher, City Lights, in 1972.

Dear Allen,

I'm a young poet, 18 in the meat, and I am reminiscing late at night about your cosmic yearnings, reading of you and remembering all your poetry. O, Allen, I guess by now you're used to young starry-eyed men, confronting you, "You're Ginsberg," and you had your literary heroes when just a boy, how strange, the ole karmic cycle.

I'm practising transcendental meditation, I've had a little beer tonight, and it's time I write. I've been so influenced by you, I'd send poetry, but it would be embarassing seeing how similar it is to yours. Your beautiful. What saddens me is you're getting old and like I have your whole pilgrimage before me, spiritual manuals that bring me comfort and I can take it from there, this whole log of experience, and now me a media baby, cosmic consciousness in ten years or so? Anything is possible.

I hope we meet some day.

Love,

Marc

Marc Olmsted
608 National St.
Santa Cruz, Ca. 95060

JAI GURU DEV.

This time I received a postcard from him.

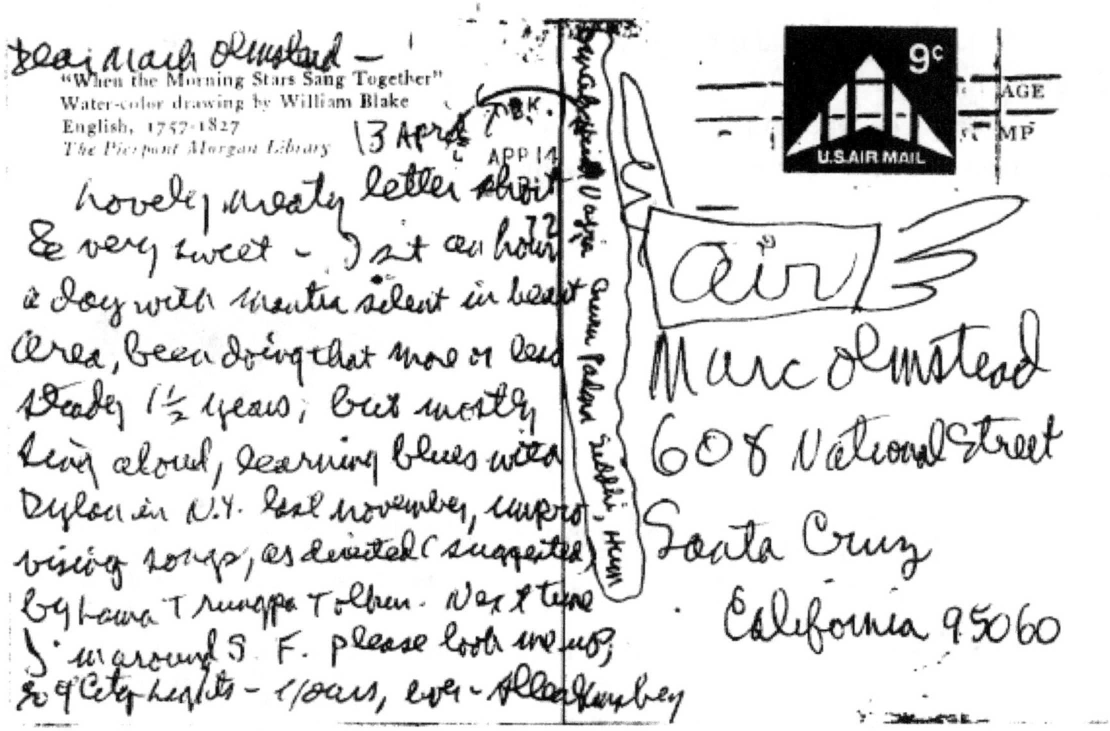
Dear Marc Olmstead —
"When the Morning Stars Sang Together"
Water-color drawing by William Blake
English, 1757-1827
The Pierpont Morgan Library
13 Apr 72
Lovely neatly letter short & very sweet — I sit an hour a day with mantra silent in heart area, been doing that more or less steady 1½ years; but mostly sing aloud, learning blues with Dylan in N.Y. last November, improvising songs, as directed (suggested) by Lama Trungpa Tolkun. Next time I'm around S.F. please look me up, c/o City Lights — Yours, ever — Allen Ginsberg

air
Marc Olmstead
608 National Street
Santa Cruz
California 95060

A year and a half later, dropping out of T.M., I tried the same tactic and basically wrote a pale imitation of the same letter, with only an interesting fragment…

Now faced with crucial thoughts, losing faith in my guru of last $3\frac{1}{2}$ years, and frightened, yet thrilled at what new growth this may mean, I wrote this poem in courage and hossana, wanting you to have it. I hope we meet someday.

I'm too embarrassed to show you the poem, and in any case he didn't reply.

Finally, I sent a letter to him in 1974 when I saw he was coming to San Francisco for a reading.

Colmsted, Marc
[ca. 1974 Oct. 4

Dear Allen,

I'll come right to the point. I'm dying to meet you. I've followed your poetry since I first became aware of you in highschool '71. Since then I've tried to read everything you've written, even tracking down such obscure works as "Leafy Scribbles". I went through Bolinas in '71 only to find out a year later that you were there, too. I missed you in Shambala's once by a couple of hours. Another time in Berkeley I heard you were in town, managing to track down an address where you were supposed to be staying, only to find out you hadn't been there for five years. I've doted on your every word in interviews, and let me explain why. Largely it's just your nakedness, the way you"wear your heart on your sleeve" as you said in one interview.

Allen, I've been trying for that Breakthrough in the Grey Room ever since I became aware of such possibilities (it all began when someone slipped me Alan Watts at age 13). Now I'll soon be 21, and I really want to talk to you about methods of consciousness expansion, as well as discussing the work of Kerouac and Burroughs. For instance, I'm dying to know how you see Kerouac's seeming right-wing politics at the end of his life (you casually mentioned in the "Gay Sunshine" interview that this was just another lesson from him, but did not elaborate). I need a clearer explanation of Burrough's cut up and tape recorder techniques as means of breaking through pre-programming. I've tried some cut-up experiments with uneven results, and I can never tell how serious Burroughs is to plan any tape experiments (for instance, his surreal instructions about holding tape parties in "Ticket That Exploded"). Also, I've been unable to find any in depth reportage of the recent PILL meeting you were in. As an admirer of Leary's, I have to get the real story. But mainly, I want to discuss your work and insights.

I'm not rying to put a heavy guru trip on you, because I realize you are still struggling, too. But there seems to have been such an obvious development of your heart since you were my age (I can really identify with "Empty Mirror",)that I'd like some advice. I really want to expand my heart and it just feels like a little dried up raisin sometimes. Your growth is a hopeful sign in the cold universe.

I'm uncertain whether I'll be able to attend your Monday night reading due to conflicts with school and my financial status. If I

(please turn over)

don't manage to work my way back stage and introduce myself (which strikes me as a horrible way to meet you, engulfed in all the rest of your fans), I can't tell you how much it would mean to me if you could possibly drop me a lign telling me how I might reach you. I hope you'll remain in S.F. a little while longer. I've never written this sort of letter to any other "well-know personality", I can't help but think of your young days walking in Paterson with W.C. Williams and want to do the same with you.

Love and HARI OM NAMO SHIVAYA
Marc
Marc Olmsted
4182 17th St.
S.F., 94114
863-9382

P.S. Enclosed are a few poems that I've written in the last few years. I'm afraid the influence is obvious, but I'd still like you to see them.

A couple were ok…

Another element of this T.M. trip was celibacy (though It's never discussed outside of the "Inner Circle". I made it a total of two weeks without jacking off, a remarkable mecord. The concern was in the loss of energy in orgasm. Well, I was still a horny motherfucker but very disturbed about my "priestly vows". The poem's to McClure because of the borrowing of a few of his images, as well as yearning for his sexy and holy vision, as opposed to this dressed up Puritan shit that was being layed on me. The poem was to a particular girl I couldn't get out of my would be monk's mind.

SEXUS COSMOS
for Michael McClure's reality

that wanting you is enough
to have you here
your meat the angels
would allow to grace
my bed
as if there were no curse
of mammals
and sex was not invented
for the ruin of man
would Shiva really tremble at his
mad cub's love?

shhhh! let me forget Yogananda
for a night

Finally, one for the psychoanalysts…

O blear
Mom is grinned
by Death
Father eaten
his mind mad
with jelly
dad, daddy darling
will you come
back to us,
to me
breath that cracked art
now
bitter
where do you move,
your brain 60 year. old
fog of valium &
empren-codine
emptying your black gut worm
like the yelp
of an old
poodle
"Gaaaaaa!" making Mom
dream of drink
and other men
while your son
in drugs, broke
Mom pays 95
shame on the flat, woe
Aggh! Father, lover
what has happend to us all

ah bleak or worse dull
the cry meat of neighbor's babe
and in here
I cry
for spoiled teet
or cock
of you

No response this time.

I remember walking the Berkeley streets and seeing a new book of interviews with Ginsberg in Cody's Bookstore window. It depressed the hell out of me. I assumed he had found something irritating or false in my letter and chose not to reply, even though I'd read he answered all of his mail. Such dark somber thoughts for a 20-year-old, certain of his lack of worth. I was going over to the UC campus that night to see a friend who worked in the library, despondent, when someone stopped me and asked where the main auditorium was. I was walking that way and offered to show him, noting that he was reading a book by Chogyam Trungpa Rinpoche, Ginsberg's guru, and remarked on it.

"I'm going to see Chogyam Trungpa right now. He's lecturing in the Hall."

"Really? I wonder if Allen Ginsberg will be there."

"Yeah, he will, I saw him just before I came over."

I hurried over to the crowded hall, paid my admission, and sat on the floor.

So as you saw, I was just coming off of T.M., meaning I had just quit Transcendental Meditation after 3 and a half years, even going to Spain to become an "initiator" at age 19 and still not finding it a spiritual (let alone emotional) solution. I had started dabbling in drugs and alcohol again. I wondered what this new Tibetan teacher would be like. I had no real understanding of Buddhism, though I'd read Alan Watts and a few other Zen books. Eastern mysticism I thought to be one big glop. I had been struck by Ginsberg's description of his change from Hinduism to Buddhism in an interview - it involved the recognition of suffering. It seemed impossible to stay high and love God. At just age 20, I was in a lot of pain, the seed of alcoholism stirring in me like a beast that had just found its teeth.

I remember waiting for Chogyam Trungpa and suddenly having a sense of the room lighting up, as if golden, a subtle effect, yet distinct. He entered shortly after, apparently drunk (as I had read about), being led to the stage by Ginsberg and another disciple.

He proceeded to give a fascinating talk in an Oxford accent, smoking cigarettes and drinking a suspicious clear liquid from a decanter. He also wore a suit. His overall appearance was that of a Japanese detective or James Bond villain.

I asked Allen about Trungpa's drinking. "I don't think it interferes with his teaching," he answered.

He talked about the Dharma or Path upholding you, when he slid back drunkenly in his chair. It came within an inch of toppling off the platform stage. His attendants rushed up to catch him, but it stopped like a Bugs Bunny cartoon. Chogyam Trungpa just turned around and smiled. He later talked about Don Juan the sorcerer and his trickstery coyote teachings. Once more the chair slid back, once more the attendants leaped up as it came within an inch of toppling. Once more Chogyam Trungpa smiled.

Someone asked about UFOs. Trungpa replied, "If I saw one I'd think that was very interesting, but I wouldn't necessarily follow it."

The talk came to an end and Chogyam Trungpa was ushered out. To my delight, Allen Ginsberg remained behind and I went up to talk to him.

"I always wanted to meet you."

"Well, now you have."

We began walking out of the hall together while I chattered away. The only thing I remember was asking if Trungpa's teachings were similar to Burroughs' notion of "living in conflict," where a Nova agent must act without knowing if his orders are coming from his superiors or his enemies. Ginsberg said it had been a long time since he read *The Soft Machine,* or anything from Burroughs' "middle period."

My appearance, age 20, was nearly feminine, and I probably looked about 17 at most. I had long hair parted in the middle, my Indian blood in me giving the look of a young brave. Ginsberg was homosexual and I knew from his writings that I was probably his type. I'd had one panicky homosexual experience before this, but felt I'd very likely offer myself to Ginsberg if he was interested. I wrote this just months before we met.

I'd be your
mistress
Allen Ginsberg
or young master
thick in your
white belly -
stretching in mirror
I imagine
furry grins
school girl eyes

Why? A good question all these years later, since Ginsberg, however famous, was still a 48-year-old balding man with a gut. A gay friend wondered if I found Allen attractive. I certainly did, but much as I found actor Claude Rains attractive when I was a kid - seeing the brave scientist of *The Lost World* or *Battle of the Worlds*.

We stopped on the sidewalk.

"Wanna talk some more another time?" asked Ginsberg.

I did very much. He gave me his number in San Francisco where he was staying and disappeared into a car where friends waited to drive him back. They were smiling.

Ok. The sex thing. Some years later I came across a quote from Plato about Socrates: "I saw he was taken with the bloom of my youth and decided to give myself to him and learn all he knew." I admired Ginsberg enormously as poet and mystic, but I think I was also looking for a safe homosexual teacher so I could check out these feelings. Darker secrets: what ambitions? Did I think myself likely to advance my career? Frankly I didn't have enough confidence in my writing. That didn't seem a driving force to connect with him. I *was* starstruck. I *did* want to be close to the great man.

Anyway, I called him and we wound up a sexual item for 6 years - mostly his visits to San Francisco.

This "first date" consisted of meeting him in North Beach, and we wandered into a bar which was terribly exciting in itself, because I was still 20 and thus without a hope of ordinarily getting served. At the back of the bar was Bob Kaufman, legendary black Beat poet that I'm not sure I was aware of yet. He was quite loaded and seemed quite mad. "Allen! Allen!" he shouted across the room, and sat down on the floor of the bar, reciting a poem from memory. It was mostly incoherent to me, except for something about the ancient pagan god Dagon. Ginsberg listened attentively with one finger raised and pressed against his lips. It was a characteristic gesture I would see countless times. When Bob was done, Allen turned to me and said, "Good poem." Kaufman suddenly leered at me, "You're with Big Daddy, huh?" I probably blushed, but in fact I was terrified.

We walked in the cool North Beach night. Allen said, "I'd kinda like to sleep with you." I confessed that I'd "never experienced sodomy." He said not to worry. He later told me that hearing me use the word "sodomy" gave him quite a thrill.

"I don't get to feel good very often," he said. I had the sense of his self-imposed bodhisattvic burden, yet it startled me, given his chickenhawk cocksman reputation.

I arrived with Allen in Shig Murao's apartment on Grant Street. Shig had been busted for being behind the cash register at City Lights bookstore when *Howl* was initially confiscated. He was a very kindly Japanese hippie who made himself scarce in the second floor apartment. The place was mostly bookcases full of first editions. Also there upon our arrival, a lover of Allen's that Ginsberg had forgotten he invited. It was more than a little embarrassing, and Allen tried to make up for it by inviting Brad to join us. I girded my loins, so to speak, for a homosexual threesome. But Brad, a few years older than me and clearly a comfortably gay young man, begged off, though he appeared somewhat hurt. After looking at some of my poems and making kind remarks, Allen signed *Yage Letters* for me as an intro to Burroughs (who was coming to town to read) and suggested I touch his heart when I met him.

Allen and I retired. He showed me how Neal Cassady would let him screw him, which was facing me and thrusting between my legs. He also showed me how to suck cock, which was go down, hold my breath and take in as much as I could, breathing as I came up. This turned out to be very useful instructions to pass on to future girlfriends. Afterwards we lay together. "Don't be mean to me," he said. And we slept.

In the morning, he taught me Buddhist sitting, awareness of my outbreath dissolving into space, both of us naked and facing the bookcase. We sat for a while, maybe 20 minutes. I liked it. It was very different from T.M. As we dressed, I found his eyes appreciating me from across the room. It was like a reincarnational flash of being a beautiful Asian courtesan in some previous life, maybe in part because of Shig's tatami mats. I do not recall ever getting such a physically appreciative look from anyone else, gay or straight.

As we left the apartment, I still couldn't help asking: "Would you have me even if we didn't sleep together?" The fact, time-tested, was yes; yet I remember his own confusion in trying to answer honestly all those years ago - "That's like saying 'would you have me if I weren't me,'" he replied. No, Allen, not exactly.

Before he left town, Allen invited me to see him tape a TV show. The guy asked a lot of Buddhist questions, which pleased the old poet. I was introduced as a "William Burroughs scholar", and the woman manager at the TV station eyed my too-young face with confusion. Later, she asked us both who we might suggest for future shows. I suggested Brother Antoninus (William Everson), whom I studied with in UC Santa Cruz. I didn't really think he was so good, but I wanted to suggest someone (and he had perfected this great mountain man holy look – which meant Everson could get away with a lot, or at least for 30 minutes). Allen said afterward he didn't think that was the greatest suggestion, either.

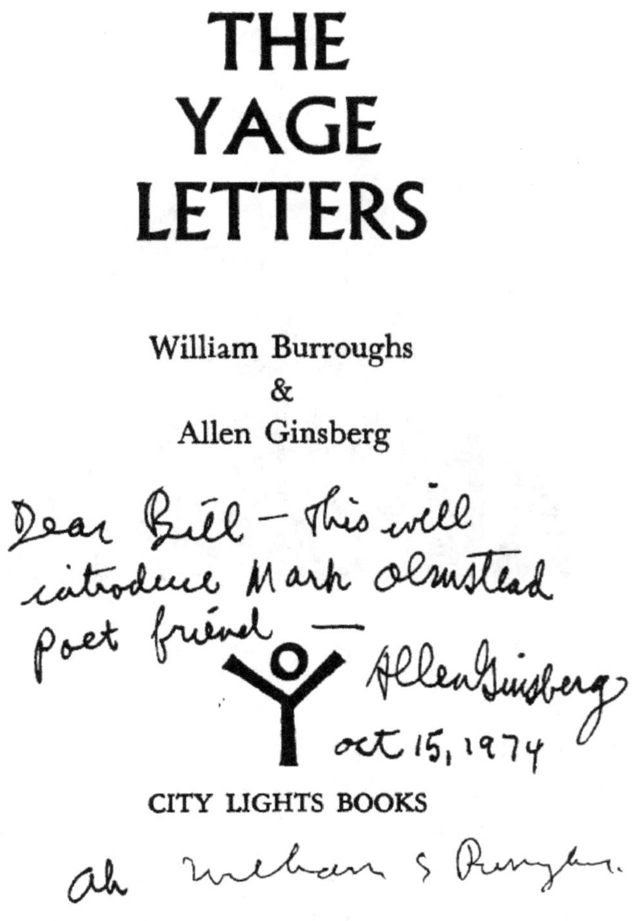

THE YAGE LETTERS

William Burroughs
&
Allen Ginsberg

Dear Bill – this will introduce Mark Olmstead poet friend — Allen Ginsberg Oct 15, 1974

CITY LIGHTS BOOKS

ah William S Burroughs

William S. Burroughs read at the First Unitarian Church, San Francisco, on November 4, 1974. I went up to him along with the usual suspects to get my book signed. I was too shy to say anything. Burroughs looked at the inscription and said, "Oh, Allen signed this." He was probably shy, too. I didn't touch his heart. The guy behind me - young, gay, bespectacled, pushy - insisted that Burroughs take his manuscript. Burroughs put out his hand in a refusing gesture and the guy literally forced it into his hand. That was the sum total of our first contact. At some point later Allen asked me about touching his heart. No, I said. "Didja touch his cock?" No, I said. "Yeah, I understand, he is kind of reptilian. I found him that way, too." Allen was concerned about Burroughs being lonely. But if I was a starfucker, it was limited to Allen.

Allen came into town again and called, "Do you love me a little? Honey?"

I was too freaked to respond warmly. Still, we were going to get together.

(Also worth noting: Years later, my copy of *The Yage Letters*, signed by both authors, was stolen.)

Ginsberg read at Lone Mountain College November 21, 1974. I took a girl I had met in acting class, Claire. Some people said Claire looked like French actress Isabel Adjani. But then I'd hear I looked like Romeo in that 60s Zeffirelli film. Both comments were equally generous. We left intoxicated by Ginsberg's harmonium-accompanied group chant of the Prajnaparamita Heart Sutra, singing "GATÉ GATÉ PARAGATÉ PARASAMGATÉ BODHI SVAHA!" like school kids, virtually skipping all the way home to her place in the Haight.

Claire and I had a vague understanding that our relationship was not going to be exclusive, and she didn't know I was making it with Allen. Yet.

When I ran into Brad (the accidentally double-booked other boy of my first night with Ginsberg), I learned Allen had abruptly left the city already.

Dear Allen,   ~ / 4

I'm leaving for L.A. today, the 20th of December, be back around the beginning of January. I have no idea when you'll be in town, so sorry to have missed you, Brad told me you had to leave quickly to L.A. yourself to see Leary's lawyer, so no blame. I'm writing mainly because I'm sorry I was so cold to you on the phone (or shy or whatever), I was still hastling out what this new chapter meant. But now, I feel resolved and at peace and wish you peace for this Christmas season and all time, and I love you very much and when you're back in town please look me up because I want to be one of your lovers and have you love me. I see no impediment to our relationship unless I fall in love with a possessive girl who insists I sleep only with her. No sign of this now, so HARE KRISHNA and GATE' GATE' PARAGATE' PARASAMGATE' BODHI SVAHA!

Love,
Marc
O.

To Allen

I slept with Socrates
wouldn't you
memory of goat hair chest
and everyone's father
I lay with the great mind
and stroked his balding skull

this is another one:

what made you think
I'd cry like snow
my condition based on
time's old yellow way
magnetic
storms
and how they count the bones

Allen noted the second with brackets and it found its way into Beatitude #37 two years later.

28 Dec 1974

Dear Marc —
Ah what a doll you are! Merry
Xmas Happy New Year see you
some time Spring I guess whenever I
get to S.F. or you ever get here or
halfway if youre passing thru Boulder
next summer. Too much to write
letters! — Still I do love you, & love
your poetry as much as you & all
ways we're both OK knowing death —
So I'll be sitting a month January
meditating simultaneous with teethbonegum
blood operation fix my moaf —.
Supper X-mas eve last nite with
Burroughs & New Years with Gregory Corso
& Bill B. old nostalgias purified last
nite by looking in eachother's eyes for

I'll teach Poetastics, Corso Burroughs Olson 'til past then
Sanders Waldman Di Prima

half an hour's time trying to see
eachother — empty headed both of us.

The soul world is open totally
for us (whether there is a soul or not)
because we're not afraid of loving
eachother forever — so love me forever
and I'll love you & the soul
won't worry (even if the body knits
its brow) — When love wears out there's free-
restful open empty space (not bitter claustrophobia)
I think of you often & your
letter was heart thrill as your
frankness + extra energy + generosity
taking the chance, writing like a lover like you did always is —
it's all one your own beauty + your
poetry's in your dose anyway — But
if you was a dwarf cripple your language
would be prettier than Pope, or almost —
Love + Play — As ever Allen

Write me more! Send poems too!

Show up. Poems to Whalen + him @ here. 264 Beaver St. Zen Center

Before this letter arrived, I was already on my way to my first mental ward.

Part 2 – Going Crazy

The moon behind the wire?

Do you believe everything moves 360°?

I stood in the white sheet of the mental ward talking to the black man who thought himself Satan. I thought I was Buddha.

I walked into the L.A. police station having taken mushrooms, and this fed the PCP messiah breakdown; the full moon directly above with two rainbow rings of condensing mist. I was wearing a Bogart felt hat, one tennis shoe and one rubber thong, a towel as a sort of Hindu skirt, an Indian pajama - shirt and love beads - pre-punk shades, a mop in my hand as a yippie staff, and a plastic flight bag full of books and trinkets I intended to show Chief Davis and the inevitable media god. First step in changing the world: enlighten the cops.

I sat down in the police station followed by three friends who had driven me there.

They thought it was a prank. Mort thought I might even be enlightened. The cops gave me half an hour to leave. A black man asked for change and I handed him a $20 bill. I chanted Hare Krishna in the cold white of the station, finally taken away in cuffs.

"You're playing right into my hands," I said.

As a teenager, I'd been initiated into the secrets of American Hindu. I joined that Mantra Club and after several years of devout mantra chanting flew to my guru and learned to teach it, finally giving up after a year when I felt as dumb as those who paid $35 a mantra (of which I got $17.50). But now, in the days of acid, I found myself suddenly as great as my guru, greater! Now the guru would clap his hands, so proud (for he undoubtedly knew all along, being a clever guru, that I was the Buddha to come, Maitreya), and the manic surge filled me like a slow motion atom cloud spreading over the Mojave in an orange flash, v-rooooooomm the dust spread out and I didn't have to worry anymore. I was God and Krishna and Buddha back on Earth to help with the Marvel Comic war of Good vs. Evil Bhagavad Gita slug-out where angels and demons, Olympian, Set and mighty Isis, the whole Justice League of America, Super-Jagger, Jaws, every last archetype returned to XX Century to pummel each other into shadow or light, the bone of the dice with the black hole cavities of luck, Shiva would win because all was Shiva, all a dream even if the planet went up in neutron dust, Shiva lit his joint in the void and took a galaxy.

rediscovered, original Santa Cruz mad ward document...

in Harlem's
sweet
Sphinx room in
Atlantic
George's
BROOM
YEAH O YEAH MICK
PICKED HIS
OWN NOISE
AND
ATE
THE PRANIC PRAKRITIS
TWOSOME
GRUESOME
BUDDHA

1/24/74

(meticulously signed and dated from the Santa Cruz nut ward, I hadn't gotten clear that it was now 1975)

Don't Hesitate

Still more acid, for school holiday wasn't up, throwing wine in girlfriend Claire's face and smashing the glass to the ground when she wouldn't believe I was the messiah.

The trips got uglier. I saw everyone as a demon on the streets. I finally stopped the acid as if a last spark of sanity deep in my brain knew that to pursue this any further would end in my death, or someone else's.

"Was it the divorce?" Dad said over the phone. I shrugged in San Francisco, the depression so great by this point that when I came home from school I'd go straight to bed and try to sleep until morning, then going to the streetcar and wishing some crazed Latino would put a random bullet in my brain the way the papers said it happened.

I saw a therapist, one the city provided. six months later I stared out over the horizon as it purpled at 6 and wondered what had happened. Was there any truth at all to what I had seen, now able to function and yet wondering just who had I been as the Chemical Man?

~~76~~
75

Friday, Feb. 21

Dear Allen,

Writing in the chill, sunny afternoon, feeling good, been doing regularly mediation (closed eye T.M. mantra kundalini, suits me best). Would like to do the Sanskrit puja I know(to Maharishi's Guru Dev, Swami Bramhananda Saraswati) for you next vist to S.F.

Bad news, but all cleared up now...I've been in two mental wards since last writing. Nether serious. Drugs got me into Messiahnic radiant sanity, harmless to all, but happened to be in right place at wrong time. Trips were something of the order of Leary's chronicle of your early acid experience in High Priest. 7 days in L.A., 5 days in Santa Cruz, both times I was stupid. A sort of mini-Leary experience, as well as realization of Messiah Trap and how to stay out of a mental ward. Insight into politica shut-down of sainthod. Every one of patients in L.A. Medical Ward was on the Nod, heavily tranquilized. S.C. Medical Ward prefers a more cheerful, active lunatic. Gave us something like ritalin. As for the exact details of the holy manic behavior that got me in, I'll tell you in person. To top it off U.C. Santa Cruz (the school I was visiting) seemed to be over-run with government narcs looking for big dealers. I seemed to be suspect, due to my friendship with several campus dealers and recent arrival from the City. Ah, Allen, times have been harsh in their lessons.

Still in school, (on Dean's List from last semester with straight A's) also got into the Film Dept.. I find myself writing much more poetry and just watching film rather than making it these days. Your comment about the impermanence of film (its immediate loss with technology's death) is precisely what interests me; the white-light-karmic-shadow-play. Also found a harmonica in Santa Cruz foothills, played a lot in S.C. Mental Ward like a Cagney or Corso mad cub. So been composing songs. Enclosed are some poems, some rhyme-lyrics, two short stories in spontaneous bop prosody. You may keep all ot it. I'm also preparing one "serious" big manuscript of 8 years poetry to give you in Spring.

Sexually, I've been very active, largely with steady lover Claire, other lovers come and go. Hetero-sex still my main interest, but you still on my list, Big Daddy. I, like Yogananda, like sleeping with gurus (don't really see you that way), but my own lovers will limit our meetings. Sever times a month, O.K.? But when you're back in town I'd like to invite you and Brad over for dinner and mantra chanting. Brad is in my Judo class, Greecian boys spar in the Tao. Full circle.

I love you, greybeard,

Marc

This letter was a complete whitewash of the messianic breakdown I'd had. Nude photos my first cousin roommate Viv had taken of me (not her real name – we were also having sex) show in my expression just how nuts I was right before landing in that first mental ward. I'd own up to how terrifying it was in my next letter. But first, Allen replied.

Dear Marc — (1) April 15, 1975
P.O.B. 582 Stuyvesant Sta.
N.Y. 10009

Forgive long delay replying — inundation
of paper on my desk — I'm that far behind
mail — and my own poems untyped. You would
love to hear your puja practice. I've begun
some more intensive Buddhist daily practice
including 100–300 prostrations (1 to 3 malas
a day depending on time) —

Amazing adventures you had on acid —
I would've thought yr. meditation clarity would
leave you immune to Messianic delusions &
sloppiness of Conduct — but maybe that's
just atheist Buddhist idea — Still you
seem to have center strong enough to experience
Cosmic-social adventures & land on your
feet like good Cat you are.

Don't worry about our love life, it's
alright, I don't want to <u>own</u> you (I'm not
around anyway) all I want to be baby is friends
with you. We'll make it. I'll be in S.F.
only briefly in May toward the last half of
month, I don't know when, I'll try to phone you
in advance when — I'll be in Seattle ~~[illegible]~~ mid-May
doing Buddhist benefits. Give my love to Brad, glad
you see eachother. Show yr. Poetry mss to
Ferlinghetti if it's ready. He <u>also</u> is interested
in Prose the last few years.

The tone of your writing (the poems
clearest) is always strong & natural &

(2) Poignantly you + your mouth + heart so ~~just~~ don't worry just have faith in your own genius and allow yourself to write all the poetry you ~~get~~ want or get inspired to. I really like reading your broken-line writing — to see what your adventures + inventions are — completely natural almost always.

I read them the prose when I first got it months ago + enjoyed reading it. Carrying on an attitude (slightly macho hip-wise + mind wise) is harder in prose than poetry — because humorous exaggeration in poetry is a mind-jump, in prose it gets more tedious unless you have a solid universe to present — well it is semisolid the prose I'd say — still live stuff of yr genius mind but younger sounding than the formal ~~poetry~~ poetry — aw — we'll talk —

Love as ever always — Allen

3) — Should I send you back
the mss or leave them in
my files? gather dust, or
rare occasion show them
to anybody accidental
of that special interest —
Anne Waldman or someone —

Here's what I'll be doing
tomorrow — see reverse page
Columbia reading w/ friends —
I love you really do — from
distance & thru time, I guess it's
your cheery poet's soul —
so enjoy that — Confidence —
Work hard I mean, write
a lot freely about real things
with straight eyes —
Sorry long wait silence
— just the fate of my desk, & mess —

Allen Ginsberg

RETURN OF THE POETS

Another night at Columbia

APRIL 17, 1975 8 P.M.
McMILLAN HALL, 116th & B'WAY.

McMILLAN HALL FEBRUARY 5, 1959

PHOTO BY FRED W. McDARRAH.

GREGORY CORSO
PETER ORLOVSKY
ALLEN GINSBERG
REINFORCED THRU DECADES BY
WILLIAM S. BURROUGHS

AN EVENING OF POETIC LITERATURE FOR BENEFIT OF ALL SENTIENT BEINGS.
WITH BLESSING OF BUDDHIST POETIC LINEAGE OF MARPA & MILAREPA &
CHÖGYAM TRUNGPA. PROCEEDS TO DHARMADHATU MEDITATION CENTER.
SPONSORED BY DHARMADHATU & UNMUZZLED OX & McAC. DONATION $2.50.

I had sent Allen a short story called *Working Out Karma*, based on my dropping out of college and holing up in Lincoln, Nebraska for a summer. A year earlier, it had actually gotten a favorable response from *Oui*, which was *Playboy*'s attempt at a younger, hipper audience, rather like *Spin*'s answer to *Rolling Stone*. The editor liked the writing, but thought it fell apart at the end. Here's a fragment from the middle:

> **One day when I was just learning how to file, a group of men and women were getting their pictures taken. Something was odd about them. They moved strangely. Their faces were pale and crushed. All of them were somehow not right as they received their ID badges affixed with the little portraits of their caved-in faces.**
>
> **When they had gone back up the elevator I whispered to Johnny the Dwarf.**
>
> **"Hey, what's with those people?"**
>
> **"O, they're from the State Mental Institution. After they're in there long enough the State finds them jobs."**

The *Oui* editor asked to see something else. I sent him *Bloody Orgy of the Space Zombies*, based on a hitchhiking misadventure where four drunken blacks picked me. It was about as politically correct as R. Crumb, whom I'd been pouring over in Zap Comix. The editor was horrified and sent a terse response begging off.

Dear Allen,

I didn't expect you to answer, knowing how busy you are, thought you'd be out here and no letter'd be necessary. In the future don't feel you gotta return a note each time, I'll probably always be sending you a little something. You don't haveta answer this one, I'll wait for your arrival.

You are a sensitive dear old being, you know, always picking up on my nervousness and soothing me. I was still too close to the mental ward experiences last letter to really relate them, but my winding up there was more than just drug illusions. Been under lotta pressure, divorce of parents and general lost in Kali Yuga feeling, not liking school, and those depressions I sorta hinted at in our visits, really quite moody and hurting alot finally all surfaced and boom! Messiah! So that was all very heavy and scarey but good also because it forced me to integrate, look into what was not harmonious in the cellar, so been doing that with the help of a little free counseling through the City, a sweet old Jungian woman psychologist not at all opposed to meditation or gayness quite lucky for me actually because I was blindly suffering and just sought help randomly. Staying away from drugs at this time, sticking to T.M. discipline in search of a center which I still don't have yet, which helped me into acid flip-outs.

But things are not like this now, sense of getting it together and writing in my tablet every day. Keep the short stories. They <u>are</u> actually younger, written at least a year ago, just wanted you to see. Also you're right about the macho sound, Bukowski inspired and trying to build strong manly loner self, now abandoned into feeling body's tenderness and heart's own natural telling of things. Your encouragements have been the best thing of recent months, very uplifting and faith-giving. I'm working hard at it, poesy desire now strongest of any...

OVER

SO FEAR NOT! Back on my good cat feet as you say. Your acceptance of me means more than I can say. I love you dearly. Enclosed are some recent poems, very pained but you know about that, just somehow not wanting you to worry...

P.S. Heard you ran into Richard Modiano at April 17th N.Y. reading, my good friend black beard short hair, was my first crazy wisdom teacher of teenage days...

JAI GURU DEV,

Marc

A couple of the poems I gave him were of interest…

lions order out
the sad mind
they sleep with even breaths
yellow grins on their
dumb-knowledgeable
skulls of
soft eternity connections

I'm human
and grind my teeth asleep
like wheels
money comes from Father
saliva guilt
nirvana's lost in Africa

If I ever am a lion
I'll chase what darkness
I can
heal things
sing

That poem wound up in Beatitude #37 in 1976. The next wound up in City Lights Journal #4 in 1978(!) – plus after my fall from heaven, I didn't feel I had a manuscript to show anymore…

Japanese cripple
bound to his machine
electric metal wheels
beyond lust's
eye or groan
he wanted a Pepsi &
meat sandwich
but the counter was too high
I helped putting the silver change
into his twisted hand
wanting to touch him remembering the
leukemia boy Mom gave a flashlight to in hospital
what he wanted most-head swollen like an undersea fish
now this broken form with a soul like mine
eyes grew wet for his pain yet grateful he
permitted me the kind
act

P.S.S. Gave up on old poesy manuscript after looking with unmanic, critical eye. Still learning, searching for the voice, don' wanna bug Larry 'til there's sumpin' real good...

I later learned my psychotic break was primarily triggered by the PCP that some seedy dealers were giving me, apparently - even if I had filled in with acid and mushrooms. I found this out 2 years later from a fellow film student who did a documentary on PCP. Messianic PCP breakdowns got less press than gouging out your grandmother's eyes and eating them. But they do happen, and last exactly the 2 weeks mine had. Some valve or something gets held down in the brain and you go nuts. Or some people do. More than once I heard that I might be predisposed to schizophrenia, but a chromosome or two saved me. You decide, I'm too tired of it all.

I *did* think that Allen's publisher would make me famous at that time - so what shadow ambition was there after all? I also thought I was the messiah, in particular, Maitreya, the Buddha to come. Within a month I was back to my miserable self.

So in 1975, a year after meeting Allen, after I wrote him more about the drug-related messianic breakdown and sheepishly told him that I hadn't found my "voice" yet (how many young poets have choked *that* out?), I got one of his most fabulous letters, a true teaching.

Dear Marc — ~~April~~ aug 1 (1) 1975

yeh anoying I didnt know you were going thru that much — maybe it's the hindu approach with a god or Self at center as a permanent entity?

It would seem to be more peaceful if there were a Budh-enlightenment of empty space awakened but no god, etc, no self, ~~that~~ just an empty center with no voice or self or thought — and around that a mandala of illusions, experiences, etc. which we live with + call a Self, Allen Ginsberg. But to get not-attached to the idea of A.G. or Marc and Marc's "center which I still dont have yet" would mean giving up search because there is no center, (neither macho ~~nor~~ non macho tender body heart) — They aint no center, no reason to be "searching for 'the' voice" — aint no real you-voice.

Instead there's the Constellation of experiences, habits + appearances to observe, welcome + living with, sport with, dig + describe and use as vehicles

to circle around
~~the~~ No-One within you —

Maybe the idea that there is
a self, pushed to limit to
test it out, led to trying
out Messiah role?

Humbler self role might
be equally silly.

Maybe you ain't no-
one at all. Just a lot of voices.

Which leaves you free
to be perfect poet observer
& transmitter of phenomenon,
with good humor & unobstructed
energy, and lots of clear voices with
no self illusion

That's a Ginsberg-Buddhist
interpretation of yr. "problem"
as posed in last letter.

Your poetry lovely & unfailing
& selfless as ever — ex. playful
with notion of self & not stuck
assertively. I'll be in S.F. some
time late May —

(2) 1979

(cont)

May 20—22 & then at Padma Jong Poetry Seminar May 23-25 — Padma Jong is part of Trungpa's organization an art colony — I've never given a seminar before like that — Up in Mendocino County, get info from them Padma Jong Dos Rios Calif 95429 or call 415-841-3242.

Would you like to come up there with me for the 3 or four days while I'm teaching? You could help me, be my secretary, maybe even set an example by yr own poetry practice — and it would give us a rare chance to stay together for that week end close & intimate — same time in an active poetry situation — I don't know what it'd be like — It'd be some security for me, having you with me & relying on your love — at least I won't be mind-wandering trying to seduce handsome students — if any —

God knows if anyone will
sign up for it anyway —
In any case a free weekend
for your food + [illegible] a
zone meditation scheduled I
think — We could be together there —
Then I go back to S.F.

26–27, then to Colorado

the 29th. Somewhere there
I'll go up visit Snyder
in Nevada City. and
spend a little time with
Brodie in the city too if
things work out —
OK — I'll leave
~~[illegible]~~ here the 11th of May
for Utah + Seattle + call
you in S.F. — Leave message
where you are with Nancy Phillips
at City Lites, or Shig at Store —
I'll get there around May 20 Tues —
Love as ever
Allen
Ginsberg

[ca. 1975 May]

Dear Allen—

It was good to get your letter but I'm afraid I can't come with you on the Padma Jong seminar. My relationship with Claire (girl of last 6 months) has grown quite monogamous without my knowing it, really, and the suggestion of being with you upset her.

What to say? She is my constant companion and lover and it just doesn't seem possible to sleep with you at this point without upsetting our relationship. I have many tender feelings for you, but need her badly right now, don't want to hurt her, right or wrong. The whole thing comes as a surprize to me, didn't know she'd feel this way. Please forgive me. I write because I'm too embarassed—guilty to tell you any other way.

O Allen, are you mad? Terribly hurt? I promise to keep in contact, if you're still interested in hearing from me. We're not finished yet.

I truly do love you. Hope you understand the situation.

Much Love &
Om Ah Hum,
Marc

Don't Hesitate

Poem fragment at the time tells all:

I told I'd slept with A.
"what did you do,
tell me, man," she shouted
wanting detailed menus of
ass fuck
then wept

(ca. 1975 May

Dear Allen-

I just called Nancy Peters at City Lights to see whether my letter prior your New York phone call had been sent. To my embarass-ment,it had. I decided since I wouldn't probably see you for a while the monogamous situation might change, no need placing that structure on you if you weren't around. But alas, it had been forwarded, leaving me feeling guilty and strange about your phone call, unable to tell you then and wondering if it even mattered, perhaps I wouldn't be with Claire when you visited S.F. next. But I felt wierd just the same since I said that work and school would have prevented me from going to Padma Jong (which were certainly factors, but surmountable ones I suppose), rather than the main reason of living out an old-fashioned if agreeable love scene. Unnerstan'? What a crummy letter to have forwarded, especially after your phone call. I felt awful. Do you think me bad? Ah, I know ya don't, but I just don't want you mad or thinking me sneaky or leading you on or somethin'.

I feel like more trouble than I'm worth, but next time you're in town, please call. I'd include some poetry but wanted to get this off right away making sure you weren't hurt or anything. I'll write a regular letter soon. No need answering this. Just...aw, you know, the whole thing felt so messy and karmic wanted to write, etc.

Love,

Marc

As it turned out, Allen couldn't go to Padma Jong anyway, because after a routine prostate check-up, he was given some antibiotics to which he was allergic. When he had a reaction, his own doctor was out of town and the substitute prescribed MORE of the same antibiotics. The result was nerve damage that left his face partially slack; unnervingly so. He regained a good deal of his original face, but one eye tended to occasionally weep and there was the slightest tendency to drool. He dabbed at eye and mouth corner with a handkerchief all the way to his death. Still, it was barely noticeable, especially considering the Quasimodo-like sag to his face right after this terrible incident. He didn't even mention it when he wrote back.

Aug 25. 75 Naropa East 1441 Bway
Boulder Colo
Dear Marc —
Stop Worrying! I doon' wanna lay no trip on you + hypnotize you in weird world — The poems you sent were Great — I mean, fine!! I read them to Class I was teaching, relating them to W.C. Williams whom I was teaching — practicing "minute particulars" — "The Natural object is always the adequate symbol" — Pound — WCW. "No ideas but in facts" — your poetic practice is the best! You're solid, + your mind's open — just too worried — But your heart + poetry are SOLID!
I'd choose Trungpa's open space if I were you — I have — Peter Orlovsky + I go to R.M.D.C. [illegible] "crazy wisdom" for a week [illegible] I sit alone there, then go to N.Y. tomorrow then [illegible] see [illegible] sooner or later — much + all love — Allen Ginsberg

Marc Olmstead
4189 17th St
SF Cal
94114

[Olmsted]
[ca. 1975 Sep]

Dear Allen,

Thanks for the reassurances. Yes, I'm too worried, general nattering of consciousness, which hopefully will wear itself out with age and meditation practice. Clear empty space is most appealing, and I have many questions for your return to S.F. I suppose I still have difficulty with Trungpa's drinking and anti-diet comments, it's hard for me to imagine a purely mental seperate enlightenment from the body's psycho-chemistry, but that's just where I have come from, Hindu orthodox tradition. The Dharmadhatu group currently working out of S.F. rubs me the wrong way, I intend to explore Tulku's Nyingma Institute, since I am dissatisfied with T.M. I imagine this approach to Tibetan Buddhism meets with a certain dissaproval on your part, since you consider Trungpa more authoratative (an old postcard mentioned you with Tulku around '72 doing work with OM AH HUM VAJRA GURU PADMA SIDDHI HUM, I guess you dropped it when you began the Trungpa association), but it draws me right now.

A recent Barb mentioned health difficulties and the Denver hospital in an article on the Jack Kerouac School of Disembodied Poetics. What's up? Are you feeling better?

I'm very busy with Film School this semester, but remain with the poetry discipline of writing a little each day. General emotional space is good these days. I do miss you, perhaps more than you'd guess from the tone of recent letters, so hurry up and get out here. I've got a new address and phone,

Love,

Marc

380 A Eureka St.

S.F. 94114

282-5787

I had now moved into an in-law cottage clearly under code – it was one step up from a converted tool shed or chicken coop. I included a bunch of poems, only one worth showing now…

1.

I forgive you now
mother
you were alone, my ribs
ache in your name
whispers of sex
hundred thousand drinks
glass teeth passed
out on the rumpled day bed
eventually pills that
could not kill your
black eyes staring from the
animal skull

2.

she wept in vodka patios
pool glittering like a hungry
blue eye, strange children
invisibly hers, a red
zipper at her
old belly memory that
they'd grown inside
like vegetables, the
black-outs more frequent
driving the car in
Buddha void of alcohol
tears perpetually hidden
from the man in the suit
with the cock
home to eat and disappear
into newspaper planet
age like a seperate vampire delerium
grinned from the mirror, wanting
to break the glass and
eat her solid
whispering for the smooth yellow pills
in the cupboard to set it free
while Jesus slept to her
radared prayers
friends becoming dreams
the world closing
up petal
in a bright
silver fog

This next note, another handwritten rarity, also shows that I seem to have gone to Allen's same calligraphy school of the nervous system.

10/5/75

Dear Allen,

Just a short note - extension of previous letter.

Could you suggest a few poetry magazines I might try sending stuff to?

I forgot to ask last letter.

Love & Ah,

Marc

AmericanAirlines

In Flight... over Utah Saltlake

Altitude;

Location; ~~#~~ Nov 18, 1975

Dear Marc

Taking a few Days off from Rolling Thunder Review Dylan tour of New England — on way to Logan Utah Poetry Reading —

My poetry is too pessimistic

— How're you —

When we ever see each other again!? — Soon —

Dylan's pronunciation of consonants vowels syllable by syllable is a work of genius — he keeps time with his mouth as well as footstomp — all well Love to you —

Allen

PS Shaved my beard in movie scene — I look like Meher Baba for next few days.

Dec. 18, 1975

Dear Allen,

A lot of time and thought has flowed past old mind bridge and here I am, presenting first: love to you and hoping for your peace, then on to what's occuring,...Spiritually, I've been investigating more of Trungpa and find a great sense of liberation in his writings, having finished Spiritual Materialism, and Meditation in Action. Have done some formal sitting and some on my own. By formal, mean hour-long sitting at the local Dharmadhatu, 57 Hartford just a couple blocks from my house, informally sitting 20 minutes or so twice a day at my flat. Achh, poor choice of words, formal and informal, I follow the practice as you related it and seem to have a good strong foundation in how sitting is to be done, have also read Suzuki's Zen Mind, Beginner's Mind. When I sit at the Dharmadhatu for an hour, this seems more under auspices of Trungpa, thus more official or "formal". Anyhow, I have not as yet dropped my T.M. practice xx making "conversion" from Hindu to Buddhist, because still feel very drawn to that Ram Dass sense of purifying energy levels etc., although the Hindu universe seems more and more of dead end futility xxxxxxxxx, ripe ground for shift to Buddhist-Trungpa attitude of no magic enlightenment, no where to go. On the other hand, the Dharmadhatu on Hartford seems very caught up in a spiritual materialist trip, one of the instructors wearing Buddhist robes, and general straightne of atmosphere is a turn off for me, comments like "Trungpa considers grass smoking super-samsara and advises against it" or general oppressive attitude that I certainly did not get from you and thus am anxious to speak with you and get your opinions. Hard for me to just sit alone at this point, just too lonely, need some guidance and can't accept the auspices of local center. Still, axxx many conflicts about leaving my old Maharishi who I've invested much love and energy in...To sum up, feelings onf conflicts about what path to choose or abandon right now, dissatisfied with T.M. yet also uncertain of leaving it, scared even of abandoning what may be true.

Conflict does seem to sum up my general state, many conflicts about you, can safely say think of you daily, whether artistically or personally. I felt very bad about those last two letters, wondering what you thought of me. I continue to see Claire, and really didn't mean that as a hetero-dodge, monogamy easy to fall into when there's noone else around to stir pot and prevent solidification. On the other hand, I felt engulfed by you into role of gay lover, which caused all kinds of new feelings hard for me to deal with in recent upset times of mental ward and general shattered emotions. Dammit I do love you and really don't mind, would even welcome another chance to bed with you, but...don't wanna be com-parmentalized, expected to be gay companion when I only feel like it sometimes. It's all so muddled, please forgive me, don't mean to be difficult or neurotic yet it happens this way, hope you understand. So I ask you agin to call me when in S.F., hoping that my scene with Claire will allow me to sneak away to at least meet during day or sumpthin', I dunno. Better really to meet again and talk about this personally, since I don't want to lose our friendship. Aw, we gotta talk...

Recently saw a psychic, the reading very interesting but also mentioned that your health might still be bad or in near future becoming so. Is this the case? Or have you completely recovered from antibiotic fiasco of hospital?

Enclosed is poetry that I am pleased with, been writing every day and consider these strong.

Love and Ah,

Marc

Allen checked off the interesting ones…

✓

~~"there's been an accident!"~~
thrilling my age 12 horror
movie brain
I ran from the house to
streetlight corner
ordinary suburban lawn
now red with this
new crab form
coughing blood
my first death outside
television
car exploded-glass & chrome,
the teeth of monsters
face a
smooth wet mask
of his juice
the kids on the block stared
some joking
when the sirens came
"he'll wreck the sheets"
they folded his violence
on the stretcher

felt evil for the wish
to see it

later the radio
said who
he'd
been

✓

matted beard & hair-filth
in a grey plastic chair
black coat pants
snowed with grime
a dozen toothpicks
weird from his lapel
like mad army brass
yellow nails curling Fu Manchu
dreaming in the
white nova
laundromat

Dorothy's Grocery
has seven black mystical
bananas
a lone onion
and no cash register
fat tongue snaking
out her bad teeth
as the blunt
fingers search
change
breasts & hips
belly
huge in the grey
smock
TV glowing on her thick lenses
and bright
animal iris

PARTICULARS

-the green coat woman
lost in her gloves
and old thought
-the blue hair skull
of the Japanese boy
-the strange
newly-hatched
lizard-furred
doves
on fire-escape

12/20/73

Dear Allen,

Here are Christmas poems, not to be mistaken with some karma manuscript you gotta do something with, just heart gift because I love you deep, miss your beard, there's much talking that letters can't do,maybe much silence also as in strong hugs, so anyway, this poesy is recent stuff of last coupla months, the best I think.

Lot of it's related to prostatitis health. The score on that: some men my age have difficulty shaking it because the gland's particularly active, causing congestion. This info comes from two different Dr.s, one of them had same trouble at 21-22 like me. Recent hospital trip, ½ day of tests and dilation of urethra-prostate has had enromous good effect, so now no pain and off antibiotics, still awhile before completely cleared but not infectious and much better.

Also greater calm-clarity under Lama Tarthang Tulku's wisdom-advice, serious daily meditation practice and fierce study of Tibetan Buddhism, so we can have lofty dialogs over Marpa, Milarepa, Naropa and the rest of Heaven Gang next meeting.

Not much else, want you to see my latest film, James Bond Sutra, only 3 minutes but condensed montage visuals similar to condensation of word in spontaneous bop poetics, very ritualized and influenced by Anger and

Duer

Bailey.

Anyway, more love, AH, TATYATA OM MUNI MUNI MAHA MUNI SHAKYAMUNIYE SOHA, OM MANI PADME HUM HRI, new year's and Christmas-Winter Solstice blessings to you and all your loves,

Marc

The Gotham Book Mart and Full Court Press
cordially invite you to celebrate the publication of

COLLECTED POEMS, by Edwin Denby
I REMEMBER, by Joe Brainard
FIRST BLUES: Rags, Ballads & Harmonium Songs 1971-74
by Allen Ginsberg

Monday, December 15, 1975 from 5 to 7 pm
Gotham Book Mart Gallery
41 West 47th Street
New York City

Dear Mark Just a note to say Merry Xmas too Love as ever, Allen

I got a reply. working up a list of magazines for you + others -

The prostatitis score took quite some time to sort out, but it turned out I caught chlamydia when I was 17 with a Norwegian blonde and carried it around for 3 years – it took a really expert urologist to finally knock it out, because it would not die under regular antibiotics. By that time, my prostate was scarred. For years I labored under all kinds of New Age/Catholic notions that I had brought it on myself. Maybe I had. A Freudian-Reichian therapist (the worst combo, believe me) once made a reference to "Fear of penetration" and I thought he meant "Fear of getting fucked," a confusion he didn't correct.

Allen visited and took me to my favorite pizza place on Castro, where I demolished a pitcher of beer by myself. My alcoholism still had a couple of years to really come out on a daily basis, but when we went to bed, Allen saw my bloated belly and said "You're getting fat!" It was not lost on me that Allen was fatter, but there seemed an obvious if unspoken trade – I had to keep sexually desirable if we were going to keep doing this – i.e. the price for his intimacy. (Another time, he took inventory of my face: "Nice eyes, nice nose... o.k. lips. It seemed a bit creepy.)

Next morning I left him sleeping in my tiny in-law chicken coop of a pad (which Allen said reminded him of Gary Snyder's old cabin in Berkeley) and went to school.

10:45

Marc,
I read thru all these
poems — all have some
taste of body & actual ~~mind~~
thoughts — really dimensional & funny,
like Kerouac blues — often the
raw surprises are the best, shouldn't
be too much revised or cleaned
up — it's enough for a book because
there's a whole life situation there —
whenever I see a mass of yr. work
I think "Don't hesitate" just set
it all up on page & move on go on
ahead writing — but this is a
solid pile of reality —
Love Allen

Call me

Allen had, to my surprise, gone through a sheaf of fresh typed poems, many with my own cross-outs. There were some interesting notes on phrasing – I mentioned "drinking in the bar with other friends' women, coyness" – he suggested "eyes behind teacups" for "coyness" – which showed how particulars would make it more interesting – only we weren't drinking tea. He changed my "the rot of teeth in grins" to "rottentooth grin." I had edited my own "I want no more/ this dream" into "I want no more/dreams." He said that the original was "ok."

One poem had been completely crossed out by me, which he saved from oblivion…

mantra in chest
  walked Geary St.
    to sudden thought end
    people
  moving open under
    sky gas
      here no else

I had been hanging around a little with Swami Muktananda in Oakland. Above this crossed-out poem I had quoted a student saying, "We are invited to live like madmen and heroes."

A number of the other poems found their way into the Hawaii-based *Plumber's Ink* (1978), courtesy of Allen forwarding them, but this Muktananda-inspired one remains one of the most interesting to me. For many years I was unaware that Allen also had a connection with Muktananda, and, unusually, that this Hindu guru had many crossover aspects to the Tibetan Buddhist view of reality.

In 1976, my younger sister Stacey got leukemia.

I was greeted at the airport by Richard and Jim Butterfield ready with my *Tibetan Book of the Dead.*

"You father wants you taken directly home."

I'm pissed.

"Well, its you sister. She's sick."

"What she got?"

"We're supposed to let your father tell you."

I look Jim in the eye and:

"Is it leukemia?"

"Who told you?" says Jim, innocently, while Richard turns away.

I drew a picture of Buddha with Tibetan AH overhead and put it in her hospital room where she could see it, and chanted AH with her and Richard in the hospital. She clearly felt better and I left utterly drained, weeping.

Dear Allen,

Word has been sad up North about you & your father. AH. I love you. I have been experiencing a similar scene, now visiting my father in L.A. to discover my younger sister has leukemia. I've burned through just about every emotion one can have about it, manic laughter, surrender of tears, now calm & somewhat clear especially with optimistic news, Stacey's white count currently under control with medicene. Enclosed is a xerox of my poetic impressions of the entire incident.

Also the big stack of poesy manuscript is for Larry Fagin, a note attached explains all.

You'll be happy to know I began Trungpa's shamatha practice one hour daily, started early August. He has me, I'm afraid, though I'm too poor to attend Naropa, damn it, I've browsed the catalogue(s) extensively with heavy desire, a thousand questions for Rinpoche, plus the Kerouac School looks delicious. But, alas, must work my way through dreary S.F. State and get my financial security, one more semester and a B.A. in film, hopefully graduating magna cum laude, then continue there for graduate school, but no more bucks from Father. My hope is for an M.A. to teach on Jr. College level and support myself, a place for my ass to sit with a roof and movie junkie habit sustained, since I still love making them as much as writing poesy, to hell with your and Snyder's anti-technology! This sweetly said of course. Anyway, maybe next summer I can visit you briefly in Boulder and get a taste of that scene.

Enclosed is latest collection, I've been writing daily and much good stuff out of no hesitation, your advice as transmitted all the way back to Milarepa's cup-ped hand, thanks, in fact I hope you realize you truely saved me poetically when we first met, since I thought it hopeless then, no one digging my poetry. Now I just got some stuff in Beatitude (the Kaufman cover), and hopefully that'll open up, plus you remember my moustached pal Peter Marti who drove us around last visit to S.F., he's been putting together readings for the various poets in his mag Birthstone, myself included, so I've had a lot of oral exposure, I'm writing on a flyer I designed for one reading, helped extensively by Dick Modiano, New York buddy on a visit, he's mentioned my name to you at several N.Y. readings, glasses, black hair, moustache, short Chaplin figure of grave intelligence.

Claire and I have entered an open relationship so with your next visit no more sneakin' around. At last.

My total love to you, I miss you true and wish ya here, ah, but sweeter maybe for your mystery visits outta nowhere. Dig you, Allen. And I've been losing weight cuz you mentioned my fatness (although you hurt my feelings). Anyway, until later

LOVE
&
AH,

Marc
8/23/76

Birthstone was an interesting local poetry mag, very well done. I had met one of its editors, poet Peter Marti, at San Francisco State University Library a year or so before. We both worked as Student Assistants shelving books in "the Stacks." Peter came around the corner to find me sitting down and reading on the job. "Interested in poetry?" I asked. He nodded yes. "Take a look at this," and I handed him Ginsberg's *Wichita Vortex Sutra*. It began a friendship that remains to this day.

Allen again came to town for a museum reading with Gary Snyder. We began from City Lights in Lawrence Ferlinghetti's VW bus, first to the Zen Center to pick up Philip Whalen and Issan Dorsey (transvestite hustler-turned-Zen cook). Allen showed me around the place, which I had never seen before, suggesting it was a good place to come and sit in meditation. It was advice I would be following.

I sat in the first row with them, pretty gassed by the whole thing. Snyder had a way of reading where he held up one finger rather like a preacher. It was unfortunately a bit grating, a little like lording it over the monkeys. Allen admitted this was true. In 1972, also apparently hip to this, Chogyam Trungpa infuriated Snyder on stage at a Boulder, Colorado reading by putting a meditation gong upside down on his own head with seeming drunkeness while Gary held forth. (Trungpa then put it over Allen's and rang it.) Perhaps because of this, Snyder had little to do with Naropa until after Trungpa's death in 1987. Some people just can't take a joke.

Allen said that Trungpa later told him that “he didn’t want his students to think [Snyder] was the finished product.”

We went to a party for Gary Snyder held in a swank house in the hills and hosted by an elegant mom. Her teenage son in black top hat offered Ginsberg some hash, which Allen made sure I got some of.

“What ‘til I tell everyone I turned on Allen Ginsberg.”

“You didn’t turn on Allen Ginsberg, you turned on *me*,” said Allen.

“And we’re all one”

“No, we’re all different.”

Harold Norse came up rambling to no one in particular. “You know I was involved with the cut-up [re: text experiments of Burroughs and Brion Gysin, Norse had been around], I’m a Beat, too. Nobody knows but they will.” I was actually shocked at how strangely raw and obvious this was. I’d admired Norse’s *Hotel Nirvana* quite a bit, but I wasn’t quite prepared for his personality.

I bumped into Snyder by myself on the way to the bathroom, ”You-you’re a visionary….” stumbling over my words. Snyder smiled, detached. “Thank you, thank you so much.” Later Allen introduced me and Snyder acted like he hadn’t met me 30 minutes earlier, a strange graciousness. There seemed zero chemistry between us, nothing to talk about.

Brad came and brought a queer friend. The friend showed some interest in me and Brad warned him off, “Careful, he’s one of those HEAT-erosexuals.” It was the first time I really saw Brad’s resentment, both of slumming heteros on the down-low and of me in particular. It hurt.

Norse got my number from Allen and said he wanted to interview me for this seminar he was proposing. “Get the best young poets.” He kept saying, and tried to arrange a dinnertime conversation. I knew to avoid anything after dark, so I agreed to see him in the afternoon. I thought I had some idea where his place was, but the MUNI trolley was late and it was a much longer walk from the stop than I anticipated. I arrived half an hour late, and now Norse had to rush out and pick up his car, but he was willing to look at the work. Granted, most of it was not very good.

Norse eventually wrote up this meeting.

this beautiful young man

This beautiful young man, just 20,
brings himself and his poems
lazily one afternoon
a half-hour late
recommended by a famous poet
who told me how good he was in bed.

His looks being superior
to his poems, which imitate his recommender
badly, I am kind and tolerant.
But in one poem he speaks cruelly
of how he enjoys "making old men
cry" when he turns them down.

"Ah," I say, "would you turn *me* down?"
And the little bitch does just that!
He's *straight*, he says, has a girl
and makes it with *one* man only,
the famous poet. I fly into a rage
and scream, "If I'm not famous enough for you
go fuck Walt Whitman and drop dead!"

San Francisco, 12.vi.76

First off, my "making old men cry" poem…

This is to Helen who has
an ass like Mick Jagger
blond young thing
a white crescent scar
on the left brow
Helen
whose letter is due next week
Helen
who is either oblivious
to my silent mental devotion, or knows
and is embarrassed
I suspect it
I record it now
so you black insects
can rub hollow
spines in applause of
my ESP
wait!
wait!
time moves like a crippled
Western Union man
towards my door
while my young meat
wastes in the bathroom mirror
my nipples
and black lamb curls
of pubic hair
sleek boy body

my lips
that call to gayness
and cause grown gay
men to weep in their beds
~~isn't that a cruelty~~ — no one gets what they want
Helen your name is Edgar Allan Poe
my body is in the mirror
I pretend I'm with you in the coolness
of white sheets
red organ of my tongue dips
into your mouth
ear
snatch
I am Adonis
I am a poet
I am holy and sad
and you outrage me
the letter is coming
the last white thigh of young girls
I see it!
iron ~~skulls~~ rats are waiting
in the mailbox!

Norse picked up on my (when writ) 19-year old vanity, but I was certainly not the mean boy he described. I later changed the line "isn't that a cruelty" to the more obvious "no one gets what they want" to clarify, but I'm not sure it would have made much difference to Norse. The poem had been written to a girl I had a lot of ambivalence about until she became unavailable. She wound up marrying a senator.

Allen had seen the poem himself and only remarked that "black lamb curls of pubic hair" turned him on. He also said that the "iron skulls" line reminded him of Corso. It should have. I had accidentally borrowed it and changed the line later to "iron rats."

Norse actually didn't scream anything, let alone about Walt Whitman. As I mentioned, he very briefly went over my work, told me it was like Ginsey but said it was ok, though, because everyone said he wrote like Hart Crane when he was younger. From the sound of the story, he'd told that one often. He then mentioned that he had to hurry out and pick up his car. He literally lunged for me and tried to kiss me. His breath stank of garlic'd luncheon meat. That's when I gave him the line about being straight and making it only with Allen. "You must get over your concepts," he muttered, still trying to get into some sort of quickie, an amazingly crude pass that once more suggested to me what women went through at the hands of men. I wasn't going for it and begged off. "Call me about that writing seminar," I said as I left. "No, you call *me*," he said, and closed the door. Nothing about Whitman or fame with just a nasty hint of self-righteous anger.

I didn't call him.

Later I heard from Allen that the event was quite the local gossip. "Maybe you should apologize," he suggested. "Apologize? For what? He grabbed me and his breath stank." Allen acknowledged that breath was a big deal. The matter was dropped. I saw Norse on the street a few years later and sent him cartoon eye daggers. Norse seemed confused as to who I was.

The following came from Neeli Cherkovski's *Whitman's Wild Children*, which I actually remembered as happening around the same time as Norse, i.e. not quite 1977. Regardless, this same line of "being straight" got me typed yet again. The alternative, however, would have been to be cannibalized on the spot, from the looks these men were giving, to say nothing of their urgency to compete with Allen. I now had some idea of what being an attractive young girl trying to be taken seriously could go through.

> The first thing Allen Ginsberg ever said to me was "You're fat." I answered: "And you're bald." Things were never smooth between us after that. I was not one of "Allen's boys." He told me, soon after arriving in town one day in 1977, "I have a young friend I'd like you to meet. He's straight, and he only makes it with me. Don't try to go to bed with him." When the young man came to show me his poems, he very quickly advised me, "I only make it with Allen," and then read a few of his offerings, lightweight reflections of Jack Kerouac's "Mexico City Blues" with a little Buddhism thrown in for good measure.

Well, they weren't all that bad. Two wind up in *Beatitude #37*. Neeli was right about the *Mexico City Blues* influence, although "with a little Buddhism thrown in for good measure" was like saying I was imitating the New Testament with a little Christianity tossed in. Even so, in a relatively short time, bygones were bygones, and Neeli was a friend. He told me more on Norse's outrage concerning me, with Harold apparently saying "…and he said I was a great poet!" Like that should make me jump into bed. Neeli also told me that Norse's signiture surfer cut was actually a toupée. Funny guy. I once saw Norse read his poem "I Am Not A Man," a good poem, which has a line about having "acne and a small peter." Very compassionate gay lib poem. Norse prefaced the poem with "This is not about me." Bukowski had already written that Norse, "a tinkertoy of a man" (probably about 5 foot 1) was also horse cocked. "Small peter" was not going to get the action for Harold. Of course, the compassionate and empathetic tone of the poem went out the window with that opening disclaimer. I also ran into Norse with Allen at the De Young Beat Exhibit in the early '90s. Allen rather cautiously reintroduced me by first name only. Still, I evidently bore no resemblance to that "beautiful young man" of some 15 years earlier. Norse hadn't the faintest idea he'd met me before.

As this is the first memoir of one of Allen's "straight boys," I seem to be in the position of explaining a few things.

Although there were many reasons to get involved with Allen, I think that there are some common traits. First, as Allen himself said, "everyone is just a little bit homosexual whether they like or not." I have found that, when necessary, I'll refer to myself as "straight, or straight enough." I certainly wound up having more than a few homosexual experiences outside of my involvement with Allen, but it wasn't until I read a Masters & Johnson report that I realized that so-called bisexuals usually have a preference, and mine was women. Until then, I felt I was supposed to conform to some sort of democratic regard in terms of the objects of my desire, and actually forced myself in that direction. That may be one thing that Allen's "straight boys" don't all share – but the part about being a little homosexual certainly does, as does the fact that most of us were at or near our sexual peak and here was a very non-threatening way to orgasm in a friendly situation.

Again, it might be strictly a personal thing, but there did seem to be some desire to be physically closer to father, or even to a male friend than the chill anti-sexuality of our culture permitted.

I'm not suggesting incest, but a Whitmanic intimacy of embrace that we are probably all starved for, men in particular. Or, as I wrote then:

sigh of father
                    wouldn't hug
          me lest the
penis touch

Finally, Plato's offering to Socrates, to "…learn all he knew." The straight boys probably all shared that one.

Cats like Norse never seemed to get any of this. It was just about consuming a bon-bon to them. They figured it was fame that made Allen a straight-boy magnet. They didn't seem the permission, the generosity, the genuine interest on Allen's part. They didn't see, that at least to us, he seemed some sort of saint.

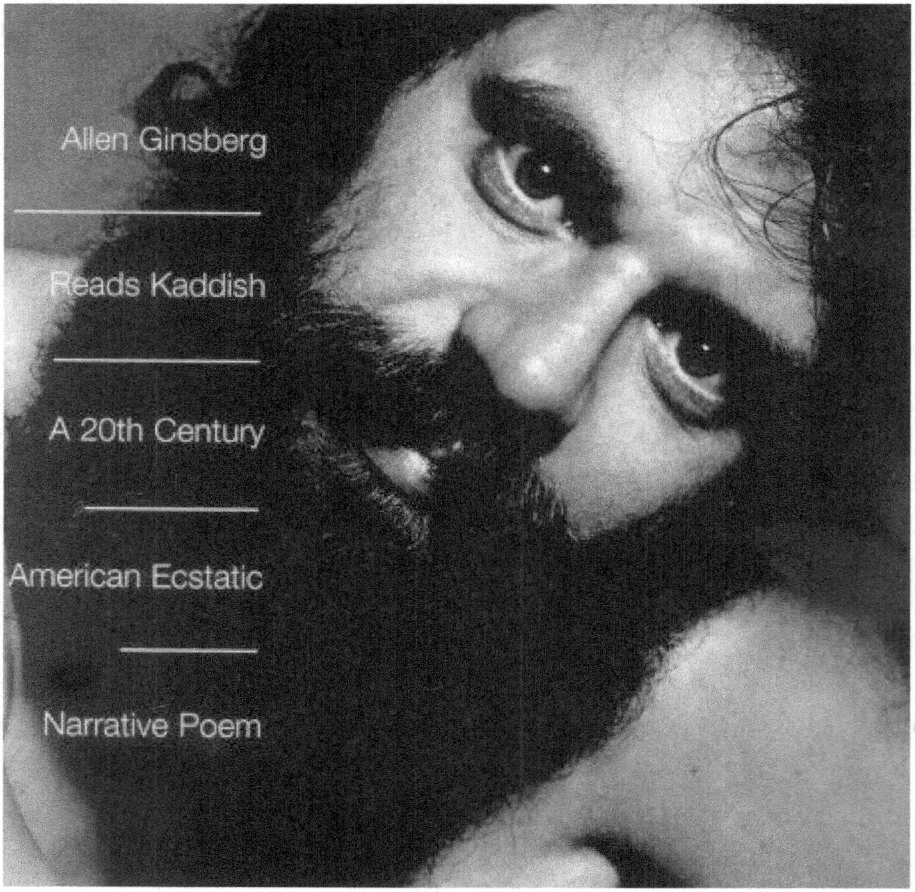

I came across this Richard Avedon photo recently and remembered how romantic I found this image in my youth. On the other hand, now I remember a near-mad, possessive intensity he'd get in his eyes while making it with me. Both are obviously true, perhaps for us all. But, to be honest, it also kinda of scared me then and it kinda scares me now.

Still, ambivalence didn't stop me from singing a cappella Allen's "Everyone's Just a Little Bit Homosexual" to my entire film class as part of an assignment. We had to present our film proposals, and I thought I could have Allen singing over images of Sammy Davis Jr. hugging Nixon, J. Edgar Hoover and a variety of other veiled or coded images of Americana. The film instructor James Goldner (who was straight) told me that rather than being a film of liberation, my proposal was homosexual panic. Not being strong enough in the face of such now-questionable logic, I junked the plan.

Dec 7, 1976
Dear Marc — I may be in Boulder Colo c/o Naropa the first week in Jan but I should be home at 437 E 12 St. Apt 23 NYC 10009. Phone 212-777-6786 after 5th or so. In any case if you're by yourself you're welcome to stay here, if I'm here or not, if you need a place in N.Y. Hope I'm there to see you. I've been with Peter Orlovsky since Oct. 10 at Vajradhatu Seminary in Wisconsin with Trungpa & a hundred others, sitting & practicing or studying all day. Just got home to N.Y. yesterday. How's yr. poesy?
Love as ever Allen Ginsberg

© 1976 the unspeakable visions of the individual
P. O. Box 439, California, Pennsylvania 15419.

P.O. Box 582 Stuyvesant Sta. NYC 10009

Marc Olmstead
380 A Eureka St.
S.F. Calif 94114

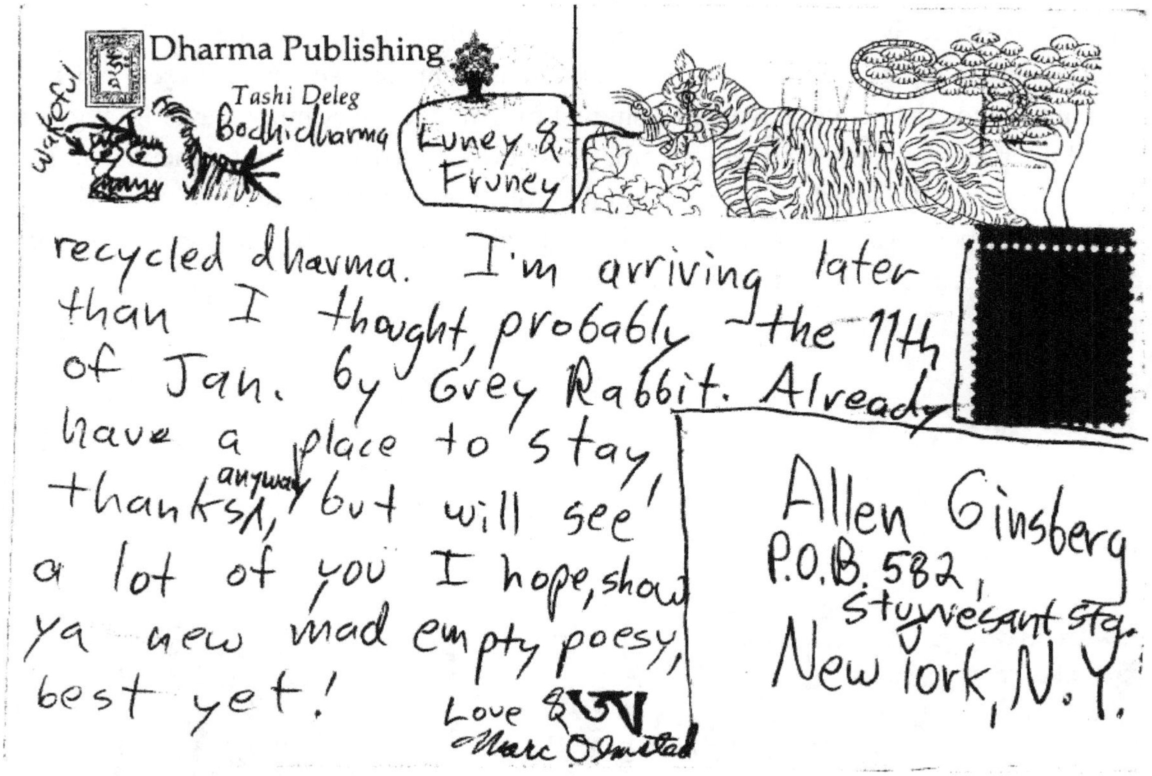
Dharma Publishing
Tashi Deleg
wakeful
Bodhidharma
Luney & Fruney

recycled dharma. I'm arriving later than I thought, probably the 11th of Jan. by Grey Rabbit. Already have a place to stay, thanks anyway, but will see a lot of you I hope, show ya new mad empty poesy, best yet!

Love &
Marc Olmsted

Allen Ginsberg
P.O.B. 582,
Stuyvesant Sta.
New York, N.Y.

And so I headed out on the Grey Rabbit, a hippie charter bus service that had torn out the seats to let you lie down and sleep on a big padded floor which, for anyone who’s taken a long trip on Greyhound, made all the difference in the world.

Part 3 – New York and Back

Road – woke dawn lone Texaco gas blink on the desert truck stop, bone waitress w/ blue lids- Chihuahua painting on the wall - Sand rain cowboys New Mex juke box diesel hum - The drunk wanted to eat her burgers - 1:30 A.M. Texas postcard scribble to assure friends of my lunacy - deer billboard Apache Gravel Mix –

It was still a very long trip on the Grey Rabbit. I surreptitiously jacked off first night in my sleeping bag.

The next day some girl flirted with me and I thought I was going to get some action. I woke up in the middle of that night to find her fucking somebody else in her sleeping bag a few feet away

The day after that some people decided to take acid. One girl looked particularly disturbed. What a terrible idea for an acid trip. Another, quite stoned, asked me whether I had been jacking off the first night. Everyone was looking at me. I think I said "yes." I was definitely not enjoying this ride.

ZERO DEGREES
sad in the Iron Ghost New York
dog blankets with their monkey tails
small black assholes

Don’t Hesitate

It turned out to be literally the coldest winter in New York City in 100 years. I met with my Aunt Marge and we drove into Manhasset on Long Island, where I grew up – I’d been born at the Rockville Centre Hospital in 1953. With me were old pal Richard Modiano, who now lived in New York, and a girl I had a crush on named Martha. I had actually brought my Super 8 camera to try and get Richard to film us having sex, though I never had sex with her before. I knew her from San Francisco and I wanted to make a movie about what you would see from the Bardo, the after-death state, where you would choose your parents when you saw them fucking. I was going to run it through this device at the Film Department which caused a kind of a color Xerox degeneration of image.

Anyway, it seemed a good way to get this arty wild chick to have sex with me, and the film itself maybe a good self-advertisement to generate a future of more offscreen willing arty chicks, but Richard also had a crush on Martha and wasn’t into it. Turned out she wasn’t either, though we did have sex. So began and ended my art porn schemes. Just prior the trip I thought I had some more venereal warts on my cock which the urologist had burned off previously, so I tore them off my shaft. Probably not a good idea for anybody but they didn’t come back. Still, I later obsessed that I might have given them to Martha anyway, wondering if I should bring it up – little knowing that years later they would later be regarded as a cause for cervical cancer. My father-confessor Richard thought it was probably ok. By the time I slept with Allen, worry had faded.

Anyway, my friends and I were stoned and Uncle Jack drove into Long Island as I scribbled in my notebook.

back to first town
babe town
first knowledge of
death, bee sting
instructions from
the Eye Box
snakey
young, hidden
naked
prank games of
cock
white smoke heavenly
death past the
winter trees
Aunt talking death
blue auto view of
N.Y. unfolding
over the bridge
roar
buzz of grating
under wheels
yellow air
train overhead
slow grey worm
of metal
Happy Bear Sign announcing
mysteries of
my childhood

Martha jerked when I touch her knee. "Mother's isolated in Tucson," she said. Uncle Jack said I'd be surprised when I saw where I once lived – how much smaller both houses would look. As he had a kind of lecturing style, I was annoyed when he was right.

first house here-
. railfoad tracks behind
father ran out
with a flaming
fry pan
now the later house
hill I slid down

& slammed
head, basement
fell
down the stairs
there garage the 20 year boy
gassed himself
for homosexuality
back porch brother went
to army from
"take a picture
heat up the flash"
brief forms
brief forms

I also visited the Museum of Natural History, which was a major experience repeated many times in my childhood.

green boned radium
Tyrannosaur
crucifixion tooth
that later
pierced me
stood here age 4
gaping at the primal
Kali secret
Father was my lover then
alert for his boy's
ecstasy

As a kid, my relationship with my Dad had a kind of psychic incest - I became his companion as Mom turned increasingly away in drink. I have no memories of him touching me improperly, but I believe I was acutely aware of his sexual frustration with my mother and it scared me. I couldn't even access that fear for a very long time. What this may have had to do with my relationship with Allen will be up to somebody else to figure out.

Allen invited me to see Burroughs.

As you may know, Burroughs' residence at 222 Bowery was nicknamed the Bunker. It was a converted YMCA, and had literally no windows. The walls were painted white with tiny minimalist art like old colleague Brion Gysin's; the door was shiny steel. I thought it was definitely a great space and safe shelter, then and now. Various young cats were hanging out with Bill at a big table like you'd see in a conference room, like James Grauerholz, his longtime secretary and now-platonic companion. I have dim memories that I may also have met Victor Bockris, hip journalist, and Raymond Foye, hip editor. Burroughs was extremely gregarious in this environment – a few drinks in him, some weed, and he was a hilarious story teller.

I told Burroughs that I had a dream about him where his face was covered with tattoos like Quequeg in *Moby Dick,* and was wearing a Hawaiian shirt like Hunter S. Thompson, and also looked like a sort of half-Thompson, which was not a stretch. In the dream, he told me he was a master of Peruvian magic. Burroughs didn't seem to like the Thompson part, scowling slightly as I told it, but then leaned forward and said, "I *am* a master of Peruvian magic, my dear." At another point he just leaned on his hands and gazed at me, openly appreciative. I felt like a young boy at the swimming hole – which was slightly unnerving when around Burroughs.

I told Burroughs about this great sci fi movie I had seen that reminded me of his work - *They Came From Within* - where man-made parasites (looking like a cross between a penis and a bloody shit) turned you into an insatiable sexual zombie. It was actually David Cronenberg's - who would later make *Naked Lunch* some 15 years later - first feature. Burroughs presented me with a signed copy of a recent chapbook.

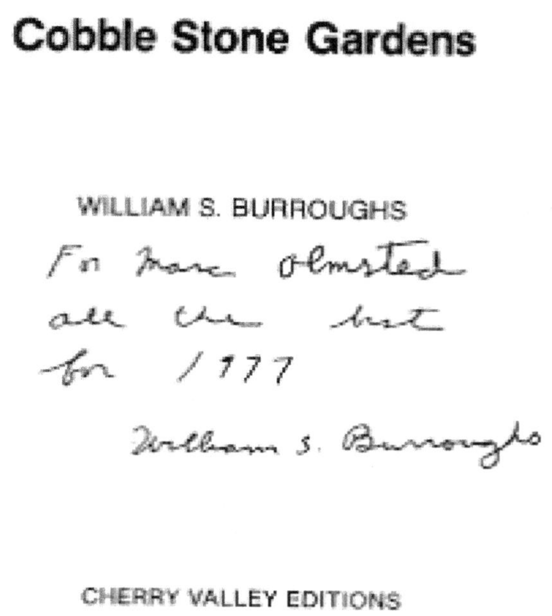
Cobble Stone Gardens

WILLIAM S. BURROUGHS

For Marc Olmsted
all the best
for 1977

William S. Burroughs

CHERRY VALLEY EDITIONS

As we began slowly gathering ourselves to leave, I had the sudden idea to use Burroughs as the subject for my rephotography experiment. I talked to James Grauerholz out of Bill's earshot and asked what he thought. James went off to Bill and came back with a positive from Bill. We'd meet for breakfast at a diner the next day and shoot Bill walking around the neighborhood.

So the next morning, I went to the diner and got to bring Richard, previously denied when I attempted to wrangle him an invitation to the Bunker from Allen. Besides my Bauer Super 8, I was also armed with a primitive cassette tape recorder.

We met at the breakfast joint, and Bill was considerably more reserved, stiff and looked a little hungover. Still, he was friendly in an otherworldly sort of way. He was also most definitely a good sport.

I turned on the cassette player, thinking I'd use it for background to the film. Our discussion turned to film itself, and I made some mention of Godard's maxim that every shot was a moral statement.

"To move the camera or not to move the camera," said Bill.

"Right," I answered.

It turned out to be the only remotely legible section of the entire tape, which was mostly a cacophony of restaurant background noise. I later used these two sentences as a loop for the film, though there were only a few mortals who could recognize the words. Basically, Bill then took a walk around the neighborhood and I filmed him.

Later I intercut the rephotographed footage with fragments shot off the TV from *Monster Zero*, *From Russia with Love,* and *White Heat*. I also shot some peep show gay porn right off its rear-projected screen where fellow film student Craig Baldwin worked. Some cruising cat wanted to join me in the booth. That Film Department device I mentioned: you spooled the Super 8 through and it would show up as a TV image, a sort of pre-VCR device the industrial world used that would allow cheap screenings of Super 8 training films. I had been introduced to this device by Craig (he was later to make the great *Tribulation '99*), because it allowed all kinds of crude rephotography off the TV screen, going in for close-ups on what was originally a full shot, and filming 2nd and 3rd generations of Super 8 footage – Craig had also introduced me to Martha. Craig had a big influence, cementing an interest in found footage and deconstruction of image. He once took me to *Texas Chainsaw Massacre* for my birthday after first blindfolding me.

Blue first Burroughs walk?
saucer-ray-crowd water
  gun window
        fence
saucer take-off

walk
flare
spider face-end

-- found poem of my own scribbles: how to edit my film *Burroughs on Bowery.*

I finished the work print in my graduate film production class, having a terrible contest of wills with instructor-filmmaker Karen Holmes. She gave me a C in the class and a D in the one unit lab, basically because I wouldn't do what she said. I had been used to a great deal more freedom and empathy in my undergraduate years. They were the worst grades of my entire film school career.

Before I left New York, my prostate was acting up, which meant I had what appeared to be symptoms of a urinary infection. These had been frequent in my history of prostatitis – but at least weren't sexually transmittable. I went to the free clinic for a prostate massage, but nobody really knew how to do it like my urologist in San Francisco, which meant that one had to press the bulb just so and it would release the built-up fluid that was swelling in it, fluid that should have been released through the walls of the gland if it weren't scarred. I couldn't even do it myself. More info than you wanted, I'm sure. Anyway, I loosened my ass for the doc at the free clinic and made some grunting noises as he entered with his finger. He was gay and later asked some questions related to my getting fucked. When I told him I had never been fucked, he almost couldn't believe it, after my little doggy-style demonstration. He said I had no urinary infection and wouldn't give me any antibiotics. He also said that whatever I tore off my cock shaft, they couldn't have been venereal warts. Sci fi man-made parasites, perhaps? I wound up cadging some antibiotics off Richard's landlord. They didn't help, as the doctor has predicted.

fucked myself up
the ass with
a finger
white flash
in chest
but I still looka girls
scared to lose em
if I opened my ass
to the feelings
of men

As for fucking Allen, my own increasing preoccupations with Aleister Crowley, 19th

Century mad genius sorcerer, gave an occult patina to our time in the bedroom.

entered him, soft buttocked,
    whiteness of back
        to the beard tufts
    grey, cock in him –
I am allowed my
  ancient breasted self of
BAPHOMET [1]
        giant prick erect
            in its own asshole

I took the Grey Rabbit back to San Francisco without event.

From reading Trungpa as well as sitting occasionally at the local center, I was aware that the head of Trungpa's Karma Kagyu lineage was the 16th Karmapa.

Werner Erhard's est [Erhard Seminar Training and Latin for "it is"] was one of the more popular of the so-called "human potential movement" of the 70s, and actor friend John Pratt told me that est Graduates (which he was) and their friends were allowed to come to a special presentation est was hosting of the Karmapa's Black Crown ceremony.

This ceremony had literally been done for centuries, as it was said that the Karmapa reincarnated again and again and performed it, placing a traditional black crown on his head while entering into a deep samadhi as the Bodhisattva of Compassion, Chenrezig. It was also said that the very sight of this ceremony guaranteed eventual enlightenment. I was particularly excited because I knew the Karmapa was coming to Ft. Mason and this would be a considerably smaller group. To my absolute shocked delight, Trungpa, on his way into personal retreat, made an unannounced surprise visit. He was hilarious and apparently once again under the influence of alcohol. "Werner is an excellent salesman. He promises you everything and he promises you nothing." He went on, "You Americans are always searching for enlightenment, satori, nirvana. I believe you in est call it 'it.' Well, you've been had. There's nothing to attain." He leaned over to Erhard who shared the stage with him and tugged on his arm, "Ladies and gentlemen, have you met Werner Erhard?" He actually had the est graduates laughing, which in itself was amazing to me. He was dismantling everything.

Years later I recalled the words of the great Zen master Dogen from his *Moon in a Dewdrop*: "Just understand that birth-and-death is itself nirvana. There is nothing such as birth and death to be avoided; there is nothing such as nirvana to be sought. Only when you realize this are you free from birth and death."

1 BAPHOMET: hermaphroditic god of the Knights Templar, depending on whom you believed, including the part about their homosexual rites in worship of that deity.

Trungpa went on to lecture them about what they were going to see in the ceremony. The Karmapa and his monk retinue came on stage and Trungpa sat in an office-style swivel chair. He visibly swayed on the chair while the monks chanted, and from their glances, they appeared astonished to see his apparent drunkenness. But when the Karmapa lifted the Black Crown to his head, Trungpa sat ramrod straight and completely still. Werner informed us that we could come up for a blessing and receive a protection cord. He said we should make an offering of something we considered valuable, money not being necessarily what was required. I almost gave away the poetry notebook I had written in extensively, but decided it would be worthless to him. Instead, I gave the finger cymbals I carried (for mantra chanting purposes in imitation of Allen). The red cord that went around my neck was unusually thick, as I would come to know from similar events over the years. I finally cut it off in a cocaine depression in 1980, but couldn't part with it. I have it to this day.

Somehow I also decided to see Kalu Rinpoche when he passed through San Francisco, probably because he was going to do the Invocation of Mahakala, and I knew this was a very significant Kagyu protector. I had hoped that Barbara, a cheerleader blonde-type and my current crush from film school, would join me on this safari, but she had zero interest. So I went alone, stoned. Kalu Rinpoche was incredibly ancient and skeletal, with close-cropped grey hair. I found the whole thing completely bewildering – what did this have to do with the sitting practice I sporadically did? I tried to visualize the face of Mahakala over the ceremony, but this didn't seem correct or even advisable. I knew nothing of the visualizations that were done with these practices. The ceremony itself was full of the Tibetan *sturm und drang* that I loved – the bells, the drums, the horns, the cymbals. *Something* was clearly happening. At the end, they gave me another protection cord. I visited Claire who was appalled I had yet another piece of red string around my neck. The thicker cord I had received from the Karmapa was already getting grimy. Claire did a little impromptu ceremony, "Nothing will happen negative when I remove this," and she snapped the thread from my throat.

April 12, 1977

HOTEL BOULDERADO

P.O. Box 319, 2115 13th street, Boulder, Colorado 80302
(303) 442-4344

Dear Marc — Poems are fine, all of a piece one season — fewer vague referential weak spots + seams than before.

You ought maybe go on + allow yrself a little longer straightforward narrative, to get out of the impressionistic confusion the style or mode Kerouacky whops up.

Have you tried recently writing very Classic Rhymes? — Campion, Wyatt, Dylan songs? I've finished reading thru Wm Blake (did I think I told you?) + writing long poem.

Dont worry about sex, I've kind of loosed hold of that obsession or thru meditation it's become more transparent + nothing to "cling to" as stereotype goes.

I shd. be in S.F. ~~then~~ May, in and out working reading preparing book for City Lights —

I'll send sheaf of poems to New Directions see if they want some for Annual.

OK — love forever + clearer
Easy Allen.

...forgiveness personality then blasted
in sister's leukemia atom, Father's
grim Willy Loman Lear insistence at bending
my head to his twisto kaima, Mother searching
for marijuana eyeballl, help+ lover going
help TV won't do, help! give up?
surrender to <u>Mars Needs Women</u>?
or the morning Times talking about a Jimson weed bad trip
of voodoo hallucinoids?

what bodhisattva, what grass high
what Tim Leary lost in space?

from PINHEAD
by Marc Olmsted
— 1976

Tim L. Lost in space line is striking ending — more definite than usual.

May 14, 1977 - Allen was reading at the outdoor Greek Theater in Berkeley with Robert Bly. I got stoned and came along. We walked around the circular rings of the place in the bright sun of the afternoon. I took his hand for a while, feeling very "out of the closet" doing it in front of so many people, but Allen asked me to stop. "It's actually embarrassing," he said, which I was quite wounded by, though in hindsight Allen walking around holding the hand of boyfriends (particularly when it was important they were "straight") was not a habit of his. I shrugged it off. He introduced me to Tom Clark, hot on the heels of his interview with Allen that had talked over an outrageous and scandalous party with Trungpa and poet W.S. Merwin. The skinny was that Trungpa might be out of control, despotic, possibly insane – though little had actually happened other than his apparent command over everyone and his wild drunkenness. Kenneth Rexroth put a blurb on the back of Clark's small press book *The Naropa Poetry Wars* to the effect that "we didn't need another Alesiter Crowley in the 20th Century." To which I thought, better two than one. Clark wanted a public debate with Allen on the subject, but Allen thought Clark just wanted to further his own career. Naropa would be denied funding and accreditation over the highly publicized incident, due ironically, at least in part, to whom Allen was reading with that very day - Robert Bly's big mouth – who hadn't even been there. The reading was memorable, remembering how he had everyone chant "Ah" and taught them all to sit.

So Allen came into San Francisco once again, reading with my old pals Harold Norse and Neeli Cherkovski, as well as John Rechy, Dennis Cooper, and some poets I didn't know.

I arrived with Allen, and a woman rushed up to him saying the C.I.A. was after her. She actually looked well-dressed and sane enough that the C.I.A. *could've* been after her as far as I could tell, but Allen told her she should meditate and cut through her own projections. I obviously wasn't on speaking terms with Norse, but I was still unaware of his poem about me. I *was* talking to Neeli, in fact never stopped, but I also didn't know what he was going to write about me. It seemed mild compared to Norse. Dennis Cooper had not yet entered his splatterpunk period of books like *Frisk*, where fantasy murders of male hustler are routine. Instead, he read one poem I particularly remember about public restroom sex with David Cassidy. Allen got the address of Cooper's *Little Caesar* poetry mag, but it was one I couldn't get into. I had read John Rechy, and enjoyed him as a kind of topgrade porn. *The Sexual Outlaw* was a little too high-falutin' but still of interest, along the lines of deceased rapper Tupac Shakur saying "thug life" was revolutionary (don't shoot me). Rechy dressed in tight denim like an aging hustler who shopped from a Tom of Finland catalog.

Peter Marti decided to go to Naropa for the summer and study. I got a letter from him that he made it with Allen. It bummed me out. [Peter's memory is that I set the whole thing up – I probably did.] To my surprise, Claire actually comforted me. "{Allen} still cares about you." She was right.

In 1977 I became aware of punk rock. First it was showing up in the media, mocked and regarded as the equivalent of Tiny Tim, that ukulele strumming freak of some years earlier who crooned in a falsetto voice and looked like he was genuinely nuts with long straggly hideous hair and powdered face. On *60 Minutes*, Mike Wallace croaked "This is punk rock." A video camera made no effort to balance the sound for the Sex Pistols, so guess what? They sounded awful. But it was all so intriguing, with *Time Magazine* showing someone wearing a suit with raw streak sewn all over it. What was up?

I asked Allen when he was in town again. "There seems to be something to it," he said. He'd already given V. Vale a check for $100.00 to help start his punkzine *Search & Destroy*. I think we even ran into the cat in North Beach right around that time, maybe the night of that very question, perhaps sparked by Vale's appearance and Allen telling me what he'd done.

Allen took me to a daytime party at Herbert Gold's. I was wearing a ragged leather jacket that was literally falling off me. Some journalist asked Ginsberg about the rumor that he had a son. "Here's my son," Ginsberg gestured to me. "In tatters." The journalist gave that predictable "is he really?" look that I was really beginning to enjoy. I wound up having an interesting talk with Michael McClure about Billy the Kid, a figure prominent in McClure's mythos and in his play "The Beard" in particular. We talked about who'd played Billy in the movies, and who was the best choice both mythically and realistically. We liked Jim Morrison for myth, Michael J. Pollard for realism. McClure then asked me about Bruce Conner, who was currently teaching in my film program. (To McClure's credit, he didn't namedrop Morrison, who I later learned he'd known.) As much as I was profoundly influenced by Conner's found-footage collage work such as in *A Movie*, he'd met with us as prospective candidates for his class by giving the list of tedious apprentice work he'd require – the dirty jobs of scraping and pasting frame ends for editing and sorting scraps. It was of zero interest to me and he'd come on quite military about it – kinda like "Now listen up, maggots!"

So I said I thought Conner was an asshole. McClure became visibly frosty and excused himself. Literally the next day I discovered in the library stacks a passage in P. Adam Sitney's *Visionary Film* about McClure's friendship with Conner since high school.

Peter Marti gave me a radio for my little shack because I literally had nothing - no turntable, TV, nada… Anyway, I now had a radio, and by accident, since my tastes were jazz after the particularly fallow rock n' roll of the early 70s, I happened on a station that was playing punk rock. In rapid (I actually typo'd "rabid") succession, I heard the Sex Pistols' "God Save the Queen," the B-52s' "Planet Claire" (you can imagine my reaction to that name), and Devo's cover of the Rolling Stones' "Satisfaction." I could not fucking believe it. It was absolutely astounding – this music was totally about where I was at. In a funny twist, evidently Bruce Conner felt the same, and wound up making a found footage collage of Devo's song "Mongoloid." A further revelation was seeing the godfather of punk, Iggy Pop, perform on the Dinah Shore TV show of all things, where David Bowie served as a kind of translator. Poet friend Chris D. (later of the band The Flesh Eaters) had played me Iggy all the way back in 1973. The music was incomprehensible to me then – totally garage and crude. But *seeing* Iggy blast Mick Jagger from his place as Lead Shaman – this was not some imitation of madness, but the *genuine* Dionysus. I was thrilled to the absolute core.

I continued working on *Burroughs on Bowery*, finally finishing and screening it for students and faculty for the San Francisco State Film Finals. In those days, they would post how everyone voted. Three-fourths of students and faculty voted against including it. I was devastated.

In November, Richard Modiano, out from New York, hitched up from L.A. after visiting his mother.

> **From his journal:**
> **...**I let myself in and took a shower. Around 4:30 phonecall from Allen Ginsberg for Marc I answered and took a message. I told Marc when he got home and he phoned back and sd we meet Ginsberg at City Lights and should leave soon (...) At the Bookstore we met Ginsberg and with Bob [Sherrard] we went to the Savoy-Tivoli to meet Neeli {Cherkovski}. {Bob and Neeli were an item then – MO}. On the way we met Jack Micheline who drunkenly stopped Ginsberg to recite a poem. Ginsey listened patiently and sd "Better write it down so you don't forget." On the way over we talked about Martin Duberman's play about Kerouac which only Bob and myself had read, both of us thought it was bad. Ginsberg had read Duberman's book about Black Mountain College, good gossip but said {Black Mountain instructor Robert} Creeley had objections.
> At the Savoy Corso was there with Lisa {then-girlfriend – MO} who had {Corso's}baby Max on her lap and Neeli there too. Corso told about

> planning to kill Ferlinghetti and than deciding to kill Ginsberg instead because then he'd get national headlines; killing Ferlinghetti would only get S. F. headlines. Bob said we ran into Jack Micheline on the way over, Corso: "Yeah, what'd that asshole have to say?" Ginsey: "He declaimed a poem with drunken gusto!" "O, man spare me," answered Corso. Neeli had poems he wanted to show Allen, but Gregory wanted all his attention to complain about Ferlinghetti not giving him money for an advance on book sales, Ginsey should reason with him, make him hand over some cash. "I'm a poet-man too!"
>
> At this point a drunken Palestinian poet joined us with his timid girl friend. We didn't know he was Palestinian at the moment. He pulled a sheaf of type-written papers out of his knapsack and read a "destroy all the Zionists" (with heavy accent) poem. "A little too angry," said Ginsberg. "Where are you from?" "Palestine." "Ah." Corso to Palestinian: "Fuck you man!" Palestinian: "Who are you?" "I'm a poet-man like Ginsey here, better." Ginsberg stood up and massaged Gregory's shoulders, Max started crying, finally Lisa spoke, "Let's go home." We all got up to leave, and the Palestinian poet and his girlfriend stayed at the table. Walked to the American Cafe for late dinner with Neeli, Bob, Ginsberg and Marc.

I was sitting with Allen at the Savoy Tivoli café in North Beach when Gregory Corso showed up – I had followed his work in my teens and was thrilled to see him – but also shocked. Gregory was unshaven and most of his teeth were gone. Those that remained stuck out of the ragged jaws of a troll. His hair was a mop of near grey. He was telling Allen some gossipy story and appeared to be quite drunk. (From then on I basically saw Gregory in two conditions – drunk or on junk. He was much more docile on junk, natch – but tonight he was fiery with an obvious alcohol binge.) If I hadn't known who he was, I would have assumed this was a mad derelict that Allen was being kind to. In fact, this *was* a mad derelict named Gregory Corso. He scared me but I was fascinated. He was also hilarious, like a genius member of the Bowery Boys. His nasal accent was one of a kind. He cursed and it was the purity of cursing itself – "That mutha-FUCKA!!" and so on. At one point, I burst into loud laughter where I had previously been invisible. Gregory stopped his story, face in a scowl with jutting lower gargoyle teeth, eyes sliding to the side and eyeballing me like "who is THIS fucka?!" I was frozen like a squirrel in a kid's aimed slingshot. But mercifully, he continued.

> We sat in booth, me, Ginsberg and Marc on one side, Neeli and Bob on the other. Ginsberg told about being in L.A. last week and visiting {Bob} Dylan in Malibu. On Halloween Dylan and Ginsberg put on masks and

> took Dylan's children trick or treating around the neighborhood, no one knew who these characters were. The last movie Ginsberg saw was the "King Kong" remake. Marc groaned, "O Allen, why don't you see a good movie for a change?" "Like what?" "Like a Fassbinder movie, great German New Wave director." Neeli finally got to read his poem, Ginsberg thought "unmoving whales" weak phrase, poem too abstract, ideas not connected to sense perceptible world. Marc sd, "I like it Neeli." Neeli didn't care, wanted Ginsberg's approval.
>
> Meal done we parted on the street. Marc and Ginsberg went to Shig's nearby apartment, Ginsberg told me to take Stockton streetcar to Market St. and gave me a quarter when I asked for change from a dollar. Instead I walked down to Market St. through Stockton tunnel thinking of Dashiell Hammett--maybe it was dangerous, but nothing happened...

Allen and I woke up and went for breakfast down the street. Gregory showed up and told the entire story over again, clearly with no memory of the previous evening. Allen listened respectfully as if he'd never heard it before.

I went to L.A. for Thanksgiving with my family. Allen was also supposed to be in town. He had been talking about maybe taking me to Bob Dylan's to see the 4-hour film *Renaldo and Clara*, which Dylan had shot while on his Rolling Thunder Tour. You might imagine how jazzed I was. Wires got crossed and I never heard from Allen this time.

By 1978 I was steeped in punk. Peter Marti and I went to the Sex Pistols in concert at Winterland, January 14, 1978. Just as it signaled an initiation for me, it turned out to be their last show ever. I didn't realize that Sid Vicious not only didn't play bass on the great *Never Mind the Bollocks, Here's the Sex Pistols* album (it was Glen Matlock), but he could barely play at all, let alone under the apparent influence of heroin. At one point, he lay down on his back to play, shirtless torso covered in razor scars. Even as a great fan, I found the show was absolutely horrible. Quite memorably, after singing Iggy's classic, "No Fun," Johnny Rotten ended by saying, "Did you evah get the feeling you're being CHEAT-ed?!"

A letter from Allen asked me out to Naropa for a visit.

July ~~8~~ 12, 78

Dear Marc —

Trungpa + Burroughs are both around then — and July begin say Burroughs Can be visited across ~~street~~.

Spare floor in my apartment probably if need be, or spare or share bed, whatever

Bring Film, we can show it to Bill or somewhere. There are no ~~[illegible]~~ regular public screenings. Have to be arranged on the spot.

Peter's here —

School Ends Aug 20 —

Love
Allen

Get 2 day visitors pass from Naropa office when you've settled in — so can see Trungpa lecture Monday Nites. Regent Thurs. Nites.

Part 4 – Naropa

White light rods pour down on my face in the gas station toilet driving for hours Ritalin eyed…

I asked Richard to join me on this pilgrimage. We worked out a ride straight to Boulder from S.F. through a ride board at S. F. State’s Student Union and we headed over to the girl’s place, an upscale house on Nob Hill. She was in the middle of writing farewell postcards and this went on for some time. We tried not to betray our impatience and get off to a bad start. The girl flirted with some jocks that were at the place – seemed she’d fucked someone there last night and was feeling frisky. She tossed her hair about like she was profoundly desirable. She wasn’t, to either of us. The girl did have big tits, though, which she was extremely proud of. I guess for those guys it was enough.

From Richard’s journal:

> Well to do rich guy’s house but inhabited by this 20 year old overweight chick shacked with handsome jock boyfriend, couldn’t figure the scene, maybe a sponger fucking her for room and board or something. Anyway, while waiting Marc took out his lid to roll a joint so the jock smoothly moved in and offered to manicure the lid and roll perfect joints which he did and then picked out three joints to keep for doing Marc the favor. Burning a joint took the edge off Marc’s resentment. Now high I was no longer impatient to get going but I didn’t like the vibe or boyfriend or Carole [the girl]…

So the deal was that we'd trade off driving and share the gas three ways. Richard didn't drive, but I agreed to pick up his slack. Unfortunately, as sunset came, she announced in a Reno, Nevada hotel casino where we stopped for a cheap all you can eat dinner that we were driving through all the way. The girl wouldn't budge on this. We knew what this meant – we'd arrive in Boulder dead meat. She offered me some ritalin to help me with the drive, which she had a prescription for. When I found out the girl also had some barbiturates to come down on, I knew I could do it.

So I got behind the wheel, the neo-Kerouacian element not lost on me, but also not my style. Richard and I were both big on getting enough sleep.

I drove and drove and drove until the sand dunes of the highway started looking like smoke, sorta like those dry ice low hanging mists of a graveyard movie. Seemed a good time to pull over, as things were in general getting a little ripply. I wrote down the fragment that started this chapter about washing up in a gas station toilet. The girl gave me the barbiturates and I curled up in the backseat and conked out for about 4 hours. It was dawn when I woke, and I swallowed more ritalin.

From Richard's journal:

> Dawn on the desert landscape I sat up front again, Marc drove, Carole slept and we talked about desert sci-fi movies, *It Came From Outer Space, Them!* Breakfast at roadside café which I insisted on—they were popping ritalin so not much of an appetite.

Richard, totally sleepless, looked like a zombie, sitting in the front seat with completely red eyes, limbs hanging listlessly at his sides like a cut marionette. She asked Richard to sort rock 'n roll cassettes in a case, which he did with slow motion exhaustion like an army experiment – keep the soldier awake and make him do routine tasks. Record the results. The girl snatched the case away from him with ritalin'd irritation. I didn't dig that at all.

As we got closer, I saw that the girl was maneuvering us into routinely picking up the gas tab – we seemed to be going over what was to be our share. Richard and I had been taking turns paying; we both kept records of our individual outlays. At a gas station piss stop just outside Boulder we conferred in the bathroom about settling up the gas bill. Back in the car we made a show of comparing our records and then I mentioned it and she said we'd sort it all out. I had a bad feeling. We were on a very threadbare budget, pretty much down to the penny. Sure enough, when we finally rolled into Denver, as I stepped from the car, I asked for her share. "Your friend didn't drive," she announced, which now meant she didn't need to pay for any gas at all. I was livid and ritalin-fueled, now completely powerless. "FUCK YOU!!" I screamed as I slammed the door as hard as I could, seriously considering snapping the antennae off. I at least had the satisfaction of her driving away with a panicked expression. With that, we had now definitely arrived at the land of the Buddhist college. Right at that moment it started raining.

We headed to the Naropa office on Pearl Street. At this point, or soon after our arrival, I heard the sound of a Buddhist monk banging his tennis racket-like drum. He was walking on the street with some banner carrying locals, beating this inscribed prayer drum (skin stretched over a rim held in one hand) with a mournful, dirge-like rhythm. I found out later they were here to protest the plutonium triggers that were being built at the nearby Rocky Flats plant. This drum beat hung over our stay like the noise of a pile driver I couldn't escape on a bad teenage mescaline trip. It seemed to say: "Your grasping ambition and desire is useless."

From Richard's journal:

> The registrar had no record of any guests like us expected by Mr. Ginsberg, she couldn't give out his address without his permission. So Marc said through gritted teeth, "Then why don't you call him and get his permission?" She did this but he wasn't there, and in fact was not expected back until the next afternoon (yesterday as I write.) "I thought you had this all worked out, Marc?" "Oh God, don't get on my case, not now." He was still bummed by the gas rip-off, the ritalin edge grating, the disappointment of no Ginsberg so I shut up.

As a counterpoint to this, we ran into Mark Fisher, a poet Peter had brought back to San Francisco for a visit. (As Richard noted: "Fisher in a dirty sleeveless t-shirt and over-sized white cotton pants also dirty and cuffless ragged, barefoot but very confident") He recognized me and in a manic Steve Buscemi style began promising the moon to me like a Hollywood agent as to all the fantastic events I was about to participate in – a public reading with my *Burroughs* movie to be screened, psychedelic mushrooms in the mountains, hints at inner connections with Trungpa and his Regent which would open into private audiences for me. I had just been published in *City Lights Journal # 4* and *New Directions #37*, both with remarks from Allen, so I thought a lion's welcome would not be unlikely. Virtually none of Fisher's ravings would pan out over the next week, with the soundtrack of that tennis racket Buddha drum pounding pounding pounding like the Telltale Heart (or the Red Death holding "illimitable dominion over all").

He took us over to Allen's place who was out of town for a day or two. I arrived to see Gregory Corso vomiting over the balcony of his second floor apartment across the way.

Playwright Miguel Pinero met us at Allen's door. He was a short, pumped up fire hydrant of a man. He eyed me with suspicious Latino disdain like I was a fag. Years later he was portrayed as bisexual in a biopic, so go figure. As Pinero had already done time in the slam, his ex-con energy made him one formidable motherfucker. Ohhhh boy.

Richard's journal:

> So he [Fisher] left us outside the door of the apt. and sd to meet him at his place after we got settled. Short Puerto Rican with suspicious attitude answered the door, opened like a dealer checking for law, it was Miguel Pinero "Short Eyes" I recognized him, knew nothing about expected guests and called to someone inside, "Allen say anything about Frisco guys coming to stay?" "Yeah, he left a note on the table" and we were in.
> Pinero relaxed a little introduced his buddies Miguel Alagrin who I also recognized from Newyorican Café NYC third world poet, curly gray hair and mustache, warmly greeted us with Latin hospitality in contrast to Pinero, and then young PR Raoul who took after Pinero but warmed up later. So where was Allen? He went to New Mexico with Peter Orlovsky to visit Georgia O'Keefe due back tomorrow afternoon, Ginsberg's bedroom and extra bedroom for us, three bedroom apt. Pinero and Raoul had one bedroom and Alagrin had his own place, summer faculty—I figured I'd get the living room couch when they got back (but it didn't work out that way.)

Richard and I took opposite sides of Allen's bed, both probably slightly nervous about this arrangement.

Richard continues:

> So I took Ginsberg's bedroom for the night, double bed, looked at the poem in his typewriter, "Plutonian Ode" already several sheets in length, saw he was reading "The Jewel Ornament of Liberation" by Gampopa and that he'd underlined passages ("the preliminary step is to make the request with a mind bent upon enlightenment") and made marginal notes ("Clarify erroneous views, origins too") I laid out my clothes and took a shower and felt refreshed, (…)

Mark Fisher came by again to announce Anne Waldman was here. "Anne Waldman!" I shouted, and frantically brushed my hair, much to Richard's amusement. Anne looked like actress Charlotte Rampling both then and now. They could still be sisters. I went out to say hello. Alas, I have no tales of making it with Anne Waldman.

Allen returned in a day, and as Miguel Pinero was on faculty, he went on to his own apartment. Student poet Robert Myers came by and Allen juggled him admirably – I don't think I even gathered they were making it. It was clear Richard would have to stay elsewhere, which I quickly arranged through Mark. Peter Orlovsky lent a gentle motherly touch, "Hello, boys," he said with genuine warmth. We then had some sense we'd be ok. Tsultrim Ewing (in the future, Allione) came over, and Allen introduced her as his meditation coach. We regarded each other with disinterest. Little did I know she would become very significant in American Buddhism, and years later sat next to her elegant now turned-silver hair at a Buddhist event, though I was too shy to mention our funny early connection.

Richard got put up nearby (below Corso in fact), and I was introduced to Ron Rodriguez, an Elvis Costello-looking writer whose surreal microfiction had also made it into those same Ginsey-edited lit journals I'd just been printed in.

That night at a Naropa lecture of Tibetan lama Chogyam Trungpa Rinpoche, Gregory Corso came with an entourage of Puerto Rican poets (including Miguel Alegrin, founder of the Nuyorican Poets Café), the retinue of visiting playwright Miguel Pinero. They were all clearly not into it. Trungpa was speaking on the Paramitas, the perfections cultivated by the Bodhisattva, and when mentioning something about "continuous panoramic awareness," Gregory called out "That's me all over, Chogyie!" Trungpa, without missing a beat, replied, "Seeing… is believing." Trungpa then asked if there were any questions and Gregory answered "Yeah, I have a question, Chogyie." But Trungpa answered other people first and Corso started heckling him much to the amusement of his pals. Corso finally said "I'm splitting" and left with the PRs in tow. Then Trungpa said, "This brings me to the next Paramita, Patience," which got a big laugh as Gregory and the others exited.

Allen took me over to a party with Anne Waldman and Robert Duncan. I had seen Duncan read earlier, found him confounding in terms of what I was interested in poetry. In the room, I kept wanting to look at his one roving eye.

Richard's notes:

> I wake early and read "Weird Trips" magazine (the cover was by Bill Stout, [buddy of our mutual friend musician Rick Fagin –MO]). George [Scrivani] comes over, takes magazine. We visit Corso upstairs, Corso reads mag, breakfast with George and Mark after going to Ginsberg's but no one there so I leave note on the door for you (later came back and saw that someone had written underneath, "Marc, please sit on my face" probably [a male student poet who was after me – MO]

Allen and I walked along Pearl Street and ran into Brad at a café! I was quite surprised and warmly greeted him – it was a delirious moment to see him suddenly transposed there from San Francisco. He was considerably less friendly; in fact he regarded me rather coldly. I had some inkling of bitterness on his part, but I never heard that story.

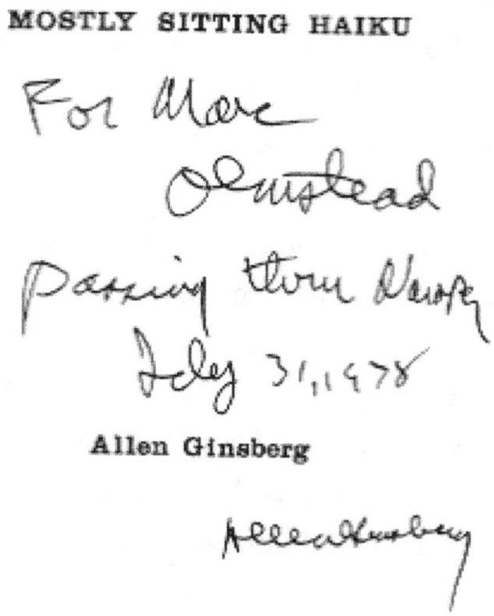
MOSTLY SITTING HAIKU

For Marc
Olmstead
passing thru Naropa
July 31, 1978

Allen Ginsberg

Allen Ginsberg

I dropped in on Corso's class a and watched with fascination as he lectured drinking a tall can of ale and passing a joint around (later I was naïve enough to think that was cool to try at my own university where I was a student teacher in Film and got into tremendous trouble for it). George Scrivani and Mark Fisher were the obvious darlings of the class, with George presiding as second-in-command to Corso. George was curly haired, bespectacled, bearded, a Jewish queer Christ. He was talking about the joys of public toilet sex, the "tea rooms," with incredible clarity and poetry like a new Genet, the surrender of being on your knees sucking cock in such squalor and stink. He then went on to extol the virtues of anal sex – "It's like a good shit," he said. Some nervous straight boy WAY out of his element said, "Yeah, but the shit's coming out, not in."

"In, out, what's the difference?" said George. The kid was speechless.

Richard's notes:

> Afternoon visit Corso's class (he talks about Ed Gein, "cunt in the frying pan" ["Weird Trips" had an article on serial killer and cannibal chef Gein, real origin for *Psycho, Texas Chainsaw Massacre* and *Silence of the Lambs* – MO]) We rode in the car with Mark and Gregory and they gossiped about some chick and then talked about the Ed Gein article that was making the rounds…ride to poetry reading at bar outside Boulder and hear Rodriguez and other student poets read, Corso went along for free drinks. Here we saw Ron Rodriguez' transformation into surreal madman at the bar when he read after working up his nerve with several glasses of wine.

In another couple of days, Trungpa's Regent, Osel Tendzin, spoke. A white guy, he looked like a banker. I was astounded at how closely he copied Trungpa's speech and general style. It was like an impressionist on late night TV, but even down to the three-piece suit, Italian shoes, and tie marked with vajras (ritual scepters). After seeing David Rome, Trungpa's secretary, dress and behave in the same way, I later asked Allen about it. "Well, they love Trungpa so much, they copy his speech. Like I do with Kerouac or like young poets who imitate me." I later worried that this might be a veiled rebuke. I hadn't heard enough Kerouac yet to realize the truth of that, until one time later Allen mentioned he was going to the dentist to "fix my mouf." It was straight from Jack.

Burroughs had this cool queer secretary at Naropa - not James Graulerholz but a new kid dressed in thrift store New Wave named Cabell, literally the quintessence of "skinny tie band" as the disdainful punks of the era referred to this refined look. I had never seen it before. Extremely short 50s hair, top button of thrift store collar buttoned, black skinny tie, natch, and a small lapel button like a Vote Ike sort of political button, only it was just a solid color with no words of any kind – a no-slogan button. Wow! This guy was one cool motherfucker. Here I was with my Jackson Browne hair and this cat was the next thing, like an alien off a spaceship or some warp into the future – the new X-man, baby! He also wrote prose that closely resembles Burroughs' cowboy porn of *The Place of Dead Roads* (as Burroughs would later jokingly refer to the dismal stretch of Highway 5 between Oakland and Los Angeles). Years later I heard he was a little tyrant at the Bunker, bringing friends home to fix while James Grauerholz tried to shoo them away. Our little tyrant apparently told James off – *he* was Burroughs' lover now, not James.

I later saw this cat read the homage cowboy porn alongside a female student - Simone, a breezy cool chick with much allure. Simone had a poem about becoming a prostitute. Also years later I heard rumors that she was actually turning tricks in Boulder. Everyone was hot for Simone except for Mark Fisher, or so he said. She was flirty but seemed to require *way* too much work to bed, that is, besides the money angle (which I knew nothing of). She was also rumored to be a consort of Gregory's.

Another night I hung with a cute girl student but she demanded that whoever might get lucky with her that night (and somebody was going to, it was obvious) had to first keep her company late into the morning. It was just too exhausting. I wound up in a room with her watching Pinero and crew play poker. I folded in her sex game to go to bed and Pinero won her probably around dawn.

Costanzo Allione, Italian documentary filmmaker and future husband of meditation teacher Tsultrim Ewing, was shooting what became a great film on '78 Naropa, *Fried Shoes, Cooked Diamonds*. Beat translator Nanda Pivano came along. She was the connection between Allione and Ginsberg, and had set up this meeting in Ginsberg's apartment. Allione was in Allen's apartment with his crew catching the conversation of Burroughs, Timothy Leary, and of course Ginsberg himself. Part of the time, I was also running around with a Super 8 camera making what would become my short collage *American Mutant*. Gregory came in with *his* 16mm camera and announced, "I'm gonna shoot everybody's feet." And proceeded to do so.

The film crew caught me over Burroughs' shoulder, above.

The new hip look came up again when this interesting (but less cool) queer had wrangled his way into Allen's kitchen to hang with Leary. The guy had a weird sort of glam look, like not quite on the money with it – but he was clearly not a hippie even with Prince Valiant hair – maybe it was vague eye make-up or his clothes, but it was some different quality that was glitter queer like the New York Dolls.

"What do you think of Crowley's *Book of the Law*?" he asked Leary.

"Not much," Leary replied.

That was interesting, since Leary had said in his writing that he considered himself to be carrying on where Aleister Crowley left off, and the queer had just mentioned Crowley's most important work. It was fairly clear Leary felt no need to be consistent about anything. Ginsberg made some reference to me being of the David Bowie generation, and Leary said, "He isn't Bowie, this guy is Bowie," pointing to the glam queer. Well, he had *that* right, and I duly noted it, even if Bowie had moved on to his Thin White Duke persona already – which was more like Burroughs' Naropa secretary. I wanted to be like Bowie or Burroughs' secretary, if not this glam queer, but not some old hippie, definitely, not anymore. This was also the influence of Craig Baldwin and Andover House, his post-hippie commune crash pad that had a lot of punk elements that were yet to be identified as such – armless mannequins, broken toys, color Xeroxes pinned to the wall – a gallows humor that was definitely post-flower power.

As for Leary's lack of consistency, Allen and I were talking with him and Allen made some reference to Leary's claim that LSD could cure homosexuality. Leary said, "Oh that was Ram Dass, not me." Apparently colleague Richard Alpert a.k.a. Ram Dass had once wall-papered a room with *Playboy* centerfolds and attempted to reprogram himself with a massive dose of LSD. Remembering how astounded I was by porn when on mescaline at age 16 (vaginas like the mandibles of strange alien fauna), I could guess this hadn't worked out. After Leary left, both Ginsberg and I recalled that Leary *had* made such pronouncements in the past, particularly in a *Playboy* interview. Ginsberg wondered if they'd done something to Leary's brain at Folsom, since Eldridge Cleaver had also come out of there as a "Moony," a follower of Sun Myung-Moon, the self-proclaimed Korean Christian Second Coming, and Cleaver later identified himself as a Republican. During Leary's Folsom stay, Tim started talking extensively about outer space travel, and in particular about alien contact, but dropped the alien bit very rapidly – a wise move, to be sure. Dolphin scientist John Lily had completely discredited himself once he began about his alien chats on LSD. Tim's new slogan was SMI^{2}LE, "Space Migration/ Intelligence Squared/Life Extension." He was also saying "Stamp Out Death." Burroughs was actually intrigued, since he saw little hope for the planet.

I think it was this same conversation with Leary about the *Book of the Law* and homosexuality that included one of Leary's typical quips that if Buddha was back today he'd be a molecular scientist or one of the Bee Gees. He also referred to Ralph Nader as an ecological fascist, which really bugged Ginsberg. "Now stop that!" he actually shouted, adding, "What does that mean, anyway?" Leary quickly backed down and said it was his position to be provocateur, not necessarily believing what he said, just stirring things up. A good gig if you can get it.

One morning I got up and saw Ginsberg and Leary both brushing their teeth in the bathroom mirror, both naked. Leary was tall with a basketball gut. He saw me and gave his characteristic conspirational wink. Tell me life isn't a dream.

I finally started to really physically crash from the Ritalin and profound lack of sleep that everyone seemed to run on partying at Naropa, with Allen at the head of the list. I was upstairs lying in bed when Allen came up and said, "Burroughs and Leary are downstairs!"

"That's ok, Allen. I'm tired."

"You're missing all the good parties," he said.

"What's the matter, you depressed?"

I *was* depressed, and hated that he could see it. It was one of those depressions where you know that what's going around you would be the envy of many, but it wasn't working for you. I really just wanted a girl like in the movies. That's why they call it *samsara*, or as my dad's favorite reference, "the vale of tears." Nobody gets what they want, Mr. Norse. Poet Amelie Frank later saw me brooding on a couch in a scene from *Fried Shoes* and said, "the little pouter." Bingo. By the way, Richard Modiano's in the movie throughout, way more than me, and he's probably one of the least ambitious people I know. More proof of Buddhism's sensible irony in a brutal world. Cue that Buddhist monk with the tennis racket drum we kept hearing all over the place.

Allen showed me a "Refuge Tree" of the Karma Kagyu Tibetan Buddhist lineage and explained how it was visualized and one did prostrations in front of it, the preliminary practice Trungpa Rinpoche required before one embarked on the "deity" visualizations of the Tantric or Vajrayana path. One had to do 100,000 prostrations and Allen was working on his. I was intrigued and impressed. Little did I know such practices would be required by my own teachers years in the future. Ginsberg also explained that at this level of the path, it was like marrying the guru, and if you felt you had to leave the teacher, you didn't want a "messy divorce." It was a very straightforward explanation of the Tantric vow with the teacher known as "samaya."

On another night, Allen was working me over sexually and I was just lying there. He suddenly said, "You're really lucky." "Huh?" He seemed a little annoyed that I got to lie there and be ravished because I had my youth and looks. Understandable. I was doing less than Paris Hilton in that sex tape.

Refuge vows are a formal commitment to Buddhism, and here I was in Boulder, visiting poet Allen when suddenly it was possible to take refuge from Trungpa (who resided there that summer), a totally unexpected situation and quite auspicious. Ginsberg encouraged us to take the refuge vows. Both Richard and I had to meet with a meditation instructor senior students who would determine if we were serious enough to take refuge (Allen arranged the appointment). Richard thinks it was Judith Zimmer-Brown. Anyway, she asked us how long we'd been meditating, who taught us, what did we understand about taking refuge. She asked us to sit on cushions and examined our posture. She thought my posture was *too* military (now that was a first) but still signed off on my aspiration for refuge. Richard was not criticized and also passed. Since our answers were satisfactory and our posture was correct enough she added us to the list and said we'd each get an individual audience with Trungpa who'd give us our refuge names. Although it may not sound like it, I had been relatively diligent with Buddhist sitting on and off since Allen taught me in '74.

Daniel Ellsberg (re: the Pentagon Papers) came to visit. He and Allen intended to go to Rocky Flats for a planned demonstration against the plutonium triggers made there. Remember the monk with the tennis-racket drum? He'd just gotten an early start. Allen intended to go sit on the railroad tracks doing his meditation practice along with Peter Orlovsky and a group of students, basically barring the train from entering the plant with its plutonium load. They would all surely get arrested. Richard and I talked it over. Who would bail us out? The idea was too unnerving to consider. So we chickened on that one.

A teaching assistant, as per Ginsberg's request, arranged the 16mm projector I needed to show *Burroughs on Bowery* to Burroughs. Cabell slipped on some white cotton gloves he'd picked up from an editing bench (this was the audio-visual classroom), prompting Burroughs to say, "Interview with the vampire, my dear." I struggled a little getting it threaded. Outside Burroughs apparently asked Richard if he smoked. He wanted a cigarette although he'd quit, and then Richard came back in to the room with the projector and said, "he's getting restless." Fortunately, I then had it and finally showed the movie to Burroughs, who chuckled enthusiastically throughout with his characteristic Renfield/Dwight Frye close-lipped "mmmmm, mmmmm, mmmmm." They say that closed lips make for a sinister laugh. They're right. "Great film, Marc," said Bill. The truly great thing was that I'd always thought the movie was very funny myself, but this seemed lost on virtually everyone who saw it. I remember asking my older brother if he thought it was funny. "In a psychotic sort of way," he had replied. Anyway, better to please Burroughs than the entire S.F. State Film Department. (In 2014, NYC MOMA requested it to screen.)

Burroughs invited me and Richard over to his apartment. He offered me a vodka tonic which I first turned down. He frowned so I took it. Gun magazines littered his place. We hung out, made small talk, sipped our drinks. Cabell was there too and joined in the drinks and pot smoking. It was actually a pleasure to talk in a low key way with the old man. I was just glad it wasn't awkward.

Allen was back by nightfall, even after being jailed, completely exuberant. "Busted again," he laughed.

As I have mentioned, Trungpa wore a suit and smoked cigarettes, as well as having a reputation for copious amounts of sake (so much sake that it killed him with liver failure ten years later). We were each to have a brief interview with him for our "dharma name" to be determined. Trungpa was rumored to have extensive psychic powers. Allen, Trungpa's student, told me to take a poem to him and I chose this one:

mind's bright suffering yammer
foolish Easter's
promise of maggots
suffocation bone,
blonde darlin -
the black leather
gloves of the
parking lot
attendant

I was proud of the poem and was ushered in to see Trungpa. He sat at a large obsidian block of a desk flanked by bodyguards, also in suits. Tibetan calligraphy in tiny frames completed a minimalist and spartan office that suggested a Japanese yakuza crime lord with his crew (though not noted until we saw a second run of *The Yakuza* at the Strand after we returned to San Francisco). "*Allen* told me to give this to you" and Trungpa grunted, unimpressed. He jotted down my name, poem unread.

So in my *American Mutant* film, now Leary was a CIA government official (when I had asked him to be in the movie he was doubtful until I told he'd be playing the head of the CIA), Allen some sort of Tibetan Mutant King, and Burroughs had already shown the proper way to handle a .357 Magnum borrowed from student poet Richard Roth, drawing "the correct way, not the bullshit way they do it in James Bond." When I tried to direct Burroughs a little more closely, he said "I am not an actor." Apparently he changed his mind, given the number of roles he wound up playing on screen, though arguably they were just about as demanding as what he did for me. Leary was even harder to direct – he kept looking in the camera and grinning idiotically. "That was great, Tim, but ah… could you not look into the camera next time?" Tim announced he *always* looked in the camera and smiled, it was a rule of his. "Well, if it's a rule…" I trailed off, obviously disgusted. "Oh fuck it," he said, and did it my way. I think I may have spared the directors who later used him (as in Wes Craven's *Shocker*, of all things – good movie; odd choice for Leary).

I tried to persuade Gregory Corso to take a part as a sci fi gangster. I had a .45 replica B.B. gun for him but when I talked to him he was very hungover, saying with disinterest "Guns are bad karma, man." I shrugged and his toddler son Max escorted me to the door, slamming it behind me while shouting "Get out!"

That night at the ceremony, I wore the over-sized suit of Peter Orlovsky and Allen's flower tie which I had admired in photos of Allen while I was still in high school a good 8 years earlier. In fact, here's a drawing of it, a cover for a Modern Lit paper I wrote as a Senior then titled ASTRAL DANCE THROUGH ATOM GRAVEYARD NEW YORK PURSUED BY SPECTRE OF MOTHER AND MOLOCH (- & I got an A!).

I received the name Jangchup Nyima, "Sun of Enlightenment" and tears came to my eyes. As I left, this guy comes up to me, "Your name 'Sun of Enlightenment'?" I nodded gravely, slightly irked by this intrusion into my holy and profound moment of having formally become a Buddhist (I typo'd "formerly" - a reincarnational flash). "That's my name, too," he said, which was quite unusual in the same ceremony. I was shocked.

Richard and I attended a party that night for the new vow takers. Leary, Ginsberg and Orlovsky were there and had also attended the ceremony. When Ginsey asked Leary what he thought of the ceremony he answered that "It was very beautiful." Osel Tendzin was at the party filling in for Trungpa. Ginsberg encouraged me to talk to him but he was being guarded by his entourage. Everyone got drunk and I ran into this guy again, "Ah, Sun of Enlightenment" and when I left the party, the guy's pulling out in a station wagon, waving from the window, "Hey, Sun of Enlightenment!" Trungpa may not have read my poem, but he had read the young poet.

When I returned, Ginsberg said, "Now Trungpa has inoculated you with his virus!" In other words, I could run from Buddhism, but I couldn't hide. Allen was right.

Ginsberg complained I hadn't come to any of his classes. It really was astonishingly rude of me. But my self-involved rationale was that I could always have poetry lessons with Allen so I used my free time to explore what else Naropa had to offer.

Leary came back from a meeting with Trungpa, expecting to be recognized as some sort of colleague, it seemed. Instead he was made to cool his heels in what he described as a dentist's waiting room, and when he was finally allowed to see Trungpa, all the lama said was "Stay out of trouble." Seemed good advice to me.

Then it was time to return to San Francisco. I asked Richard how much money he had left. He had none. I was absolutely astonished but I figured I had enough to split with him. Try as we might we couldn't swing a ride out of town, so we would have to hitch.

Richard's notes:

> It was the last night and I was leaving Ginsberg's after making departure plans with [Marc]. [Allen] saw me leaving and stepped forward to say good-bye. I thanked him for everything and he thanked me for visiting and for cooking dinner the other night and I reached out to shake his hand but he took my hand and kissed it instead.

I got out of Allen's bed in the morning and said goodbye. He opened his eyes, said, "Goodbye, Marc," rolled over, and went promptly back to sleep. I told Richard my feelings were hurt but Richard minimized it.

Richard's notes:

> Depart Boulder on city bus to Wyoming border. Ride from Latino who talks about Star Wars movie all the way to Rock Springs.

We did alright until we hit Rock Springs, Wyoming close to the Utah border. No luck. I bought a loaf of wheat bread and some bananas at a gas station venue. That's what we were going to live on until we made it home. We found an empty lot off the interstate, just dirt with tall dried yellow weeds, and figured we'd crash in it until dawn, smoking our last joint, which seemed a good idea, especially hitching. I also remembered the fake .45 I had for my *American Mutant* movie. If I'd been smart, I'd have ditched it. We'd already been rousted at one freeway ramp by a cop – motherfucker, we'd been lucky. He didn't search us, he just wanted us gone. Still, I wanted that gun and kept it. The memory turns my blood to ice. Praise the guardian angels of youth. Richard knew Rock Springs from previous Greyhound trips; it was a rest stop on the border with Utah. He'd seen the bluffs where we wound up sleeping from his previous trips and we retired there after the cop told us that it was illegal to hitchhike, that the fine was $200.00 or thirty days. "Do either of you have $200.00?" the cop asked. Then he said try asking for a ride at the gas station. We went to the gas station but it was already late. That's when I scored the bread and bananas. The next morning we returned to the gas station and Richard spotted this Native American guy and asked him for a ride. He told us to get in the truck bed. He drove with two others in the cab. They stopped at the liquor store and tossed in a six pack for us - we thought we had it made. When we arrived in Salt Lake City the driver said we'd certainly get a ride to Nevada before the day was out.

Richard's notes:

> Ride from Native American railroad workers… I get bad sun burn here; stop at railroad car and have lunch; It was a real railroad car with bunks for sleeping, painted a faded and flaking mint green, hot and fly infested and located on a side track that looped out from the main track. We shared their lunch of rice and beans and corn tortillas (no meat or cheese) and drank beers with them, stayed about an hour while they talked in Lakota or whatever their language was; ride w/Natives ends in Salt Lake City, Utah. Teenager gives ride to Bonneville Salt Flats.

Richard had started to char in the summer heat, his fair skin blistering and suppurating. He was the Hideous Sun Demon, man. A well-meaning teenager gave us a ride but turned off on a side road leaving us to hitch on Highway 80 in the middle of the Salt Flats. It was a no go, and some guy in a pick up who'd gone west hours earlier and seen us standing there was returning to Salt Lake City stopped and yelled at us from across the road that we'd never get a ride here and we should return to Salt Lake City, he'd take us back - which he did.

We began hitching at dawn with zero luck. Eventually I put Richard out of sight, which would get some pedophile to stop but then Richard would come lurching out, slouching towards Bethlehem with his running sores. The car would pull away before we could get to the door handle. Things started to look really bad for us.

We talked about jumping a train. Richard seemed confident that this could be done. I looked at a train passing on the horizon. The idea of trekking across town to try and catch a railroad car seemed a feeble plan.

I threw a fit by the side of road, ranting and raving, kicking this chain link fence. Richard looked on like a Hiroshima victim, silent and beyond flinching.

Finally, we got a ride in a van. Inside, a male nurse drove, a guy in a wheelchair where the passenger seat would've been, called himself Shaky Jake, a paraplegic Vietnam vet. They were born-again Christians. They'd also picked up some hippie. The hippie was bragging on and on about the chicks he'd conquered. He was extremely annoying, even more annoying than the born-again Christians who clearly had an agenda to save all of us. Richard and I announced we were Buddhists and fell silent. That meant the Christians would have to resort to Plan B – show us their tender mercies. The hippie asked Richard for a blue denim shirt, which Richard gave him. His name was Joey, and the male nurse went by the name of Rabbit. They took us through Nevada and put us all up in some cheap hotel with them. Richard and I immediately glommed on the complimentary food coupons and went to eat. During the van trip Richard recalls I analyzed the Naropa experience, exploring the nuances of Ginsberg's responses to me, just how important was I to him, what role did I have in his life, did I make a good impression on him, was he rebuking me when he answered, "Yeah, just like a lot of young poets imitate me."

Later I helped the nurse get the wheel chair guy into a shower, his urine bag slapping on the floor and whizzing by itself into the air. I noticed the wheel chair guy had some pain killers on the shelf and crept back in later to swipe two or three. I got up in the middle of the night to pee and found the nurse and the hippie in bed jacking each other off. It was fucking priceless. I didn't bring it up but I eyeballed them both for the remainder of the trip with a knowing "bullshitter" x-ray.

I was still exhausted and thought to pop the pain pills and maybe nod off until we were home. The pills did virtually nothing but the Christians literally drove us to my shack's door in San Francisco. Amen! Richard remembers my frustrated romantic summation as "Well, it was a completely homosexual experience."

Part 5 – Back Again

I'm a
James Dean Catholic
swallowing drugs
for the martyred
eye
fierce and numb
locked in the
body, inspired
crucifix fuck
machine death fuck
fucked in the ass
by Christ

In the autumn following the trip to Naropa, Allen breezed through San Francisco once again in a few months and offered to take me to see a video work-in-progress of *Kaddish*. I wrangled an invitation for my friends and so there were four of us crammed into the back seat: me, Ginsey, Peter Marti, and Mort Shapiro (still two years away from his debut as front man for the band Invertebrates). The other two people, one behind the wheel, I don't recall at all.

We arrived at a loft space South of Market. I was dressed in my black raincoat with broadbrim Shadow hat and Allen introduced me as "famous Italian film maker Marc Olmsted," longhaired Fellini kid I guess. The director, whose name I can't remember (and not sure he even finished the film), predictably reacted like "Maybe he is." I do remember what we saw was not particularly successful, and Allen asked my opinion when the director was out of the room. I told him and the director entered in the middle of it, eyeballs full of death rays. He demanded I start my opinion from the beginning. So I did. He was not pleased, and so then we left.

Allen had been invited to check out the Poetry Center archives at San Francisco State University. I invited Allen to come to the undergraduate film class I'd been teaching. I didn't tell the kids. We screened *Breathing Together*, an excellent documentary on late 60s phenomena by Morley Markson. There seems no way to see it on VHS or DVD, although parts were edited into Markson's later (and considerably less successful) *Growing Up in America. Breathing Together* is shot in black and white 16mm, and includes a great reading Allen gave of *Howl* sitting in the snow, very likely at his Cherry Valley farm in upstate New York. When the lights came up, there was Allen himself. I really enjoyed that one. The kids were blown out. Allen was very self-effacing, referring to his pre-Trungpa remarks in the 1971 film as "vanity." Then we watched my *Burroughs on Bowery*. Again, the lights came up, and Allen asked me if I'd "explained the Cut-Up" to the class, referring to Burroughs' technique of chopping up his own and others' texts to get surreal phrases like "dead fingers talk." It was, of course, completely pertinent to the way I'd used the collage of found footage and rephotography. Afterwards, a girl student came up to me and said, "When I first saw your movie, I thought it was shit. But after Ginsberg talked, I thought it was great." I could have used Allen during the Film Finals. I asked him privately if he'd liked the movie. "Yeah. Kinda fuzzy though. But I guess it's supposed to be like that." One of the beefs at the Film Finals had been that I hadn't focused the camera, which wasn't true. The rephotography had so denigrated the images that they began to blur. To this day I prefer it to be seen on a TV where no one needs to wonder if the projector is focused or not. I left the class with another girl student and ran into openly gay Supervisor Harvey Milk, who waved hello. He had celebrity status in town at this point and the student turned and said, "You know everybody." The truth was I had tried to get a job in his camera store on Castro Street only a year or so earlier.

Charles Bukowski came to town, and Neeli Cherkovski was one of his closest friends and soon-to-be-biographers (*Hank*). I had seen Bukowski read first at UC Santa Cruz 1972 in a tiny lounge to maybe 20 or 30 people. My brother had turned me on to his *Poems Written Before Jumping Out of an 8 Story Window* chapbook in 1968 when I was 14. I loved his work immediately. By 1978, the crowds at his readings were huge, and would get larger. Neeli had me at a party for Bukowski, but the only contact I had with him was when he came staggering into the packed kitchen. He looked at me and smiled through slitted eyes. I thought, wow, maybe he remembers me from that UCSC reading. Neeli walked up just then and said, "Hank, this is Marc Olmsted." Hank shook his head and said, "Jesus, I thought you were a woman."

One of Allen's most championed young protégées, Andy Clausen, threw a party in Berkeley. It was a wild drunken binge, and finally I left with Claire in tow, only to run into Corso just coming in. "*Who* is this *angel*?!" asked Gregory. Claire smiled, quite flattered. Gregory had not a word for me. I thought I better get her out of there fast.

But Claire was already reconsidering her options with me. What was good for the goose, etc. etc. I went to see Nick Ray, director of *Rebel Without a Cause* among many other great films, speak at Pacific Film Archive, and Claire came along with one of my better friends, musician Michael. Little did I know she'd already slept with Michael. She asked Ray which film he had the "most fun on." He leered at her looking a little boozy even behind his eyepatch, and said "I've had a ball, baby." Everyone laughed and Claire blushed. Years later it came out that he had been fucking teenager Natalie Wood on the *Rebel* set, and I remembered that look he gave Claire.

With Claire, I was beginning to have a sense of things generally swinging desperately out of my control.

I met a cat named Mitch Loch in film school – Mitch threw the most amazing parties – imagine David Bowie in Thin White Duke phase playing Z-Man in *Beyond the Valley of the Dolls*: "It's my happening and it freaks me out!" O.K., now add that Bowie's played by Peter Fonda. And remember this is Bowie's queer phase. Now you have Mitch in 1978. So Mitch throws a huge Halloween shabang – he dresses as Carrie after the pig blood's been dumped on her at the prom. I go as Iggy Pop. Claire came with me – I have no memory of what she dressed as.

I had one of those classic drug experiences. I took a Quaalude. Nothing happened. So I took another. Both kicked in with devilish force. A brief period of being vertical – so out of it I was bumping my ass against a lesbian to the music who finally said "Will you stop that?" I didn't even know she was there. James Grauerholz, was in town and dropped by. "You *do* look like Mr. Iggy Pop," he said. High praise indeed since he'd met Iggy (though I wasn't aware of that at the time, or much else). Finally I vomited (in the toilet, thankfully) and flopped onto the bed with the coats, where I held court for the remainder of the evening. I tried to kiss Claire when we left but she begged off, "Your mouth tastes like vomit."

In November of 1978 I was the sickest I'd ever been with the flu. Two weeks in bed with codeine cough syrup – long-suffering Claire was unsympathetic and barely coming around, if you can believe she hung in this long. So I was quite alone in my chicken coop shack like a dying dog with only a paperback of *Children of Dune*. I had plotted a timeline for my term papers and found now that it was impossible to complete what I needed to do in Experimental Film, as I was just too weak. I had essay questions to answer and I wound up making an audio tape of my answers (stoned out of my mind on weed at the very least). To my disbelief, my instructor Robert Bell, rest his soul, gave me an enthusiastic A and asked if he could play it for his undergrads. (Whatever happened to that tape?) When I had finally recovered enough to go outside, I dragged my carcass to the liquor store and saw a headline. Jim Jones and hundreds of his People's Temple crew had dosed themselves with poison purple Kool-Aid in Guyana, front page photo of bloated death. I went back in my shack as if in a bad dream. Then it was my birthday. I was 25. Claire didn't show – she'd run off with an admirer. It was clearly over. I crept out again in a couple days. City Supervisor Dan White had wigged out and shot Supervisor Harvey Milk and Mayor Moscone. I again crept back in my shack. It seemed the End of Days.

James Grauerholz invited me out for the Nova Convention in NYC, which was a big event for Burroughs. I was just too broke to go. It was a who's who of an event, though the no-show of Keith Richards apparently caused a near-riot. My own film, *Burroughs on Bowery,* was screened but the projector was for magnetic soundtracks, not optical, so it was shown without sound while writer Kathy Acker read some poem about "William is a good boy/William is a bad boy." I didn't know who Kathy Acker was at the time and was not pleased to receive this news from Mark Fisher. Now it seems pretty cool.

SATURDAY MATINEE

CONVERSATIONS

Host: Les Levine

Panellists: Timothy Leary, Les Levine, Susan Sontag, Robert Anton Wilson

FILMS CINE VIRUS II

Programmers: Kathryn Bigelow & Michael Oblowitz

Towers Open Fire	Antony Balch, 1963
Cut-Ups	Antony Balch, 1963
Car Crash	Eric Mitchell, 1978
Set-Up	Kathryn Bigelow, 1978
Gola Meller London	Seth Tillett, 1978
Circuits of Control: Table Conversation	Michael Oblowitz, 1978
Snake Woman	Tina Lhotski, 1978
Gordon Alien	Michael McClard, 1978
The End of the Film World	Amos Poe, 1974
Devo: The Mongoloid	Bruce Conners, 1978
Blood and Guts in High school	Kathy Acker, 1978
Burroughs	Marc Olmsted, 1977
Burroughs: Home Movies	Steven Lowe, 1976-77

SATURDAY NIGHT

PERFORMANCES

Introduction: Terry Southern

Phillip Glass — New Piece for Electric Organ

Brion Gysin — I Am That I Am

John Giorno — Grasping at Emptiness
Eating the Sky

Keith Richard

Patti Smith

William S. Burroughs

Claire gone, I finally decided I needed to get fucked in the ass.

The first time I was fucked in the ass I believe was by Peter Marti, then-young poet who has long given up such dalliances in sodomy, at least of men. We actually spread out *Penthouse* magazines in a mandala around the bed to help our visualizations. There is something grim, stupid, and typical all at once about this. Maybe even hot, but not by my memory. I got fucked but Peter yelped out with barely my cockhead in his ass, so my buggery wasn't going to be reciprocated. I wound up with a giant hemorrhoid, which I had never had before, so in typical Catholic guilt I feared maybe some part of my lower intestine has ruptured and was now hanging out. This thought from the same boy who, when he first ejaculated, thought he'd broken a pipe "up there" and some sort of spinal juice had come out instead of pee. Why I might have prostate problems in my mid-twenties might be clearer given these sex terrors.

Later I wound up with what looked like a venereal wart on my cock, probably unrelated to this particular romp, and decided to burn it off with regular wart remover. I still bear the scar of this atonement. I was now currently seeing a Reichian therapist twice a month trying to sort all this out, but I'd grab a tall beer from the liquor store as soon as I left his office.

One time Richard and I took acid and we looking at a book of H.R. Giger paintings. "That's what my prostate is about," I told Richard. He was shocked. "I didn't know it was that bad."

Part 6 – The Job

Mescaline/ age 13/ read all about it in Life Magazine
Ouija board/ Krishna Lord/ driving on acid in the family Ford
Made me American Mutant!
Made me American Mutant!

I'd heard about a gay bar called the Stud that played exclusively New Wave (which was the all-encompassing term, in 1978 at least, for punk rock and synthesizer-dominated bands) on Monday nights. "Breeders' Night," they called it – since straights were welcome. So those of us with crazy jobs, like my swing-shift at the State University Library Circulation desk, allowed for these night hours.

The amazing thing about New Wave was the permission it gave to absolute amateurs to get up and make music, regardless of any ability other than a child-like delight. This was such a profound antidote to the overproduced bloated rock of the mid-70s that had ceased to be about anything but a sort of Roman emperor conclusion to the excesses of the '60s. Suddenly there were garage bands and self-produced 45 r.p.m vinyl records that captured a raw new vision that seemed as real as the Beats to me. In its earliest days, there was absolutely nothing trendy about it. It was in fact a place for misfits and pariahs, and was generally met with contempt and ridicule by outsiders. You were not going to improve your dating life back then by being a punk rocker – it would be a couple of years before it was a staple look of clubbing chicks. What's more, bands like the Clash hinted that some sort of real revolution was even possible, a promise that 1968 had held as well.

But if you wanted to get laid, you were heading to the disco and listening to the Bee Gees. Camps were very clearly defined as to the music you listened to – which is similar to today except for the incredible melting pot of cannibalized sounds that were once stylistically and culturally at each other's throat. But it is obvious by style even today whether you're into reggae, hip hop, Goth, the Grateful Dead or the so-called "alternative rock." Visiting other tribes is somewhat more acceptable today than it was in 1978, however.

As a part of this evolution for me, my actor friend John Pratt decided to put on McClure's play *The Beard* at San Francisco State University. I was cast as Billy the Kid and an actress that looked like a drag queen (John's possibly covert intention) played Jean Harlow. We were in some sort of Heaven/Hell/Eternity. It was a play that had been busted for obscenity, in particular for Billy miming going down on Jean Harlow at the end. Pretty tame stuff now. My Jean Harlow had a crotch that smelled of old tuna fish through her leotard, so it was not so hot for me either. One of punkzine *Search & Destroy*'s premier photogs, Kamera Zie, took some pictures for our publicity – she was one of the people I had met at Craig Baldwin's punk crashpad, Andover House. John played the Dictators' cover of Iggy & the Stooges' song "Search & Destroy" to open the show. I came to the front of the stage with tight jeans unbuttoned to barely above the cock. We played a couple of dates around noon – so-called "brownbag theatre." John also cut the play's endless repetitions of the same lines (a writerly absurdist hangover, apparently) and this leaked back to McClure, whose agent sent a letter to John demanding that the play be restored and McClure be paid. John ignored both requests and nothing came of it.

Meanwhile, Peter had hooked up with some New York Naropa friends and was now shooting dope on occasion when he went back to visit. Corso apparently had something to do with the New Yorkers getting into it. As Vinnie once told Richard, Corso was cool, he was a poet man, Kerouac's friend, praised as *the* great poet of the Beats by Ginsey. He took dope so dope was cool, and what could be cooler than taking dope with Gregory Corso? I was going to join them, fighting depression and loneliness with Claire's departure, and booked a ticket. On the phone I said, "I'm rolling up my sleeves, boys." A young Candice Bergen look-a-like had seen *The Beard* and decided to have a fling with me. I sold my New York ticket and she immediately dropped me. I never did shoot up.

Not all Peter's poetic connections were so dark. He also introduced me to Bill Voigt, a serious Buddhist student who'd passed through Naropa. One night with a bunch of poets, we were all high and drunk and I was pounding on a drum leading everyone in the Hindu mantra OM NAMAH SHIVAYE, which was a favorite of Swami Muktananda. I remember Bill looking on benignly.

It was inevitable that I would address my own look in these newly self-defining times. I wanted badly to join the weirdoes I was seeing on the street, but I was scared – mostly of no longer having a sex life if I did. I mentioned to the elder gay hairdresser Peter had me seeing that I would at least like to get the bangs off my face. "We could give you a body wave," he said. I was totally naïve that this was a perm. He began wrapping up my hair in big pink curlers and I asked what that was about it. "To make it look uniform," he replied. I never saw a picture of what he intended, and when he was done I looked like Travolta's pre-*Saturday Night Fever* look in TV's *Welcome Back, Kotter.* I had the big wavy long hair of a '70s jock and my reaction was stunned horror.

I crawled home as if deformed and, remembering that the hairdresser had said not to wash it for 3 days, I washed it 3 times immediately. No luck. It didn't budge. I called my actor friend John Pratt and gushed out my dilemma. He summoned his punk hairdresser friend April to my chicken coop (coincidentally, it was also April Fool's Day, 1979) and she had at me with the shears. When she was done, I had hair like James Dean. My life was changed. I immediately went out and bought a whole new wardrobe that included black peg pants, Converse tennis shoes, skinny ties, and thrift store pastel dress shirts. I had majorly mutated! Fate had conspired where my timidity could not.

I caused an entirely different reaction on the street, sometimes positive, though when I showed up on MDA at a birthday party for Peter Marti's drunken sister-in-law. She laughed in my face and said, "You look like a convict!" It's now hard to remember that as recently as 1979, even newscasters had hair over their ears and collars.

I was already active in the local Aleister Crowley lodge, the O.T.O. (the Ordo Templi Orientis), thanks to corresponding with and visiting his foremost scholar and previous student, Israel Regardie. But in some ways this new look embraced an even deeper commitment to sex, drugs and rock 'n' roll as religion – something that Buddhism was not particularly compatible with. The O.T.O.? No problem, not when its patron saint Crowley had experimented with every drug known to man at the time and died at a ripe old age shooting six times the amount of heroin that a street junkie could take and survive. Jimmy Page, David Bowie, Ozzy Osbourne, and even now Marilyn Manson have all expressed devotion. Crowley is even one of the faces of the crowd on the cover of *Sgt. Pepper's Lonely Hearts Club Band*, shaved head in the upper left corner like a staring Mussolini. I continued with Buddhist sitting practice, but told a Naropa friend of Peter's, Vinnie, that "Crowley kicked Buddha's ass." I even changed my Buddhist shrine to a Crowley one, though it was destroyed twice when people closed my door too hard. I nervously remembered that Richard and I had done an amateur Buddhist ceremony invoking a Tantric protector when we established the Buddhist shrine. It would seem that my change of religion now was not going unnoticed on other planes as well.

As the O.T.O. suggested, I routinely kept a "magickal record" or diary of all my various rituals, meditations, dreams and drug visions. To give you an idea, here's a typical excerpt dated a little more than a month before my transforming haircut.

2/20/79
Went to punk rock night at the Stud last eve. Full of grass and booze had amyl nitrate which seemed to zap me into a kind of astral visionary space. I saw a bright golden dragon in my mind's eye that scared me, attempting to balance things by visualizing the six pointed star over my head. Later came home to banish. As I made the first pentacle in the East, saw a skull rush at me but stopped by the pentacle as if behind glass. Nonetheless it stayed. I chose to ignore it and went to sleep.

Allen was also not particularly happy about the change, and gave me a fair amount of shit about it. Still, when Dylan converted to born-again Christian for a year or two, Allen said it was the Blakean Christ Dylan was embracing. I had no such luck with his opinion. Many years later he'd mention that filmmaker friend Harry Smith was high up in the ranks of the O.T.O. "Grand Dragon" said Allen, half-seriously – there was no such post. I reminded him of my younger days and how much grief he'd given me over Crowley. "Well, do you think that it helped you?" he answered. Reflecting back, I was hard-pressed to say yes, and instead said nothing.

As for 1978, the drugs were changing, too. Quaaludes, amyl nitrate, and cocaine were regular parts of my new punk appetites. Not surprisingly, my tastes were also getting more pansexual. I was going to bed with queer friends when the mood struck.

These harder drugs were not without their consequence for any of us. One night, Peter and I went to the Stud. Some guy handed us a joint and I took a small hit. Peter, however, blasted it. "What was that?" he asked the guy. "Angel dust." At that moment, Peter said he saw the words ANGEL DUST written in the air above him. He immediately became violently ill and rushed into the bathroom. All the stalls were closed, and Peter said he pushed open one to find this guy sitting on the toilet. Peter barfed on the guy's shoes and collapsed on the floor.

Eventually Lisa, this chick we knew (a brief fling for me and later astonishingly huge disco queen in Japan and Europe), came looking for me and reported on Peter's dire condition – we would have to get him home. Peter drove a candle van for this cat named Michael – I even worked some days with Pete (we'd get drunk on beer at lunch) – you know those candles you see in the supermarket, that special display? Well, dig, some outside vendor is in charge of that display and Pete was the dude in San Francisco – so he drove this big white utility van full of candles and that's how we'd made it to the Stud that night. I was rather buzzed myself – very buzzed by some people's standards. Soon I found myself behind the wheel hurtling home trying to stamp the breaks in the oily darkness below my seat – and sometimes missing. But we made it, Pete kept his job, and his boss Michael eventually went off to a three-year Tibetan Buddhist retreat and became a lama, I shit you not.

I had already become disheartened with reading poetry – the readings in the city were made up more of poets who wanted to read than anyone who wanted to listen. Even though I prominently held up the copy of *City Lights Journal* that I appeared in whilst reading didn't seem to impress anyone. As cocaine further fueled my ambitions and alcohol became a nightly habit with Peter Marti and Mort of the soon-to-be Invertebrates (who was now living in Andover House), I decided I should form a band. I'd already met a cat at school with a synthesizer – a young reed-thin queer named Joe. Joe leaned to "Castro clone" in looks, little mustache like a cop, but he was really into New Wave. I called him up and said "Let's start a band." He liked that idea very much and we decided to get together.

I'd dropped a note to Allen mentioning that I wanted to film more for my *American Mutant* project, but by the time he'd come into town, I'd run out of stream about it.

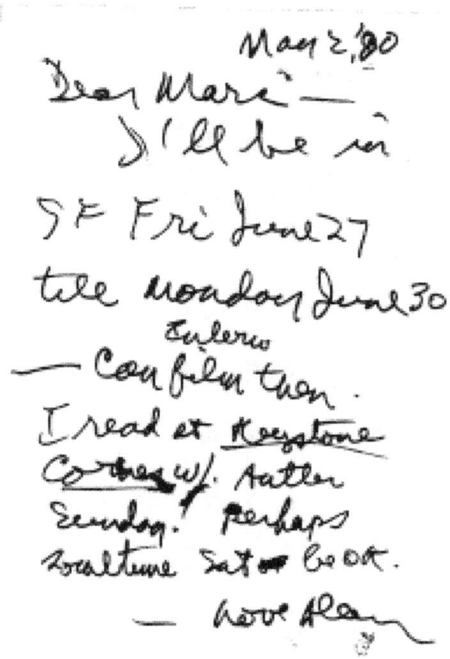

May 2, '80
Dear Marc—
I'll be in
SF Fri June 27
till Monday June 30
[illegible]
— Can film then.
I read at Keystone
Corner w/. Antler
Sunday! Perhaps
Sometime Sat be ok.
— Love Allen

The expense of 16mm, the lack of enthusiasm from my Film Department, and the disinterest of any college in hiring me as a teacher with a soon-to-be-completed (or so I thought) M.A. in Film made me seriously question this experimental film direction. Even with a letter of reference from Allen (which I'd written as he instructed, mentioned below), I didn't get a nibble from even a community college – though why I thought a letter from an albeit famous poet would help get me a film teaching job is typical of my dope-addled thinking of the time. There were soon to be tons of unemployed filmmakers with degrees. Meanwhile, Richard was beckoning for me to join him in New York if an apartment came through.

May 23, 1980

Dear Marc — Sorry I'm so slovenly returning the wrong page last time — enclosed find your letter.

I'll be at Jack Tarr Hotel

Nite of June 27, then read with Gregory C. at Keystone Corner June 28, then leave June 30 back to Naropa. See you one time or other. I'll be at Shig's the subsequent nites I guess.

Regards to Peter Marti.

You can probably use my apartment in N.Y. while I'm out here in Boulder if you need a place to crash while looking for work.

Barnes & Noble Books & Billy MacKay often has jobs — ask Bob Rosenthal.

Studying Sappho and Sapphic verse form just got around to pile of mail.

See you in S.F.

Allen

But the apartment didn't happen. Now I was thinking rock star anyway, especially with the more coke I used.

I had some lyrics and some ditties in my head, like jingles for some insecticide. Somehow I managed to communicate these to Joe and he worked them out. Joe convinced me to join him at the Baths, once. It was an off-night Tuesday, the place nearly deserted. I walked into this one room and there was a movie being screened showing a guy in his tighty whities, wrapping a length of cord around his underwear-encased dick and balls. The film was shot from the torso down. The local band Mutants was over the P.A., singing, so help me, "Insect Lounge" which had the refrain, "I'm going down (down) to the Insect Lounge…" while some guy was blowing another. No one was interested in me. I was a grower, not a shower, and I was not growing. I left Joe without being approached, and Joe and I were not interested in each other.

Meanwhile, I was hanging out at this after-hours club called Club Generic – I'd read some poetry there. The place was run by Stephen Parr, and the beer was in these white cans with big black letters saying GENERIC. After Joe and I had a few songs together, I asked Gary Schwantes, a great sax player who lived at Andover House, if he'd gig with us at Club Generic. I also talked poet Pat Reed into playing violin and got my brother Ross to come down from Northern California to play drums. Twelve years my senior, he used to be a professional drummer. He'd even gigged with Chuck Berry, but he'd wound up a librarian.

[Love, Marc]

You there
Pry this open
Vampire tomb
Young Michael Dracula
The last of his line
L.A. USA
Dog in a coffin
Black velvet box
It's Dracula's Dog!!! Arooooooo! Dracula's Dog!!! Rowwwwwwwoooooo!!!

I'd written down these notes while sitting in the St. Francis theater on Market Street watching one of the many horror movies I loved. The film was literally called *Dracula's Dog*.

So Ginsey showed, as did Claire. Ginsey put his tongue in her mouth in greeting, which she seemed to like. Allen asked me how my prostate was doing in front of my older brother, adding "How's your asshole?" Ross looked away, hopefully too drunk to later remember. "Dracula's Dog" was our last song, and I ran and crawled around the stage, Iggy-like, saying the refrain and holding the mike out for people to make their own dog noises. When I held it to Allen, he said "Ah," the sound of primordial space, ever the bodhisattva. "Oh come on," I answered and held it out again. "Woof woof," he replied.

Joe was absolutely horrified at my grandstanding. "Are you always going to do that?" he asked. He wanted no part of it and dropped out soon after, though we had made some good tapes. John Pratt played them for his cokehead dealer drummer friend Don, who immediately invited us down to where he rehearsed.

Sister Stacey came to visit me in San Francisco, now a punk with leukemian hairdo, accompanied by her girlfriend Kathy to see the Weirdos, here also with Hal Negro of the Satintones. They came to see me at the rehearsal studio, and jumped around and danced.

I spoke to her on the phone drunk a few weeks before the end in the hospital "It's all useless, without purpose," I told her, ever my useful and upbeat self.

"No I don't believe that, Marc."

"Yes, there is the path," I said in the bathroom of Peter Marti, black phone clutched in my drunk hand, resigned that in uselessness there could be peace of a sort, that bottom of the lake uncluttered mind of Zen sitting that visiting me occasionally in long sweats of trying to sit.

Then I called her back a few days later: "Yes, there is purpose, there is the dance. And it's a happy dance or a sad dance, but always dancing."

I asked to be called down when she was going to die. I was in S.F., she L.A. They spared me. My folks spared me the horror. First the labored breathing, as if she has just run up 6 flights of stars. Then, towards the end, she began to shake violently. On their last visit to the hospital, she had died minutes before, and dad and mom now divorced and strangely close again in her death, went in to see her still form, warm from the fever, and dad bent to kiss her brow and using her babyhood nickname, said "Goodbye, sweet tootie."

There was a funeral where I read Kerouac, a piece from *Scripture of the Golden Eternity* that she'd dug. Nobody got it, except Richard and our friend musician Rick Fagin. There were 500 people there.

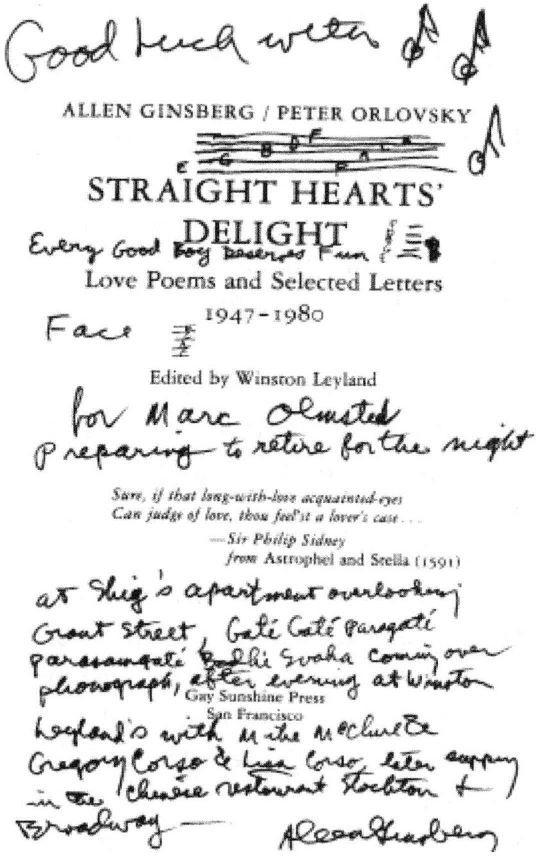
Good Luck with
ALLEN GINSBERG / PETER ORLOVSKY
STRAIGHT HEARTS'
DELIGHT
Every Good Boy Deserves Fun
Love Poems and Selected Letters
Face
1947–1980
Edited by Winston Leyland
for Marc Olmsted
preparing to retire for the night
Sure, if that long-with-love acquainted-eyes
Can judge of love, thou feel'st a lover's case . . .
—Sir Philip Sidney
from Astrophel and Stella (1591)
at Shig's apartment overlooking
Grant Street, Gate Gate Paragate
parasamgate Bodhi Svaha coming over
phonograph, after evening at Winston
Leyland's with Mike McClure &
Gregory Corso & Lisa Corso, later supping
in the Chinese restaurant Stockton &
Broadway — Allen Ginsberg
Gay Sunshine Press
San Francisco

Back in San Francisco, Allen invited me over to a small book release gathering at Winston Leyland's, publisher of *Straight Heart's Delight*, which was a collection of selected letters and poems between Ginsberg and his long time partner Peter Orlovsky. Leyland hadn't liked Allen's title, which Allen had chosen in part just to rattle the concepts of Leyland's Gay Sunshine Press readership. Leyland still snuck in a qualification on the back cover, making sure everyone knew Allen meant "straight" as in "straightforward." Allen caught it and said, "Aww, he couldn't leave it." Allen also caught that I was on coke, which he first thought was amphetamine – the tell was my revolving jaw and lip licking. He wasn't happy about it. Gregory Corso was there with his girlfriend Lisa so I nervously steered Allen off the subject. I remembered a story that Gregory had hounded Peter Marti mercilessly at an International Poetry Conference in Italy when he learned Peter had some coke. One of my oldest friends, film scholar braniac Paul Stiver, was up from L.A. and he'd driven me over. Paul was a high school friend, permanent L.A. denizen and Avis Rent-A-Car delivery man. Whenever he scored an S. F. bound car he drove it up and visited. Somehow we started talking about Sergio Leone's Italian western *Once Upon A Time in the West* with Gregory, who loved it as much as we did. McClure was also there and excused himself early, somewhat frosty with me if memory serves.

Allen had already noted that Reichian therapy seemed to have loosened me up sexually, and back at Shig's, the coke did more of the same. It was still an early stage in my using the drug, where it made coming difficult but didn't affect the hard-on. The result was that the orgasm was intensified, a blast of white light in the head. The Reichian work had paved the way for a full body orgasm (sometimes with an inner blue light). Allen thought he might even try coke with me next time – though he was still strongly opposed to the drug itself. I told him "You just haven't had good coke." "Yes, I have," he insisted. Actually, he'd probably had better coke than me. Next morning, feeling frisky, I rolled over and said, "I wanna come." "Don't be gross," he admonished, but was accommodating. I was certainly more into it than the Naropa days, and I was also letting him fuck me.

Still, I was not doing very well. Too much booze and coke. I was depressed a lot. I slept with a trendy New Wave girl I had schemed on for months. She wanted to eat at this ribs place and the beans made us fart horribly and odiferously throughout the night. I don't think it had anything to do with obeying her Bacall-voiced command "Fuck me in the *ass*." If we had any real connection it might have been a thrill. I had done coke probably cut with speed and couldn't sleep. I wound up sitting in her front room until dawn, astounded to hear Tibetan horns and clashing cymbals in the early morn. We were near a meditation center, what would turn out to be KDK - Kagyu Droden Kunchab as founded by the skeletal and ancient Kalu Rinpoche I saw perform the Invocation to Mahakala in 1977. The sound filled me with both profound yearning and despair. But I was still far from ready to quit drugs and alcohol. I saw her one more time and wound up drunk in the back of a pickup truck with her. The driver of that truck later married her.

Not long after that, I ran into Peter's Naropa poet friend Bill Voigt at the San Francisco State University library where I worked. Bill had a distinctly enviable vibe of mystical peace and wholesomeness that I rubbed my aura against like a cat. He told me he was living at that KDK meditation center. Again, that yearning and despair welled up in me.

I was dealing grass mostly, but I pulled off a big wholesale deal of Quaaludes and made enough to buy a color TV and a trip to New York. There I visited Richard with his mad, promiscuous and oh-so-fascinating artist roommate, "A." A was an incest survivor, something no one knew at the time, which she didn't even acknowledge to herself until years later after she'd gotten sober. She wasn't just some crazy alcoholic party girl without reason as Richard later explained, who he'd met in Urbana, Illinois in 1976. By 1979 she had decided to live in NYC and study at the Art Students League (she was quite good) and that's when she wanted Richard to move in with her in the Queens apartment. A brown skinned, lithe brunette, she looked like some exotic and mysterious mix of white, Native American, and Latina, with a dash of East Indian. A was making it with Richard and anyone else who caught her fancy, male or female – and on this visit, she picked me, a deal brokered by Richard himself. The back story as Richard later said: she told him she wanted to sleep with me, "Arrange it for me." Richard was reminded of Marlene Dietrich telling Col. Lionel Atwill to fix her up with the young cadet in *The Devil Is A Woman,* and he does it because he has to if he wants to keep on fucking her himself, just like the Sternberg-Dietrich relationship in real life as we know from her daughter's biography. I got up the morning after and Richard was vigorously masturbating in his room without a door. Whether a conscious or unconscious invitation, it seemed to me Richard wanted to join us. As Richard explained: "The whole situation was like a *Venus in Furs* scenario. Forced into a masochistic scene, I embraced it. I'm sure I didn't know I'd be seen, but masturbating in that situation was what I could do to make my exclusion bearable until I had her to myself again."

But I was foolish enough, like many of her paramours past and future, to believe I could possess her and began finagling upon my return to San Francisco exactly how to do that. (And making it with Richard then or later was pushing the envelope beyond even my own experiments – we never went there. It seemed incestuous.)

This particular visit, Allen was out of town, but Peter's friend Vinnie did take me to the Mudd Club, Danceteria, and CBGB - the quintessential New York City punk clubs of the day. We also went into Alphabet City to score more coke, which Vinnie knew like his own bathroom in the dark. Vinnie and I entered a burned out building. He'd tried to dress down my New Wave look – "You're a *real* bad boy now," he said. He donned some aviator shades. Vinnie pushed cash through a wooden hole in a bolted door. The Puerto Rican on the other side checked us both out and then pushed the money back. No sale. I guess I looked like some kid that Vinnie the plain clothes narc had gotten to squeal.

Before returning to S.F. I also met up with Mark Fisher and had an ego clash when he said "I'm the best young poet on the scene today. Gregory thinks so too." Later Vinnie told Richard that Fisher was baiting me and I took the bait.

I returned to San Francisco obsessed with A.

I love your eyeballs
I love your neck
I love your clit
I'm a nervous wreck
Venus rises
In the nighttime sky
Sending love light
To my open eye

Now you're 3000 miles away
Now you're millions of miles away
Now you're 3000 miles away
3000 Away!

Gary - the Andover House sax player of our "Dracula's Dog" gig - was as enthusiastic as I was to start a New Wave band. He'd just bought a synthesizer, and was a good enough musician to magnetize a great bass player, Tom Latta, whose instrument was fretless. I named the band The Job, after a collection of Burroughs interviews. Don the drummer had joined us, and we talked Steve Parr into letting us play at the Club Generic again.

A and Richard had just gotten in from New York and were at my pad, recovering from a train ride in the cheap seats, a two day trip. It was an exploratory trip to see if they'd like living here.

To get into the spirit, my band somehow wound up at a party where Claire used to live. Richard and A declined, saying they'd meet us later at the club. But it was time for the gig, so we began to leave down the stairs. Former roommates of Claire's were throwing the party, Belinda and Gretchen. Gretchen was a beautiful Kim Novak blonde nurse whose last name (anglicized from German and withheld here) made her sound like a Bond girl or porn star, then came up to me and asked if I'd sleep with her. Believe me, I was not used to this, and it was certainly one of the most dream-like moments of my erotic history. I said we had to go to a gig, knowing that A would also be showing up to it. "Pleeeeeease?" she said. Then said it again! Jezuz, what now? I said I had to call Richard and let him know I wouldn't be coming home. "Richard," I whispered in the phone, "are you guys coming?" "No, we're too tired, Marc." "O.K., tell A I'll see her in the morning." After all, A had hardly declared fidelity and HERE was Gretchen Hotbabe! (her last name really was like that). "Come with me, Gretchen, our band is playing." Briefly I was a rock god.

I saw yet another girl I had just started to sleep with at the Generic. I was juggling like mad. But we did well, and a booker from the prestigious I Beam club asked for my number. It would lead to opening to the Offs. It was also one of only a handful of small successes that would come from the next 4 years of brutal gigging. But I was high as you could get, then going home with Gretchen, who blurted out "I love you," while we screwed. She admitted she'd pored over Claire's copies of the mad nude photos my cousin Viv had taken. Clearly she wasn't a size queen.

I returned in the morning to my pad where Richard and A had crashed. Any ambivalence I might have had as to who to be with romantically would be solved by A drunkenly masturbating an equally blitzed Richard under the covers in front of me and a couple of my friends that very afternoon. I got how it was going to be with her then.

Gretchen was terrific in bed, matching my appetites, which had always been a big problem for Claire. In a very short time, we moved in together into her place. I decided to cool all extraneous affairs, including with Allen. They would never resume with him.

Meanwhile, Peter Marti was hosting Gregory Corso in his pad, as Peter well chronicles in his great poem 'Heard The Old Poet Corso Died." I've included some highlights below:

Back in SF, Vinny's phone call: "Gregory wants to see you, he's broke, needs a place to hang out, needs cheap drugs, told him you'd fix him up..."

And so: The Visit.

I pick him up at Embarcadero YMCA,...

His room was rank with him. Overflowing trash ciggie butts and dirty clothes. [...] We sit hours at big kitchen table smoking my home-grown pot, cooking up dilaudid. Gregory, unlike Vinny, wouldn't help shoot me up mainline. "I don't give nobody their first drugs; I don't shoot people up." So he's in the tiny bathroom hunting un-collapsed veins in his feet, spritzing pink bloodwater from the cleaned needle on my flyer plastered walls

I'm in the kitchen jabbing a too-large gauge needle into my asscheek trying to skin pop, once actually see inside the muscle—the glutei sinewy black somehow like a hole opened up into Void—[...]

Gregory would quote himself to me: "I met a man/ who died" about Kerouac then riff on what he meant, how he edited. Waves of language of sublime Mind slithering forth on clouds of grass and cigarette smoke. I was rapt, was stoned, could hardly follow sometimes (he could take so many drugs and be energized!)

I grew mute, stultified while he Sang.

I said something about my ambition once: "Watch Out for Ambition!" he shouted, "and don't think Ginsberg's shit doesn't stink!" followed.

[...]

Gregory would often say: "what about the Poet? you gotta pay the Poet." Desperate for money once, he was challenged by R. Rodgers to write a poem on the spot, which was bought by poet Richard Modiano for $20

You'll never die
because when you're dead
you won't know it

[...]

Fall, 1980 my basement apartment was cozy for Gregory

I doled out the drugs and cooked, Gregory held forth. we'd stroll to Cafe Floré to drink beer or coffee (where cute counter girl/friend of mine named B. worked)

"Getting laid... It's all about pheromones"

he whispered confidentially, eyeing B.

"any woman'll go for you if she gets a whiff of your pheromones," And with that, he reached into his pants and, as he narrated: "rubbed under the foreskin cause that's where the pheromones are," then proceeded to go pick up our order, first passing his fingers beneath B.'s nose, then patting her face to make sure she got the full-on Gregory Experience. He asked her out, but she declined him...maybe next time...

[…]Corso could turn mean on you, turned on Allen more than once, turned on benefactors, turned on drug buddies and me too.

[...]

Gregory took about 30 dollars and the pills I'd "hidden" in the house. I had dozens more securely stashed for his hopeful extended visit, now cut short by his urge to move on. I was indignant, calling everyone "did you hear what Corso did?[...''"]

Ginsberg: "I never understood how smart guys like you and Marc and Gregory could get hooked…"

[…]And I never saw him again after that Fall of My Youth...

(By the way, the "B." Peter mentions was actually Belinda, Gretchen's former roommate. Now she's a cop.)

Peter was manager of the Job for a time, his effectiveness best summed up by the time I was trying to get a new guitarist to join us. The guitarist came to our gig and was unimpressed, I felt him begging off, and as we turned the corner of the club, there was Peter passed out slumped over a table, one hand holding the beer glass he had vomited into, a string of brown regurgitation trailing all the way back into his mouth. "And this," I announced with a cynical flourish, "is our manager. Peter, you haven't finished your chocolate shake." Needless to say, I never saw the guitarist again and that night I collected what was owed us from the club, dragging Peter home by pouring him into the back seat of Gretchen's car.

June 17, '81

Dear Allen,

Well, the band continues to move along. look forward to you seeing us again next time you're out, you'll be surprised at the improvement. I've had a change of address, living with a girlfriend now (first domestic scene for me). Hope you'll be able to come over for dinner. Still writing, still sitting, sanity prevails...

Love,

Marc

new address & phone
Marc Olmsted
3830 A 18th
S.F., CA 94114
(415)621-1049

usually home 5:30-6:30 PM Wed.-Sat.

Ironically, once I had a working New Wave band, then I really began seeing Allen as a possible help in climbing the ladder of success – yet I had also terminated my sexual relations with him. So I can honestly say that it was not ambition that had motivated my sleeping with Allen.

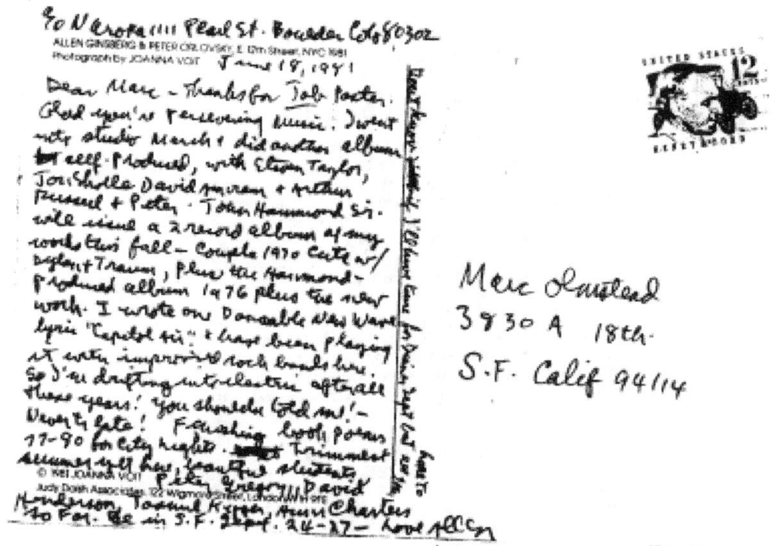

Ginsberg himself was now attempting to write pop songs. He had shown some great ability with tuning Blake, and further encouraged by Dylan, came up with some hilarious ditties of his own like "Gospel Nobel Truths" or "Do the Meditation."

However, his entry into rock 'n' roll was not really successful, particularly with "Capitol Air," which was an interminable long series of verses with no chorus. The song might have worked if the length had been truncated – he'd have musicians play various solos to break up the monotony – but the lack of chorus was deadly. He actually performed it on stage with the Clash, which one can hear on the "Holy Soul Jelly Roll," collection, but I think besides the novelty of it being with the Clash, there is not much to recommend it other than the lyrics. At Le Disque, Peter Marti, probably coked out and drunk, was actually quite blunt about it with

Allen – "That was terrible." Allen was miffed and apparently made some catty remark about Peter's heterosexual preferences, but he gave us a nice quote to use: "These sexy, intellectual, distinguished rhythmed, sharp harmoniced baby sounds of the 80's in poetry/music do The Job."

We went on to perform again at Peter Belsito's fire trap, Valenica Tool & Die, a storefront where you'd go down to the basement for the bands. Belsito later chronicled the scene in his excellent *Hardcore California* book, though we were barely given a nod. Gretchen brought her friend Kitty to the show, who was visiting from her current home in Washington D.C. Kitty wandered away before she saw Ginsberg. Later, when she saw that Allen was on the Clash's *Combat Rock* LP, she was properly horrified at the plummeting of her stock in hip.

HERB CAEN

Much Ado About Something

I HAVE A PUNK pen pal who signs herself Pheno Barbidol and tries to keep me clued in to what's happening on the new wave scene around here. I assume Pheno is a she since the letters, generally chiding in tone, include a red lipstick imprint under the signature. Of course, in San Francisco, one never knows, but in my mind, Pheno is all girl and also literate. Her latest screed begins:

"Well, you did it again, you culturally disoriented old reprobate. You really missed the boat with your weekend activities. What did you do ... go to some incredibly boring cocktail party? Or maybe you hobnobbed at another one of your mindless middle class galas? Ugh. What you could have been doing instead — if you'd pay attention to the flyers you see splashed like pimples on S.F.'s fragile face — is see history in the making on Friday night at the Tool & Die on Valencia. That's right, bucko. History! ... Allen Ginsberg was there singing his own new wave song, 'Capitol Air,' with new wave band extraordinaire, The Job. It was not to be missed. Even a Rolling Stone photographer was there." And so on.

★ ★ ★

San Francisco Chronicle — Tues., September 29, 1981

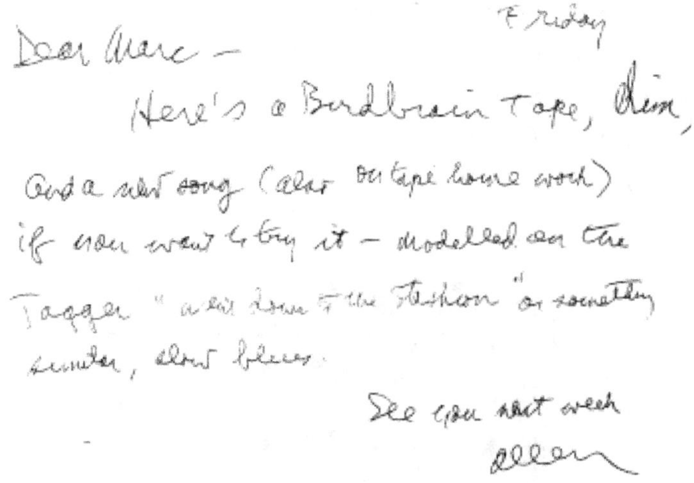
Dear Marc — Friday
Here's a Birdbrain tape, dim,
and a new song (also on tape home work)
if you want to try it — modelled on the
Jagger "went down to the station" or something
similar, slow blues.
See you next week
Allen

We'd lost our drummer Don, who'd flipped out when his wife, the bass player in an all-girl band, began an affair with the very butch lead guitarist. Don was also not happy that we'd replaced extremely competent but Van Halenesque guitarist Jeff Nathanson with surf punk Dan Rielly. Dan was great but he broke strings virtually every gig. I managed to recruit former Dead Kennedys drummer Bruce Slesinger (a.k.a. "Ted"). We rehearsed with Allen at my little cottage that I now lived at with Gretchen. Through my curtains, I could see the neighbors staring down from the next door apartment building: "What hath God wrought?!!" Even turned down, the vibrations were so intense that a vase flew off the shelf and landed on the couch where Allen had just been sitting. I watched him pick it up and put it back with Zen mindfulness.

"Capitol Air" was musically notated, but "Birdbrain" (on tape only in a "dim" mix, as Allen put it) was somewhat more successful, recorded by the Glu-ons as a '45. I suspect the Glu-ons had created the refrain, since this structural element seemed lost on Allen. My band members to a man hated the melody of this refrain for "Birdbrain," which was the only melody whatsoever. It sounded a lot like the mid-60's Neal Hefti TV "Batman" theme. So they created a significantly wilder and post-Miles "On the Corner" sound – which sounded terrific but was lost on Allen's pop aspirations. After we did it, he said, "I don't understand your aesthetic." But to his credit, he never tried to make us change it. Even if a little confused this time, Ginsberg's connection to punk persisted because of his always open and inquisitive mind for new and valuable cultural trends and developments - how many other 50-something people could make a connection to something like punk? Ginsberg was never behind the times, he wasn't stuck in the Beat Generation, and even at the end of his life he was following Beck and the Beastie Boys. I remember looking over his shoulder as he showed me a letter from Bono. He'd hoped to do an *MTV Unplugged* with Beck right before death took him.

Back in 1981, the Job regularly put out a program with the lyrics printed up. Here's one from around that time w/ Bruce Slesinger a.k.a. "Ted," the drummer who had stepped in to replace Don on a few gigs. I will point out the interesting prescience of the line written in 1981: "madonna is a whore in the new aeon" (from 'What's Going On in the New Aeon'). The notes on it are Allen's (wish I could tell you more, I found this in the Stanford U. Special Collections archive)…

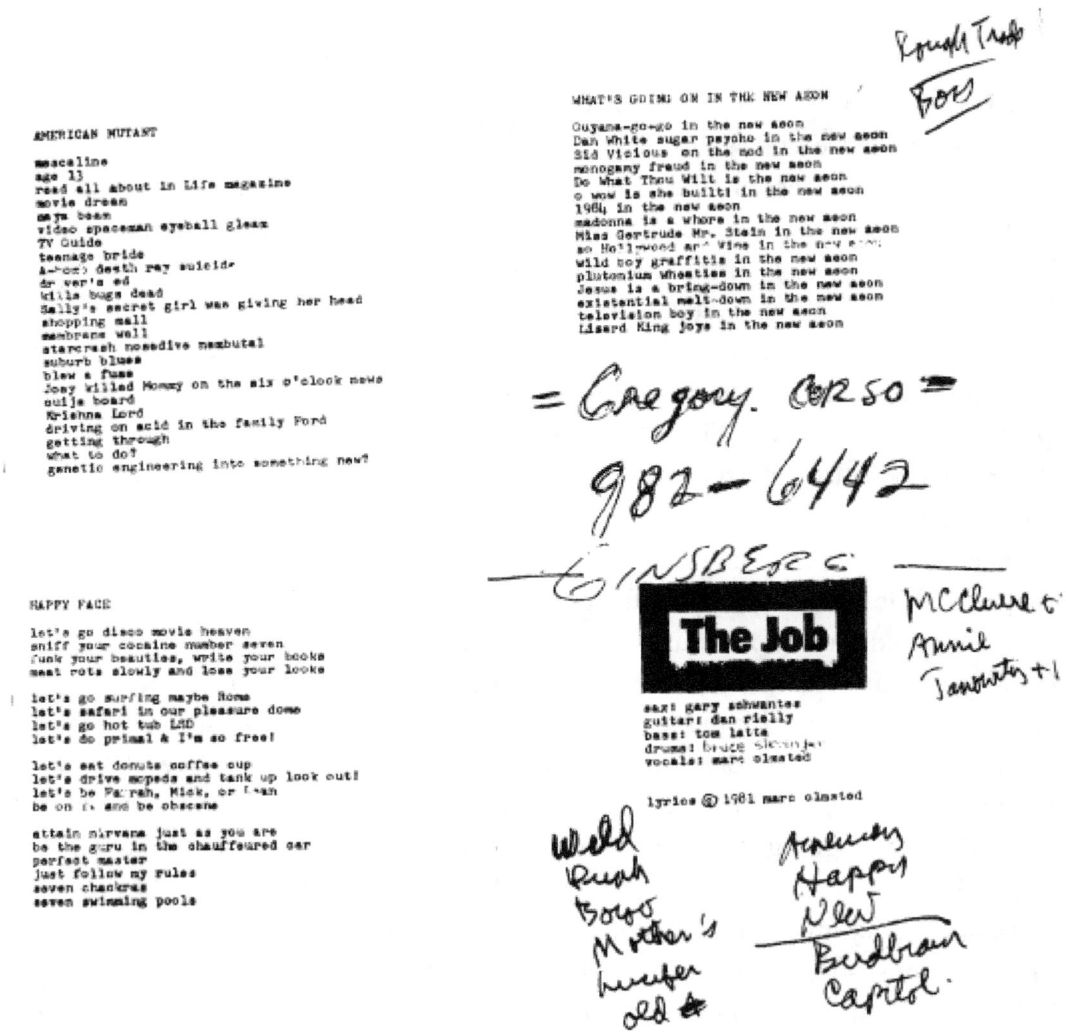
AMERICAN MUTANT

mescaline
age 13
read all about in Life magazine
movie dream
maya beam
video spaceman eyeball gleam
TV Guide
teenage bride
A-bomb death ray suicide
dr ver's ed
kills bugs dead
Sally's secret girl was giving her head
shopping mall
membrane wall
starcrash nosedive nembutal
suburb blues
blew a fuse
Joey killed Mommy on the six o'clock news
ouija board
Krishna Lord
driving on acid in the family Ford
getting through
what to do?
genetic engineering into something new?

WHAT'S GOING ON IN THE NEW AEON

Guyana-go-go in the new aeon
Dan White sugar psycho in the new aeon
Sid Vicious on the nod in the new aeon
monogamy freud in the new aeon
Do What Thou Wilt is the new aeon
o wow is she built! in the new aeon
1984 in the new aeon
madonna is a whore in the new aeon
Miss Gertrude Mr. Stein in the new aeon
so Hollywood and Vine in the new aeon
wild boy graffitis in the new aeon
plutonium Wheaties in the new aeon
Jesus is a bring-down in the new aeon
existential melt-down in the new aeon
television boy in the new aeon
Lizard King joys in the new aeon

HAPPY FACE

let's go disco movie heaven
sniff your cocaine number seven
funk your beauties, write your books
meat rots slowly and lose your looks

let's go surfing maybe Rome
let's safari in our pleasure dome
let's go hot tub LSD
let's do primal & I'm so free!

let's eat donuts coffee cup
let's drive mopeds and tank up look out!
let's be Farrah, Mick, or [illegible]
be on TV and be obscene

attain nirvana just as you are
be the guru in the chauffeured car
perfect master
just follow my rules
seven chackras
seven swimming pools

The Job

sax: gary schwantes
guitar: dan rielly
bass: tom latta
drums: bruce [illegible]
vocals: marc olmsted

lyrics © 1981 marc olmsted

= Gregory Corso =
982-6442
Ginsberg
McClure &
Annie
Janowitz +1

In San Francisco, November 1981, Ginsberg was going to read at On Broadway in North Beach, (directly above the legendary punk club, Mabuhay Gardens) and invited my New Wave band The Job to back him up. Gregory Corso was also on the bill. Bob Kaufman, the black poet of the North Beach bar Dagon poem recitation of my "first date" with Allen some years prior, had come along with Gregory. Kaufman shuffled about like an electroshock causality, barely speaking. Kaufman was beaten particularly badly by the police years earlier and may have suffered some brain damage as a result. By all accounts he was functioning normally until that police roust.

We all met backstage and Corso was cantankerous, "You young rock and rollers are just in it for the gold." I thought to myself, "If we are, I've yet to see it." I was splitting $90.00 between 5 band members, and that was more money than we usually saw. He thought my friend Paul Stiver was a "Rolling Stone [magazine] shmuck," as we stood back stage with the girl interviewer who shrank into the corner during this tirade. I worried that Gregory might do anything, wander onstage, disrupt the band etc. Allen agreed this could very well happen with Gregory, but it would be alright. I only half-got this “crazy wisdom” teaching, but I accepted it. And Gregory behaved himself (special thanks to Richard Modiano’s journal in getting the details of this memory correct).

Allen told the band last minute that we could go on after his reading and play a few songs. I had gotten completely soused (as opposed to functionally soused) thinking I was done for the night. On top of that, the drummer had wandered away, clearly bored with the poetry. He was found downstairs in the Mab. At one point I was rushing down those stairs to run into Michael McClure walking up and he paid me a compliment about the band and I thanked him but told him I had to find the drummer pronto. McClure frowned that I didn’t stop to chat – I had apparently fucked up with him yet again.

When we opened with a song I was so drunk that I forgot the lyrics. I could only make up phonetic noises with vowels and consonants. No one noticed. After Allen and Gregory left, the energy of the remaining mob was barely containable anyway. We did 3 or 4 songs and stopped. While Richard watched the pre-show with Paul and the show itself and the final aftermath, Paul told him, "this would make a great Robert Altman film."

Gretchen wasn’t there. She did come to most of my gigs, took most of the same drugs, and ran around the scene with me. One night the two of us went to a party at filmmaker Curt McDowell’s – the party was pretty dead, except for the memorable image of Bruce Conner, literally unrecognizable until pointed out, now with bleached blonde hair in some sort of Air Force khaki blazer, pogoing to the music while manically saluting. Gretchen and I danced for a while just for the hell of it, and then started to split. Curt pleaded with us to stay – I gather we’d done well as fixtures – but Gretchen wanted out so we split.

The Job’s most successful crowd pleasure was the doom and gloom synth-based “Lucifer Rising,” the title of which I’d taken from Kenneth Anger’s last prominent underground film.

LUCIFER RISING

pagan holy moly
Satan holy roller
golden eyes aglitter
kick out old Jehovah

ain’t no heavy judger
ain’t no doom of flesh
sin is just restriction
soul – I haven’t got one

give me strange new visions
meat is just a spirit
shake my ass so girly
blue electric orgone

here comes Mr. Anger
streaming force and fire
time of the magicians
Horus is appearing

Lucifer Rising – Lord of Light!
Lucifer Rising – Light Bringer!
Lucifer Rising – Light Ray! Into my eye!

It would have appeared on a *Live at Le Disque* compilation LP back in 1981 (when Don was still our drummer) but the tape actually mysteriously slowed down when our set reached that particular song. I shit you not! Then it sped back up when the song was over. This didn't happen to any other band. So we wound up using "Happy Face" for that LP because it was the second-best take of our set that night (and included a charming moment where I shouted "Look out!" at Peter Marti who drunkenly nearly collided into the mike stand – it sounds intentional on the song). "Happy Face" was a bizarre fake-funk pseudo James Brown send-up of samsara, but cynically without a solution, which Allen took me to task for. Some of the lyrics, like "attain nirvana just as you are/be the guru in the chauffered car" suggested to Allen that was I was also rejecting Buddhism. I wasn't, but he was right that it was sloppy and glib in message. He also didn't like how I bent "Happy Faaaa—aaceeee" in the refrain. "You're doing some British thing. You can't hear the word." Dylan's vocals were Allen's model of perfection – and he was right again. The secret was in Dylan's enunciation of consonants, Allen pointed out. Not vowels, as in "British" style.

We still wanted to release "Lucifer Rising" and decided to do so as a self-produced 45, now with Tom Stamper as drummer.

Hymenaeus Alpha (a.k.a. Grady McMurtry), the Caliph of the O.T.O. knew Anger personally. At his suggestion, I got an address from the Caliph to send a demo to Kenneth Anger. Anger responded with this angry letter:

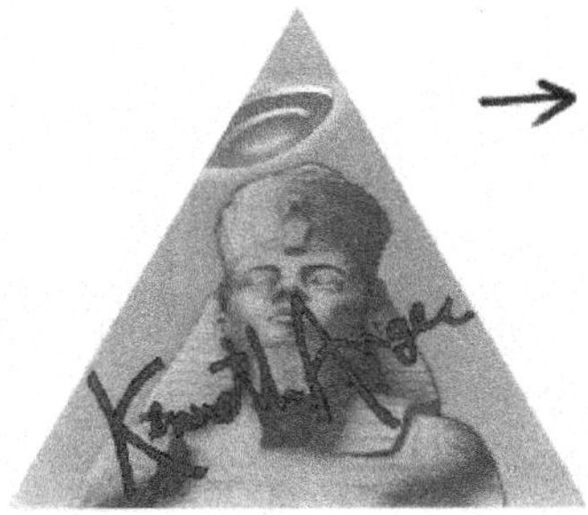

Lucifer Rising
→ © 1980 Kenneth Anger

354 East 91st Street, Apt. 9
New York, N.Y. 10028

May 22, 1982

Dear Mr. Olmsted:

I am amazed at your naiveté in recording a song using my copyright title "LUCIFER RISING" without first asking my permission and feelings on the subject.

I dislike your lyrics intensely, and on that basis alone would never grant permission that you use my title. "LUCIFER RISING" is copyright 1980, and I expressly forbid you to release the song on your album, with the title you have ursurped, and the references to me. If you persist in releasing the song on an album after this warning, I will be forced to take legal action against you. You misjudge my character, if you think you can get away with this.

Sincerely,

Kenneth Anger

Kenneth Anger

Needless to say there was no way I was going to "persist." As I drowsed into sleep that night, I lucid-dreamed some shadowy figure putting a spell on me. I remembered Sitney's *Visionary Film*, the same book that told me Conner and McClure were high school buddies. It also had Anger saying that one of his hobbies was hexing enemies. I had no trouble talking Gary Schwantes, my main music partner, into re-recording. "It isn't worth cancer of the liver," he said.

I was crestfallen. I talked to Caliph Hymenaeus Alpha and he shrugged. Getting a reaction like that with Kenneth was apparently the luck of the draw, which is why he thought we should send it to Anger BEFORE pressing the record. Anger had already fired Jimmy Page from the soundtrack of *Lucifer Rising* (though Page had finished it) and replaced him with former lover Bobby Beausoleil, the bisexual Charles Manson follower who was doing life for murder. Beausoliel recorded his tracks from prison.

So we went back into the studio and changed the vocal, and "Mr. Anger" became "Mr. Alpha." The Caliph, "Mr. Alpha" himself, liked the song, giving us a blurb: "Has an uncanny ability to capture the Thelemic Current at its crest." *Thelema* was Greek for Will. Ray Bradbury, old friend of the family actually said, "The Job! Bravo!" But now there was just the guitar riff in the hook where "Lucifer Rising" had been, but "Light Bringer" etc. remained. It seemed pretty gutted. Worse, we had been completely unaware of Bauhaus' "Bela Lugosi's Dead," and the exact chords opened that song as well – it was now a big New Wave hit (and remains so to this day). What's more, the 4-song vinyl EP had now virtually taken over as a marketing strategy for indie releases, so our 45 was almost completely ignored and sold abysmally in spite of a decent review here and there, like S.F. Music Calendar's "A very fine post-wave dirge."

Allen replied to my letter 10/11/82, now lost…

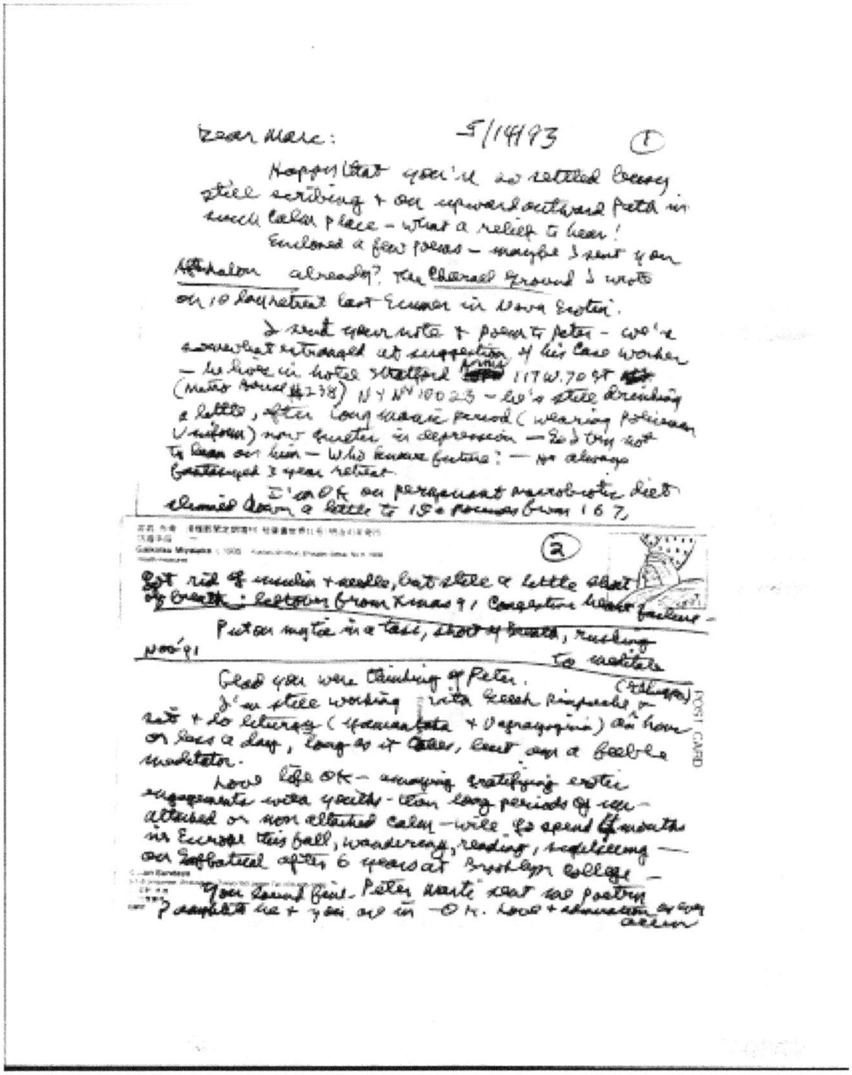

Dear Marc: 5/14/93 (1)

Happy that you're so settled [illegible] still scribing + on upward outward path in [illegible] place – what a relief to hear!

Enclosed a few poems – maybe I sent you [illegible] already? The Charnel Ground I wrote on 10 day retreat last summer in Nova Scotia.

I sent your note + poem to Peter – we're somewhat estranged at suggestion of his case worker – he lives in hotel Stratford [illegible] 117 W. 70 St (Metro [illegible] #238) N Y NY 10023 – he's still drinking a little, after long manic period (wearing policeman uniform) now quieter in depression – so I try not to lean on him – who knows future? – he always [illegible] your letter.

I'm OK on permanent macrobiotic diet [illegible] down a little to 150 pounds from 167,

(2)

got rid of insulin + needles, but still a little short of breath: leftover from Kansas 91 congestive heart failure – Peter [illegible] in a taxi, short of breath, rushing to [illegible] Nov '91

Glad you were thinking of Peter.

I'm still working with Gelek Rinpoche [illegible] + do liturgy ([illegible] + [illegible]) an hour or less a day, long as it takes, [illegible] at feeble meditation.

Love life OK – [illegible] gratifying erotic engagements with youths – then long periods of [illegible] attached or non attached calm – will go spend 6 months in Europe this fall, wandering, reading, [illegible] – on sabbatical after 6 years at Brooklyn College –

Your sound fine. Peter wrote [illegible] poetry [illegible] + you [illegible] – OK. Love + admiration as ever

Allen

O Poe

sad-eyed nymphet
told in
    ocean's rhyme
laudanum's
 glass eye
   fixed on
     future's
      crypt
journalist of
   secret fact
mind's morbid
   clime

raven-brow!
razor hanging
 pendulum
        o'er
 all heads
the Symbolists
  kiss
gather
 corpses into
arms in
Tantric charnel
  grounds
o Poe
 binged out
in the back
  alley
still as
  a pill-head
   done
w/ his revelry

What gossip from
the worms?

So I added "What gossip from the worms?"

This would be a grimly appropriate segue into the appearance of the word "AIDS," first spoken in mid-1982, now a storm cloud on the horizon of San Francisco. My friend Thom Iwatsubo talked me out of using amyl nitrate, which the first questions about AIDS were looking at as a possible immunosuppressant. You could walk into the Jaguar Bookstore on 18th St. near Castro and there were these sets of unmarked amber bottles of liquid. The more expensive bottles were the bootleg amyl nitrate, which a heart patient needed a prescription for in the legal world. The cheap bottles were the butyl nitrate, which also were sold in brand labeled bottles like Rush and Locker Room. They were legal and hardly worth the effort of inhaling. The amyl was often used to enhance orgasm in the gay community, though I never had any erotic reaction. I even tried masturbating to the point of coming and then taking a whiff. For me, amyl was such an out-of-body reaction, my cock would wilt immediately. It reminded me of nitrous oxide, under which I once wrote the words: "slay my body/consciousness remains." (How Bhagavad Gita, my dear.) But I begrudgingly gave it up, taking my amyl bottle out of the freezer and dumping the dregs, never to buy it again.

The Job went back into the studio, this time only with Jonny V as guitarist, myself, and Gary Schwantes. Jonny was the guitaritst I'd always been searching for. An incredible post-psychedelic feedback stylist hampered only by heroin, which didn't effect his playing, but eventually did affect his showing up. We were now working with taped drums and occasional taped bass lines, when Gary wasn't playing them on keyboard live but had switched over to his sax.

But it didn't stop me from moving out of Gretchen's because she was continually hounding me about my drinking. The boozing had gotten terrible even by my friends' standards. One time I passed out in the recording studio while we were doing some preliminary mixing and woke up after 45 minutes without even knowing I'd been out. Gary told me hours later to my absolute horror.

Fellow film student (and occasional sex partner) Mitch Loch told me about the Squaw Valley Screenwriter's Conference and suggested I submit my just-completed thesis, a horror film screenplay called *Snakejohn*. Mitch was also submitting. I got in, he didn't; he literally came in as first alternate in a list of 12 accepted applicants. He threw an incredible fit along the lines of it "not being fair" and out-and-out said he should never have told me about it. Mercifully, one of the 12 dropped out and Mitch would be joining me. Every applicant would put up $200 for expenses, and we were fed and housed – getting to hang with Frank Pierson (Oscar'd writer of *Dog Day Afternoon* among many other greats) and Alvin Sargent (Oscar'd for *Julia* and *Ordinary People*). For two weeks I drank like an animal and behaved like an absolute wild man, including a drunken affair with writer and performance artist Milo Johnson. We actually found our way into a Squaw Valley auditorium at night and screwed on the stage, which included her apparently being "body slammed." It was the first affair I had while being with Gretchen, but it seemed my days with her were numbered (and indeed they were). Milo was also the first to mention AIDS to me – she was concerned about her past as an intravenous drug user. Explained to me while in I was in a drunken stupor, I apparently told her I had a bisexual history anyway... so what the hell.

Mitch and I roomed together, took mushrooms, smoked pot, and he watched my brain swim in alcohol. Once we crashed a nearby resort at night, stripped and joined these hetero couples in an outdoor hot tub. They instantly left, their bathing suits now obvious.

Mitch was also sniffing some terrible white powder he'd ordered from the back of a magazine, probably the equivalent of crushed-up No-doz. I did some because there wasn't anything else. Towards the end of our conference days, Mitch announced an idea to me – a video collaboration, a fictional account of our relationship as friends. I said I was game. It would become something called *Bardo of Dreams*, which is the Tibetan name for the dream realm, *bardo* meaning "gap" or "intermediate state."

Pierson really liked *Snakejohn* and told me he would show it to top agent Rhonda Gomez and try to place it at Warner Brothers, where he was pounding out a script for De Palma.

For six months after the Conference I prayed that every time the phone rang, it was Hollywood. It never was. Richard had brought the script to a party at Gina Shock's (of the Go Go's) and our mutual bass player pal Rick Fagin gave it to Jodie Foster to read. When Jodie returned it to Rick at Gina's, Jodie apparently said she loved it and then pronounced it unproduceable. *Snakejohn*'s zeitgeist - a demon cult leader, an all-girl punk band with the singer as butch-femme female action hero, her dysfunctional cop brother trying to solve murders with a supernatural edge, over-the-top gore - would get sucked into the pop culture lexicon within the decade, rendering the script retro. It had been so extreme in 1984 that (prior the Squaw Valley Screenwriters' Conference) my Zionist thesis advisor, perhaps a bit touchy to gratuitous, sexualized violence, refused to sign off unless two scenes were toned down. Ritual pedaphilic rape and masturbation on a parchment soaked in blood were both removed.

I was supposed to cement a connection for S.F. State University's Extended Education (new job) out at California Academy of Sciences in Golden Gate Park. After I was done, I had some wine for lunch in the cafeteria and went outside to smoke a joint. Across the way was the Asian Art Museum and I wandered in. I was immediately mesmerized by the huge stone buddha statue of Amida (the Japanese name for Amitabha). There was a rush into my heart, and I truly felt a trance come over me, yet it seemed almost unclean to be experiencing it high. It was as if I was being initiated. Still, the unclean feeling that came on after that first rush made me try to step back. But the statue seemed to have a hold on me. I waited until it felt ok to walk on. My own spiritual practice had been in such a dark despairing place, one of the greatest dry spells I had ever experienced. This now was a relief. I continued in the museum and noticed that Bodhisattva of Compassion, Avalokiteshvara, which also seemed to have a hold. When I returned to the first statue, I closed my eyes and felt swept away, "a swimming upward and outward like the spins, but pleasant, no nausea, beginning to dissolve, watery" as my magickal diary recorded it. I also wrote that Amida seemed to almost say "take heart!" Outside a strong heart sensation lingered. I didn't know what to make of the experience.

By 1985, our music was the most refined it had been in the 4 years we were together, the closest to what I wanted to make. But when Jonny, having gone to score, didn't show up at a gig at the Mab until halfway through it (walking on stage and plugging in), Gary was so sick of all the abysmal club gigs that he called me and told me he just didn't want to go on. The Job without Gary seemed meaningless. I also threw in the towel, and the 5 songs we'd recorded weren't completely mixed until 2007.

I went to see Allen Ginsberg read in Marin with a French girl I was sure I was going to screw, especially when Allen called me to come up on stage to help him with his harmonium. "I'm too loaded!" I yelled out. It was true. "Come up here," he demanded, so I did. He showed me where to put my fingers on the keys while I pumped the bellows with the other hand. He held a wooden clave, clacking it with the other clave. He was singing "Put Down Your Cigarette Rag." The girl was impressed, but not enough to sleep with me.

It also happened that the last time I saw Gregory Corso (in a dapper suit, no less) was that same night at the after-reading party for Allen. I was astounded to see how put together Gregory was. In fact, I reflected how many times I'd seem him rise phoenix-like out of the depths of the most harrowing binges over the years - chasms that many, even most, did not return from. "I think Gregory is too aware of his own genius," I overheard Allen say. On another occasion, Allen said, "Gregory Corso has a lot of prajna but very little skillful means." Prajna is a Buddhist Sanskrit term that translates as "Transcendent Knowing." "Skillful means": the ability to apply it. Gregory pinged off life like a blind pinball. It had cost him fame and position. Sometimes he seemed to care.

As for myself, the fear of what would happen from drinking to such excess would soon eclipse the terror of quitting.

Part 7 – Sober To L.A.

it is all a movie, it is all show biz for better or worse it is one vast Wild Kingdom of shiny klieg lights and pouty starlets and old haggard character actors in the night with neckties askew

Apparently, unlike Gregory, drinking was scaring me shitless. I was now trying to control it. Richard had suggested I get my liver routinely checked. It turned out to already be swollen at age 31. "Drink a lot? Cut your drinking in half," said the doctor. This was even before moving out of Gretchen's. My effort at cutting my drinking in half was to drink only on the weekend, but the binge would then be so severe Gretchen had actually asked me to go back to drinking every day.

Some days I just didn't bother. I was invited along to lunch when Allen was again in town, which included legendary anthologist Don Allen (*New American Poetry*) and great Zen poet Philip Whalen, now a sensei. I drank a half-liter of wine and ate nothing. Being 5'6" and still looking barely in my 20s, Don Allen was somewhat astonished and wondered if I wanted any coffee before we left. Coffee, I thought, heavens no. I've worked for this buzz. But my tolerance was a great deal more than Don could've guessed. Only Philip actually reached me while talking of a friend's illness, turning to me at one point and looking pointedly in my eyes, "Like cirrhosis of the liver, it is a very painful death."

We went out to Whalen's in the Mission, where a second satellite Zen Center practice space was then being maintained. On the wall in the kitchen, I was thunderstruck to see a color pencil portrait of Whalen by Kerouac, "Buddha Red Ears." Oh my gods! Why I could barely keep from doing prostrations, my dear! Ginsey asked if I had any grass. Of course, Allen. Whalen wanted us to smoke in the backyard, which we did, though I don't remember Philip joining us.

I still remembered Whalen vividly from the first time I met him – that time we'd gone to see Allen read with Gary Snyder. Later, on a acid trip with John Pratt (but prior this outer Mission encounter), I saw Whalen going into Golden Gate Park with Issan Dorsey and wanted to run up to him, get some blessing, something. I thought better of it at the time – which showed some sense, probably. Given Whalen's somewhat cranky sarcasm, I might have been in for a Zen pig roast.

Not long after this particular visit at the satellite Zen Center, I showed up again and was literally the only one to sit there with Whalen, besides a giant life-sized golden statue of Bodhisattva Manjushri, hefting his sword of transcendental knowledge. (Given the lack of attendance, it was little wonder this Zen satellite was destined to be shut down soon after.) After sitting, I asked him if he remembered me. "Yeah, you've got that band, right? Punko Acido or something."

Like any alcoholic who decides to control his drinking, I went through the usual routines. Drink two beers a day, count the number of beers, don't drink at all on certain days etc. One time I visited Allen at a book signing at City Lights, sober for the day. Even when we went out with Michael McClure and his then-wife Joanna, I didn't drink. We were all trying to be good, it seemed. Michael and Joanna barely disguised their annoyance that they couldn't have Allen to themselves. McClure asked Allen to write the intro for *Rebel Lions* and Allen rather crankily answered he was too busy (Dennis Hopper wound up doing those honors for McClure). Joanna took Allen's camera and shot a photo of the three of us, a rose in Michael's teeth from the tabletop of the North Beach café we sat in.

Mitch was coming over to my new apartment sans Gretchen about once a week to discuss the script of what was now being called *Bardo of Dreams*. The plot was about this young man with a brain tumor, played by Mitch, who'd stopped dreaming. His friend (me) nurses him in his final days. I wrote a tarot scene and dialog for a Roger Ebert parody. We discussed a lot of plot points and Mitch would go back and write them up. Tibetan Buddhism and Aleister Crowley leaked their way in as a result.

It turned out to be a tremendously ambitious project for Mitch. He dropped $12,000 of his own money on the video production. The 45-minute tale had a great deal of Mitch's fondness for mushrooms in the production values, a sort of Pee Wee Herman sensibility to the décor of the loft where all the action occurred. It also affected the tone, which never clarified just how seriously we were to take any of it. Add to this Mitch's insistence on playing a hetero character, when the first sentence out of his mouth was as sissified as the day was long. The apparent AIDS metaphor became equally clouded. Mitch told me he had no interest in being labeled a gay filmmaker. But the movie was completely a gay aesthetic in a flamboyant, glam and campy sense.

I was drinking on the set and, since the character was a drunk, this was only a problem between takes. Mitch was not happy. The acting coach was not happy. In particular, the coach saw me light a real joint for a scene where I was smoking a joint. "Look man," I told him, "I'm of the Dennis Hopper School of Acting." Never mind that Brando wouldn't appear in the same shot with him in *Apocalypse Now*. I might have added that I was of the Monty Clift School as well. In fact, my Reichian therapist has added fuel to the fire in saying "What is it about you that makes me think of Montgomery Clift?" Duh. [For those of you who may not know Clift's work, much of his later period was quite under the influence. And much of it was fucking great.] I had even asked the Reichian if he thought that a 12-step group was inevitable for me. "No, they're too dumb, too redneck. Not unless you fell in with someone really smart. I think we just need to work with your screwed-up orality." Whatever the fuck that meant. Suck on *this*, Sigmund.

So anyway, the cameraman (a professional) was doing drunk imitations of me. Mitch was telling me I was ruining his movie. But I was thinking, what do they expect? I *need* to fucking drink. I even wrestled Mitch to the ground after everyone had left the set in some sort of Norman Maileresque "let's come to terms with our power differences."

But the next day, having once again found a newspaper reporter's bar nearby the set before coming in, I had a serious buzz again by the afternoon. I called my dad on a payphone to wish him a Happy Father's Day. "Your brother's in the hospital. Vomiting blood!" he tells me. "Jesus Christ, Dad, I'm next." "But you don't have a drinking problem," he said. I was drunk as I talked to him.

I hung up and went back to the set, considerably subdued. Mitch noticed, but didn't ask. We finished shooting and I went home to my apartment. On the phone I talked to my brother in the hospital. I didn't understand at the time, but he had vomited blood because of an ulcer, not the sort of stomach hemorrhage that had killed Kerouac as the result of liver dysfunction. My brother Ross was 12 years my senior – I figured he was the litmus test to hang my alcoholism on. When *he* started to wear out the parts, it was time to quit. His style of drinking around my father had been very overt – he drank *at* my dad. Mine had been secretive, like my mother's, who drank for 30 years in the marriage, got sober, and 5 years later divorced my father. Ross would bring in cases of beer like a military operation when he visited my dad for Christmas. I hid fifths of vodka (the cheapest brand I could find was called Vodka of the Gods) and padded around the house sipping screwdrivers, smoking dope in the backyard, and snorting coke in my room. I had done this for years and my dad would say upon my arrival, "Now Marc, do we have enough orange juice for you? I know you love that orange juice." Yeah, Dad, just enough orange juice. Trust me on that.

Ross said from his hospital bed that he was quitting drinking. Ask not for whom the bell tolls.

On Monday, I woke up and called in sick at work. I went down to the liquor store and bought a single tall beer. Today's method of control, I thought, would be buying beers one at a time. No doubt that would slow me down. Down the apartment stairs and around the corner for a single beer. Back up the stairs to drink it. So I had my single tall beer, smoked a joint and read the paper. A day of rest, recovery, and contemplation.

Done with the initial buzz, I went to take a shower. As I was showering, there was a sensation in my heart like a hammer to a mirror. At the same time, the thought: "You're an alcoholic, and you need to get to a meeting NOW!"

I didn't want to go to a 12-step meeting loaded and I almost talked myself into waiting until I was sober. However, I had more than once talked myself out of going (usually in the depths of hangover) and when I felt better, I didn't go. So whatever force was impelling me won out this time. I marched myself into a noon meeting within walking distance of the pad.

I called Mitch and told him about what I had done and he walked me into another meeting that night. I have to give him credit for that. I needed someone with me. I left clutching a copy of the official 12-step book like a raft on a molten lava sea and came home to my new cat, Flatears. While still living with Gretchen, she'd asked if we could feed Flatears when it appeared one day with xylophone ribs and torn-up bloody earmeat seen from our window. Flatears was maybe a Scottish fold with traditional droopy ears or maybe a regular cat whose ears had been ripped up from so many disasters he looked like a dog. What a heaven beast - I could weep now at the thought of his divine sadsack hangdog mug - he *was* me.

I was then doing the recommended 90 meetings in 90 days. Within two days, Richard called and said simply, "What's up?" I usually was the one calling Richard, since I was part of a ring of friends who used phone card numbers we hadn't paid for (the trick was to get a group of people dialing the time long distance, systematically making up numbers until one clicked – much easier than it sounds). So it was quite mind blowing for my dear friend to be so atuned to where I was at from all the way down in L.A. He had felt a disturbance in the Force. But then we did have that history of more than a few telepathic acid trips.

I clued him in and he gave his support.

We finished shooting Mitch's film on the following weekend. I found out when he was giving the wrap party that he had decided to take sole credit for the writing, having zero memory that he offered me co-writing credit at Squaw Valley, an agreement I had labored under up to seeing the wrap party poster. We fought bitterly over the credit and eventually I got second bill, as I felt I had contributed at least a quarter of the content whether by brainstorming with him or writing up my own dialog. Such were Screen Writer's Guild guidelines. (Mitch told me after it was all over that he still didn't believe it was true.) Mitch believed *Bardo* was his ticket to Hollywood. Gary Schwantes, my old sax player, scored the video, but as for a ticket to Hollywood, he said "Better luck with Greyhound." *Bardo* did win some awards, like "Best Dramatic Video," Atlanta Film & Video Festival, 1st Prize, Palo Alto Film Festival, and

"Best of Festival" Award, Video Refuses, San Francisco. It was also later chosen for the Valley Film Festival Videofest and 10th Annual BACA Film & Video Exhibition, NYC.

Still, Gary was right. Like with *Snakejohn*, Hollywood remained silent.

But to return to the point where I only had a week clean and sober, I flicked on the TV to see my stoner actor-director hero, Dennis Hopper, proclaiming his own sobriety. It was the first I'd heard of this and I literally wept. Now he's also a Republican which is another reason to weep.

I called my mom after two weeks, because she'd been sober and doing 12-step since I was 13. "Mom, I waited to tell you until I thought I could do it, but I'm two weeks sober." "That's great, Marc," she said in that sweet smoker's croak of hers. "Didja give up the cocaine, too?" I have never mentioned using coke to her. "Yes, mom." I'd given up all of it – weed/LSD/whatever.

I finally saw some *Bardo* footage three weeks after being sober. It was good I hadn't seen it earlier. Contrary to Mitch's fears, I was fine on camera. In one shot, I opened a champagne bottle with a flourish and perfect timing. And of course, I was supposed to be drunk. So it all proved to be usable. But at three weeks sobriety, there was no way I wanted to go back to drinking.

Peter Marti and I were not speaking each other even before I got sober. He'd gone on to form a rock band himself and used some of my musicians (starting Arms of Venus with his wife, and later joining Barking Spiders, gods help him, where his wife left him on his own). I thought it was clear I'd loaned Peter this oil portrait of Kerouac I'd done. He'd then put it in a Kerouac bio book promotion at his brother Paul's store and someone offered to buy it after seeing it in the store window. Peter magnanimously offered to split the profits 50/50. I hit the roof. The guy who wanted to buy the painting backed out anyway, so I marched into the book store and reclaimed it.

Peter had also fallen under the spell of a house painter and coke head guitarist who later married and was divorced by Diane di Prima's daughter (same girl who grew up on LSD with poet mom at Tim Leary's upstate New York ashram). Peter was Dennis Hopper to this guy's Col. Kurtz/Brando at the end of the river. Cocaine had Peter convinced that musical world dominion was in the picture, especially on the coat tails of this guitarist. He became increasingly mercenary, even trying to involve me in a plan to trick a family member into buying severely-cut coke (stepped on by Peter himself). Gone was the sweet, somewhat femme hippy I'd met in 1975 (and the same could be said of me, even sober). Peter then switched over to the cheaper speed and got *really* weird. Gary Schwantes, my old sax player, recounted how Pete went to his place to pick him up for some gig. A neighbor asked Gary as he left his place in the apartment complex if he knew "who that was pounding on the mail boxes." Gary arrived to find Pete rattling drumsticks on the boxes' metal wall (Pete didn't play drums). As Gary put it, "His hair was pointy, his shoes were pointy, everything about him was pointy." Peter would drink and drug for another couple of years, minus my friendship.

As a drunk, I had also lost touch with poet Bill Voigt, who had been Peter's friend primarily. When first sober, I felt compelled to track him down. It began with a search for the Bodhisattva Vow - a pledge of service in the Buddhist tradition. In 1985 I was practicing Buddhist meditation about once a week at the local Zen center and usually after a couple of glasses of wine at the University bar. I had already taken the commitment of Refuge 7 years earlier with Chogyam Trungpa at Naropa. After sobering, the 12-step emphasis on "carrying the message" to other alcoholics and addicts inspired me to take the Bodhisattva Vow but first I had to track down where it was given, usually by a Buddhist master.

Alas, the Bill Voigt in the phonebook was somebody else, a friendly old man. Calls to the Zen Center requesting the B. Vow led to a phone number at KDK, Kagyu Droden Kunchab (Al-Pervasive Whisper Transmission that Benefits All Beings). I called the number.

"I'm looking for the Bodhisattva Vow."

"Yes, well that should be available when Kalu Rinpoche comes into town. Why don't I put you on our mailing list?"

"Sounds good. This is Marc Olmsted..."

"Hi, Marc. It's me, Bill Voigt."

So many blessings in those early days of sobriety; so easy to forgot years later in the seeming hard gloom of a world that doesn't do what I want. Bill invited me over to the Center where he lived.

I sat down to witness the practice of Mahakala, a black six-armed manifestation of enlightened mind with a wrathful demonic appearance reserved for protectors of the teachings. This was the same practice I'd seen Kalu Rinpoche do in 1977. Now, 8 years later, in came Lama Lodu, a middle-aged man of stocky frame, burgundy robes, mustached, salt and pepper hair shorn close. His wide cheekbones gave him the look of a whalebone mask, a virility

I later learned was nearly irresistible to women. He reminded me of the Japanese actor, Toshiro Mifune, particularly in his samurai classic *Yojimbo*. Various students knew the ritual instruments associated with Black Mahakala: horns and a large drum. Lama himself rang the cymbals in the curious pattern I would soon find very familiar. The energy was enormous. I thought I had visions of the Black One. They occurred a few times in those early days and were never repeated, as if I saw a sort of mind's eye projection over the shrine room. The scene itself - statues that could easily rest in a museum. Silk paintings of "deities," thankas, hung from the walls. Colorful ritual objects symbolizing deity and palace/home, *torma*, crowded the altar. The brass shrine bowls glistened in candle-light. When the practice was done, Lama continued to sit bolt upright, open eyes staring off straight ahead like a warrior waiting for a battle charge. I was hooked.

One of the last projects I had done while drinking and using still had a life in sobriety. Richard and I had decided to try improvising a movie script into a tape recorder. This became what is now known as our sci fi radio play *Cold Heaven*, but it went through a weird mutation as the screenplay *Winter Science*. The dialog we improvised was mostly under the influence of alcohol, cocaine, and weed. Friends dropped over and we would include them in the hi-jinks. Some of the most memorable dialog one friend contributed in an alcoholic blackout. Richard faithfully transcribed the tapes and I cobbled it into a screenplay. The result was, as you might guess, hardly commercial. Now in sobriety, I fell under the influence of some advice and attempted to introduce a more action-oriented thread. The result pleased only a few. Friend Paul Stiver put it most astutely: Which was it? A character piece or an action film? It was, of course, first and foremost character-driven, and would probably make a pretty hilarious indie sci fi picture to this day.

```
            RENO
I got tanned from the radioactive face.
          (gesturing to Drinker)
And he's Mr. Tarantula.

            EDDIE
Man, I though you guys were weird.

            DRINKER
I saw a cat and then I spat, and then I
kick you in the shitter, and then I go
wiggle, wiggle, wiggle, wiggle.

            EDDIE
Hey, you guys been turning on!  I'll
go upstairs and put on a record.

            DRINKER
Put on the groove, man, put that record
down and let it spin around and go whugh,
weegh, eegh, eegh, eegh, ahg...

            EDDIE
O.K., I can see you guys don't know how to
handle good times, man.  I'll see you guys
later.
```

I later went back sober and took out everything that I'd added in an attempt to sell the thing. But not before seriously considering and executing a safari to L.A. that would take 2 years of my life, with *Snakejohn* and *Winter Science* under arm.

L.A.: Vajrayana monastery, an expiation of sins, a joke shop, a brothel of mannequins, Satan's desert, Buddha's wild kingdom.

I had met Ken McLeod, the white Tibetan Buddhist teacher my lama had told me to see down here, a sort of graduate student who had done two 3-year retreats and so was well-schooled but hardly the trained-from-childhood heavy my brown Tibetan guru was. But still there was a peace in his kitchen and once more I had a sense of the miraculous, the miraculous world without God, meaning the sort of shining miracle of it all even without the personal salvation of self, no reward for the ego in the universe of the spider, rat and tornado, how weird to pick up the Tibetan thread of the lineage I had previously studied now in this giant town, hidden and mysterious. Ken was in his early 40s, handsome in a vaguely Monty Clift way, with a slight British accent and a giant IQ to go with it. How soothing Ken's intelligent voice in that miracle kitchen of perfectly ordinary mind.

Allen never visited L.A. in the two years I was there. Virtually nothing happened that was connected to him. In 1983, I'd been asked to contribute to a special 60th birthday tribute to him. The book arrived when I was just two months into L.A., a very odd reminder.

> Teenager 20 - nearly gave up writing after running into academy wall of college - same old story: your mind ain't o.k. as is - met Allen Ginsberg who gave permission - sanctity of the ordinary-basic haiku moment, H. Miller's matchstick in gutter, Howl's holy bum and asshole refined through Buddhist practice - everything's o.k. but we still need discipline - I was big confused pain early 20's, later relaxed due mainly to that original permission, a meadow for me to see I didn't have to be tortured, though took a good 10 years and will always be a mess, probably, still in better shape than that kid who first saw him lead drunken Trungpa Rinpoche to stage - Ginsberg's contribution: beyond poetry, politics, to show the space of mind both exist in, where problems unravel, poetry rises and self lets go - a chance for us all to the last outbreath.
>
> From Best Minds: A Tribute to Allen Ginsberg, 1986

Friday the 13th leaning in with a full moon, I learned that the previous night my L.A. denizen nephew Steve had committed suicide by sleeping pills. Private writings in the temp job office, seizing a scrap of moment because I was spooked, making arrangements with Lama Ken for a ceremony, who said: "Get a lock of his hair, a few dollars for an offering." I then called his work place and told his boss, who said: "I'm shaking, he was so happy, he had a new girlfriend." "I know, Micky, I know."

Prayers prayers prayers, o Void, o hole of the world that swallowed my sister in leukemia, now this, God we *were* the House of Usher, a big play of grief. And thinking: you have your *Wild Kingdom* now, don't you? (My title for the novel on L.A. I was writing as it all unfolded.) I heard a producer at a 12 Step meeting call L.A. Snake City. Snake City you bet, the monastery for me, naw, who knew now? My taxes after going over them showed no money coming back, maybe even paying the Feds. L.A. would be very hard to leave. But easy for Steve, o you fucking doomster, you bonehead, you bonehead for real. Paul Stiver was downtown on jury duty, blessing! We walked the streets of Broadway staring at the movie marquees, maybe we'd even go see *Wanted Dead or Alive* Rutger Hauer violence film, we liked the director, but that would wait for another day, though we turned to see the woman in the ticket booth brandishing a switchblade, polishing it, very shiny, impressing the drunk bugging her at the window hole.

I often thought of Bill Voigt, who I was to have "replaced" in S.F. with Lama, that one opportunity that haunted me over and over when L.A. became so dense, stressful, and my spiritual practice faltered, all for some hideous ambition unrealized and perhaps never realized, but such regrets were folly. Now Bill was away on a 3-year retreat in Oregon. Perhaps he would emerge a lama like Ken. Yeah, Bill would certainly be a lama some day. (2007: he's known as Lama Jinpa.) I wanted to be a lama. 3 years in Oregon sounded much better than 3 in L.A. What would we both be like when we met again?

Thinking: Should I go back to San Francisco, live with Lama as invited, renouncing my VCR?

Marc Olmsted the Great Screenwriter Dharma Practitioner Celebrated Ex-Alcoholic Cute Beyond Words? Brilliant Endless Talker of Bullshit.

The only real highlight of my two year stay in L.A. was a ten-day retreat with Kalu Rinpoche in Big Bear. At one point, a student from some previous retreat asked Rinpoche if he intended to make it snow again.

The last night: after Vajrasattva empowerment, flashes of lighting, geese over the lake crying out in supernatural tongues, I stood on the balcony, snow coming down.

Ken told me he ran into Allen at a conference out of state, and Allen, hearing my name when Ken mentioned it, said I was "a good poet." Ken decided I should have a poetry column in his newsletter.

in the middle
 of nowhere
with everybody
 else
redhaired punk
 youths walking

asphalt
w/ cigarettes
Valley children
difficult Buddhism
remembering
jewel ornament
of liberation
jewel in the
lotus w/ grey
sky, concrete
LUBE & OIL
Tarzana
Centre
classic nail
wraps

There never was a second column.

Richard had returned to New York but still came out for a visit from time to time. On one occasion, I'd read Francis Ford Coppola still hadn't found a script he liked for his optioned *On the Road.* I'd mentioned this to an agent with whom I was friendly, Michael Hamilburg, and he literally called Coppola's producer and asked if he'd be interested in a treatment showing how we'd do it. The producer, Fred Roos, said yes.

The problem with *On the Road* as a film was it was a sprawling one-act play. The trick, it seemed to Richard and me, was to find the hidden three acts that would make it work on screen. We worked and worked and worked, and at one point I asked Richard, "Why are we doing this?" He answered, "Because we love the movies and we want to be a part of them." That was it, that it explained it all, these Stations of the Cross called show business that my character actor dad said "will break your heart again and again." We came up with an interesting interpretation, at least to us. We framed it as a platonic romance between Jack Kerouac and Neal Cassady, or as they're known in the book, Sal and Dean. Boy Meets Boy/ Boy Loses Boy/Boy Gets & Loses Boy: for Neal abandons Jack twice in the book. Hamilburg sent it off where it was met with the Great Silence with which Hollywood rather consistently responded to me. On top of that, *Snakejohn*, the script Frank Pierson has praised, found me in the office with the story editor of Empire Studios, a cheapie horror film company notorious for delaying its payments. Flanked by movie posters of *I Was a Teenage Sex Mutant* and *Sorority Babes in the Slimeball Bowl-a-rama*, he told me that "although it wasn't *badly* written, it didn't transcend the genre."

Another bad haircut, this time revealing to me that I was going bald at the crown, again needed an emergency mutation. My old James Dean New Wave 'do had grown out into a kind of mullet and was chopped off by some crazed queer barber into…gods know what. A lukewarm 12-Step girlfriend got me to another hairdresser, and we turned it into a flat top and dyed it jet black with some glistening German cellophane rinse. Strangers asked to touch it in elevators. With shades on I was mistaken for Korean.

The lukewarm girlfriend also demanded an AIDS test from me. It was my first. Negative. I sweated that one like waiting for a cancer biopsy result.

A shocker in the midst of my stay in "Hollywood": Tibetan lama Chogyam Trungpa Rinpoche had died. This was the guru I had originally committed to Buddhism with, the Refuge Vow in Boulder, wearing Allen Ginsberg's flower tie and Peter Orlovsky's suit.

His final days were in Nova Scotia, a vajra mansion, and when he died, emaciated skeleton from internal bleeding, lips writhed back in skull grin, they dressed him in his ceremonial robes and propped him up on a throne. People flew in from across the world for a final "audience." they entered the room one by one and "practiced with him". This macabre bone story cut through my own dull bullshit like a ninja star.

Mitch Loch came to visit, and we went over to Christopher Isherwood's old place in the Santa Monica foothills, where his widowed lover Don Bacardy now lived. I've forgotten how Mitch connected with Don, a great portrait artist, but I think that Mitch had met him wanting to write a script out of Isherwood's *My Guru and His Disciple*. I never fully understood what Mitch thought he'd do with this book, since his understanding of its core, the Hindu philosophy Advaita Vedanta, was limited at best. But Mitch liked Isherwood's struggle with incorporating sexuality with spirituality.

Isherwood's old place was a dream-like god realm in L.A. From its magnificent view of the ocean, it seemed some alternate universe to the horrid smogville I knew. The walls were filled with amazing paintings and photos, like the one of a painfully teenage Bacardy in tuxedo running around with Marilyn Monroe. Don announced one alcove as "Hockney Hall," which was a mini-museum collection of David Hockney paintings. The collected value of this hall alone, not to mention the quality of the work, was dazzling. Bacardy praised Mitch as "very photogenic" in *Bardo of Dreams* (he would later paint Mitch), and asked me if *Bardo* was "my first time acting." Swell.

Meanwhile, I had one more failed romance. As a drunk and drug addict, my relationships had lasted years. Now they sometimes lasted days.

In all this grimness, I did have the pleasure of connecting with Hubert Selby, Jr. - "Cubby" as his friends called him. Selby is best known for having written *Last Exit to Brooklyn* and *Requiem for a Dream*. I met him in a 12-Step context and would call him for wisdom, since he had a strange saintly vibe like an old junkie, sorta like I imagined Mickey Rourke's dad might be, whispering in this flickering pilot light voice. He once told me as I stood mentally crucified in a phone booth calling him in desperation, "Buddha said, 'There is no why.'" Now I think you'd probably have some trouble tracking down that particular scriptural reference, but he was right just the same. Some of Cubby's spiritual ideas were quite bizarre, like his dead father "telling" him that he was going to 12-Step meetings in Heaven. I couldn't ask Cubby's advice very easily after that.

I attended Ken's last class on Bodhichitta (the current of Buddha mind whose cultivation of attitude led to enlightenment - at some point, at least). He was headed off for India and I wanted him to ask Kalu Rinpoche for a Mo. This was a divination, and my question was whether I would be successful in show business in the next few years. That seemed to cover screenwriting, acting, story development, whatever. In short, if there was no show business career waiting for me soon, I would leave this godforsaken town. The impact would be heavy, indeed, and perhaps the reader questions why I had faith in the divination. I did, that's all.

The results of the Mo - Ken was due back from Bodh Gaya so I called his girlfriend - Ken was delayed, but had sent on a letter. The girlfriend knew the Mo's answer to my Hollywood fate.

"Didn't Sam tell you?" Sam the Tibetan Center secretary had not. "Well, it's negative. I guess you wondered why you were so successful." She never liked me much. The loud traffic outside shrank to a whisper, to a high-pitched ringing in my ears. Just like in the movies. I stood with the phone, frozen. The street sounds slowly returned.

I had the sense that my return to San Francisco would be easy as my departure.

"Frisco, that's really a gasser," said Cubby over the phone.

Tears choking, helicopter roar above L.A. Wilshire steel, sports car roar of show biz.

Dead lizard on the road. L.A.'s a desert. Thrifty Drugs shouts with L.A., thrift fashion, vodka models, hopeless fame of the magazine rack.

Thinking: Lama Lodu, o vajra master, I return to you now in thought and tears.

Part 8 – KDK

gaps in suffering
sometimes
big as Mt. Fuji
chatting with
the Buddhist nuns
over tea

In a day before everyone I knew was on anti-depressants, in a time before the Web, in a year where we had forgotten about the atomic bomb, in a world of my own mind where I was still young enough to chase my fantasies with the same optimism that an alcoholic picks up the next drink, the century’s close felt near...

Now I was a punk writer, age 35, living with a Tibetan lama, recovering from Hollywood and alcoholism in a San Francisco late 80s landscape of rock clubs, tattoos, piercings, 12-step meetings, and personal ads.

I looked over the RULES AND PROCEDURES FOR RESIDENTS. I would primarily be required to practice Chenrezig 5 times a week, morning or evening. On the weekend I would be required to do one morning practice, either Ngundro - a text preparing the student for advanced teachings, particularly the 3-year retreat Bill Voigt was now on up in Oregon - or Green Tara - a liturgy invoking a voluptuous green "goddess" who was virtually naked, Marilyn Monroe playing Virgin Mary as a belly dancer, a marvelous generous Big Mom. Exceedingly un-Catholic. Especially so, since these "deities" were regarded more as principles of enlightenment than heavenly beings, for Buddhism is fundamentally non-theist. Here essentially non-existent gods and goddess were vehicles to realize (and annihilate) the fiction of our separate ego-clinging selves. Still with me? Yet no practitioner could deny that these figures, paradoxically, also had a life of Their own.

I'd be given a household chore of some sort. There were no group meals. Guests were allowed, but the perimeters were vague, probably so Lama could decide who stayed and who didn't. We actually signed a lease that basically gave Lama permission to throw us out. This was no conventional landlord you could sue.

Finally, I would also be required to shine the brass shrine bowls about every two months, after getting up at dawn and filling them for that week. Mmmmmm. Could be a problem.

I came back to my room after a visit to the nearby Haight. Christiane had shoved a note under the door, another resident of KDK who was French, into Burroughs – a really sharp Buddhist student. The famous old poet I admired, Allen Ginsberg, was coming to town for a book signing! This seemed incredibly auspicious, it was just two weeks since I was back in town and three years since Allen had been in San Francisco. It made me feel confident in my move out of Hollywood and my efforts to restore myself as a poet, for Allen had helped get me published in a few prestigious journals and had been a longtime champion and teacher. I had nearly stopped writing poetry completely at age 20 when I met him, frustrated with a college scene that wasn't particularly supportive of the crude aesthetic I was honing, directly out of the tradition of writers like Jack Kerouac, but without the refinement that would come with Allen Ginsberg's tutelage.

And now Allen was coming into town, our sexual relationship done for 8 years, but our friendship intact. I had broken off sex with him when I moved in with Gretchen and never resumed it in the horror of AIDS.

Above all, he had taught me Buddhist meditation, awareness of the outbreath dissolving into space, sitting together naked in his San Francisco room. It began my interest - I was at the Meditation Center because of him.

Ginsberg would be reading at the Jewish Community Center and I got Christiane, the French writer, to accompany me. First thing I saw was author Michael McClure, who looked remarkably fit after his last boozy appearance. Turned out he'd quit coke and had either stopped the drinking or cut back considerably. McClure was amazingly handsome - even James Dean might not have made such a stately appearance in his 50s if he'd survived. "You look great,"I said, having met him a number of times. "So do you," meaning he liked my ninja flattop. I briefly talked to Ginsberg beforehand and he saw that I got in free. As usual, people swarmed him. What a good feeling to see his bald pate again, like an emanation of the writing muse come to reassure me - it's ok to be a poet - fuck Hollywood - we'll work something out.

The reading was a strong one. I can remember my own tears rather than actual poems. Much of the material I had heard - some I was familiar with as early as age 17 - all of it resonating with association, with a guidance I had chosen to this very moment - with a sense of the preciousness that I knew this man - great bard, teacher, social activist, mystic, lion of dharma, peace heart...

Afterwards I hung out and met another young fellow poet, Andy Clausen, gravel-throated construction worker and number one on Ginsberg's up-and-coming list - someone he never even had sex with. As Clausen was rather paunchy and slightly ravaged from drink, he was not precisely Allen's type anyway. Above all, Clausen did deserve the spot as lead on the list. There were a couple of others Allen promoted in interviews. I tended to be on the B-list, getting a mention and a helping hand now and then. Of course I yearned to be on that A list, but I really didn't have the confidence in my work. It wasn't deserving of the A list and I knew it. I also met Chris Funkhouser, a young mover-and-shaker poet from Santa Cruz. We had pictures taken with Ginsberg. Amazingly, there was also an old high school poet friend, Jerome, hanging around by coincidence - someone I knew from L.A. and who disappeared in a couple of mental wards. His head was still not quite screwed on, which I could detect from a brief conversation. I went off with Allen after the reading to a chain coffee shop. I asked Christiane to come with me but she was too shy. Jerome wanted to come, and I would've welcomed him except he was just too crazy. I remember hanging out at a big table at the coffee shop and Clausen drunkenly dominating the evening, though he was quite amusing. McClure had brought his young girlfriend and seemed a little annoyed. Ginsberg propositioned me in the bathroom when we both took a piss. "I thought I was too old for you now, Allen." "You're still cute."

I would've slept with him but the fear of AIDS was too great. Actually, it was more the fear of not being able to be honest with women I went out with (sure, I sleep with men - let's fuck). The question did come up - I had been tested for HIV - and just wanted to stay out of homosexual activity at least until this horrid plague had come under some sort of control. It was "the Red Death held illiminitable dominion over all" as Poe said.

I wound up getting a ride home with a couple of women - one a cute artist/ Tibetan Buddhist practitioner in the Nyingma tradition, Susan Rashkis, but still not a rail-thin punk vampira, to my folly. A great evening though. I made arrangements to have breakfast with Allen in North Beach next morning.

I remember one last thing Clausen said as we were heading from the coffee shop: "Marc Olmsted. You were such a promising poet 10 years ago. What happened?" What happened was trying to write for Hollywood and never sending my poetry out anymore. What happened was trying to be a rock'n'roll star. What happened was an alcoholic habit that had bit to the bone. What happened was I didn't know what happened.

I met Allen for breakfast in North Beach. My work assignment had come to an end and I had the day free. It was Friday. Sitting in earnest brooding conversation with Allen was Kush - someone who videotaped a lot of readings and had quite an archive - though much of it was unwatchable. Kush had met me a number of times and ignored me. I was apparently regarded as one of Allen's boys and not worth acknowledging. Branch left. Allen was going to get a ride from a journalist down to San Jose: "Why don't you come along?" I told him I'd have to get back that evening - "We'll get a ride back for you." The journalist would be driving back.

So along comes Steve Silberman, the journalist who strikingly resembled a young pudgy Allen. With him was a photographer, Mark Geller, and another male friend. Everyone turned out to be gay. I felt a little uncomfortable, a pretender. We all piled into the photographer's Citron station wagon and headed down the freeway to San Jose. Allen put his hand on my thigh. Strange, it didn't seem possessive or even have to lead to anything. It felt good. I thought back to our sexual days. Some of them had been as good as any heterosexual times. Other times, I woke up and looked at the bald old man - he'd shaved his famous beard at one point and then it was really a shocker to wake up next him - he could've been my urologist. Back in those days I had trouble scoring with women because I looked so young, yet chicken-hawked in the gay world. A grim joke at times, or, in Buddhist terms, business as usual.

The road spun on in front of us. We talked about Jesse Jackson. Allen felt he couldn't support his Presidential nomination because of Jackson's heavy drug war stance. Allen confided that even the top aides within the White House were coming to him and saying "What can we do? This is not working." We discussed the possibility of total legalization. I imagined the freeway if everyone had access to coke. Not a pretty picture - a definite *Death Race 2000*. We talked about Allen's long-time lover Peter Orlovsky who was in and out of the loony bin from drink and shooting up street drugs in New York. Sad, since he was a remarkably gentle poet himself. We discussed 12-Step programs. Allen himself had been going to Al-Anon. He had quite a history of attracting drunks and drug addicts into his emotional arena and, at 63, was beginning to check out why. Mark the photographer held up his camera over his shoulder and snapped photos into the back.

We arrived at Ginsberg's motel, Best Western, which was decent enough but also utterly generic. Ginsberg moved his room to get a better view, of what I'm not certain, maybe the tree in the front yard, as there wasn't much else to see. The place was also virtually deserted. The man behind the counter checked in Allen cordially, also gay, and eyeing this entourage of young men Allen had accumulated around him. I felt a fundamental pressure - glad to be close to Allen but remembering something I'd said to him the first night we made it, 14 years earlier: "Would you have me even if we didn't sleep together?" What was that feeling, as now the TV station host arrived to take us off for a taped interview. I got to ride in the car with Allen - I had special treatment and it made me nervous - what was that about? Of not being a colleague, of being a whore of some sort, even though this didn't seem to lead to sex. The feeling I'm getting as I write is a profound tension - a tightening in the face and neck - I wanted to be accepted like Andy Clausen - remove the physical thing altogether - I want to convince you Allen had me along as a friend and not as someone who might give in sexually even though it had been

8 years - Jesus, I wasn't *that* desirable and it wasn't that hard to get someone new - funny how Allen specialized in straight boys. They really wanted it from him.

So what did Allen think? I had an opportunity to make amends to him privately - a 12-Step thing. I thought I'd caused him a lot of grief in my early years with a possessive girlfriend and a conflicted brain - a real hot-and-cold kid like I was later paid back with some of the women I dated. He smiled. “You don't have anything to apologize for. You were a gem, a real find.” Still, was that the answer I sought? I leave it to you - he seemed to like me and enjoy my company, especially the Buddhist and poetic thoughts - and I didn't have to sleep with him anymore for it.

OK, we're in the studio, and Steve Silberman is talking to me now, obviously wondering about my connection with Allen - and we watch the talk show unfold. It's pretty funny. The TV host is goofy amd Allen says what he wants. The thing wraps up and Allen gets ready for the next item - arrival at a book store for a signing and impromptu conversation with the populace.

There's a chair and microphone on top of a stage. It throws Allen a little as he thought he was just signing books, but shrugs and gives up. He's famous now. He’s met all the Beatles, Jagger, Dylan, Joe Strummer of the Clash. Who's new? People start to filter in, including some blond kid - a cute bookwormish boy who asks me how long I've known Allen. “14 years,” I say. Is it possible? And of course the kid's me, I've never grown up and yet I have - blessings and rain of sorrow - ancient, even, I watch the event unfold - the room gets packed - finally it gets started with the bookstore owner giving a little pitch - always rather embarrassing “Allen Ginsberg meant this and that to me when I was blah blah blah...” it gets old very fast - but what else are they going to say?

When asked as to what kind of Buddhism he practices, Allen teaches everyone how to sit and breathe. One older guy tries to get a private conversation going with Allen and he gets cranky: “Overcome your shyness instead of engaging in a solipsistic dialogue!” The place gets too crowded amd people can't get in, so he berates those sitting in the aisles. “Part of being aware of the space around you is consideration of the other sentient beings in the room!” He's pretty cranky.

Time for signing books. There's a big line, and Allen is autographing but there are also sunflower drawings, skulls, buddhas, flying saucers, big third eyes in triangles. Everyone's excited. I note a posturing James Dean type over in the corner, looking like he wants to take his shirt off for attention. What does any of it mean, I want attention, too. Allen had been asked who he reads: “...Clausen. Marc Olmsted, who's with us today.” Was it possible to ever get enough?

As I’ve repeatedly mentioned, the acceptance of Allen really eased my basic discomfort of being a fucked up character, or a lousy Buddhist practitioner with easy irritability, emotionally overwrought, although when we had briefly had a moment together walking in San Jose, he complemented my poetry but added, "Have you ever considered therapy?" He was in therapy now. Seems the same stuff I was attached to 14 years ago was still there on the page, even if it was "more transparent," as Allen put it, meaning less solid iron habit. It got me thinking. 12-Steps, it seemed, were going to keep me sober. Period. Tibetan Buddhism was a way of stepping beyond personality, but didn't particularly address the problems of personality itself.

Now it's time to go on this big honorary dinner that is private and sort of yuppie art community. Everyone's dressed up. I have only a sleeveless t-shirt - Allen makes room for me, adds a chair at the table, joking with those present: "This is my manager." The meal was kind of boring, I couldn't drink the wine anyway.

Off to the reading on San Jose campus. How can one describe a poetry reading - I can't give you his books through this page - he read about sleeping between a bride and bride-groom, giving them kisses as he heads off in the dawn - a poem on LSD written in 1959(!) when Ginsberg was given the drug as part of a CIA research project - a famous poem to America asking for tenderness and nudity of physical meat and heart - finally a poem about a Blakean sunflower found in the junkyard with Jack Duluoz - alas, if I could give up my own shame as requested.

It is coming to an end - once more the book signing, cupid boys with shirts off address the poet shaking their charms - one asks for his stomach to be autographed - was I so bold? Naw. The photographer Mark will give me a ride back into the city. It's over, greatest day in a long time - I plan to see Allen Sunday in the city when he'll be back - now the streets are dark, it's a 45 minute drive - I feel the fatigue hit me - the photographer asks intimate questions and I answer - I confess I don't make it with men anymore and why - he doesn't seem to think much of my answer and I'm embarrassed - still, that's what I do - too timid, perhaps now without drugs and booze to fortify my courage - but also, I just like women more - it's not worth sacrificing them, and I doubted even the most sympathetic hearts would be able to stifle their own sex horror - here's the vampire boy of sodomy, look out! Forlorn, back to the Center. Just gimme a girl and I'll keep quiet.

I went down to see Allen sign books at City Lights next day, early evening. It made me remember 3 years earlier, when I'd done the same - set up a sort of test while I was at it. I'd arranged a note to get to him through the bookstore when he had arrived - giving my new number - would he call me or would I have to look him up? - a very indirect "adult child of an alcoholic" thing to do - he didn't call - so I showed to the signing and confronted him in a low key way - "You didn't call," the hurt look on my own face too practiced, I'm sure. "Didn't have time yet." Would he have called? Maybe, maybe not - the wasted speculations of a drunk, sober or otherwise. Too many tests...but it established the way I would handle Allen from then on. I'd seek him out when he got into town and not wait for that call, afraid he might not make it. Who *would* he call? Old, old friends, new boyfriend - that's it? - again I felt on the B-list, fearful I might be a pest - but he never treated me that way. Later, when he visited San

Francisco, his call often came before mine.

So with this whirlpool of thoughts I approached City Lights and found it an absolute nightmare, completely packed with people, an impossible scene. But it didn't matter. I'd see Allen in a week and a half, after he returned from Northern California. I rode the bus home admiring the boots of an aging punk.

Ginsberg was now back into town for a benefit to "Save the Coral Reef." I talked with Steve Silberman on the phone and we made arrangements to go - Mitch would also come - and here I had a car and could collect my share of bodies. How often I had been chauffeured in my drinking days? 11 years in San Francisco - now I was Dad.

Poet Kenward Elmslie was also reading in town, and Allen had been invited to the reading. We went with Shig's nephew, who was studying to be a doctor. I drove the leased Honda I had from L.A. Elmslie's poetry was fun, surreal, I decided I wanted to get a copy of his *Moving Right Along* but hesitated, money tight. Shig's nephew picked up on this and bought it for me graciously.

The "Coral Reef" benefit included Allen, eco-poet legend Gary Snyder, Japanese wild man Nanao Sakaki, McClure, and Snyder's old lover Joanne Kyger - a huge event with a huge turnout at the Palace of Fine Arts. Steve was writing an article for the Sunday paper, and he asked me if I minded if I got included. "No problem," said the ambition-hungry poet. I saw photos taken that fun day down in San Jose - one in particular showed Ginsberg with his hand on my thigh, though it was almost cropped out. Mitch caught it immediately. I remember there being some attractive women in front of us - here I was with all gay men - and I could see them trying to figure out our preference as so often happened in this town. I yearned to be with those women - they listened with that eavesdropping straight ahead stare to our stories of obvious interactions with Allen and the other poets. I'd also met Gary a number of times though never with any real connection. Steve and I slipped backstage and talked with Allen before the show. McClure was friendly. I looked up and saw his girlfriend, who was amazed that I remembered her name, which obviously pleased her. There was to be a party afterwards in the Aquarium at the park - *that* sounded like fun.

We arrived early. Well-wishers had restrained the great writers back at the reading site. The idea of a party in the Aquarium was certainly bizarre. I remembered, stoned in bygone days, how I'd think mantras at the dolphins. I'd always felt badly for the dolphins in particular. Eventually others drifted in. We wandered the corridors of the Aquarium in a lonely dream, waiting for the "Event" to start.

Then they were here, and food was served, bottles of booze emptied. Dinner was sushi, so positively ghoulish you'd think it a cannibal joke worthy of weird novelist Willaim Burroughs. Alas, it was just upscale insensitivity. Everyone ate ravenously in front of the docile fish. The dolphins were at least downstairs. I glanced up at a fairly attractive woman in a tux who poured me a Calistoga water. "Are you a poet?" she asked. I nodded with some embarrassment.

"You look like one. You look like you have a lot on your mind." Ah, the melancholy Dane, consuming sushi as the fish wiggled in their blue-lit oblivion.

Allen talked to me for a while, attentive. We discussed the recent sheath of poems I'd given. After a long hit-and-miss attempt to meet Allen's push for William Carlos Williams' objectivism, he felt I'd finally nailed it in a poem called "in a park" than ended with

the old iron
  cross with
        rivets on
  the brick
church across
    the street
unmoved by
 a siren's wail

The funny short lines were duplicated straight out of my Kerouacian spiral-bound pocket notebook - an exhaustive practice that was so rarely followed by editors I eventually dropped it.

"Now's the time to publish," he said, which meant put out my own book, or bombard the magazines, but just get it out there. My poetry practice had become quite solitary, masturbatory in fact - I had trouble justifying a lot of time sending to magazines because rarely was there money in it – but it led to funny friendships with editors and poets (I've yet to even meet David Cope of *Big Scream*). I got to know Jim Cohn of *Napalm Health Spa* and Eliot Katz who had a brief involvement with *Long Shot*. [Like Andy Clausen and a homosexual mountain man who called himself Antler, these guys were all post-Beats, the real heartsons of Allen.]

I chatted with Amy, McClure's girlfriend, but he came up from behind and grabbed her, whispering into her ear, paranoid it seemed - not that I felt like any particular threat - but the conversation abruptly ended. There was actor Peter Coyote, who'd graduated from local plays to the world of film. His girlfriend flirted with McClure rather openly in front of Amy. There was also Gary Snyder with his new Japanese wife - I didn't go up to him because it would've been the same interaction we'd had before. "You're a great poet." "Thank you." "You're really a great poet, a...a visionary." "Thank you." Next. The evening wound down as I eyed various women, feeling like I was in one of those big water tanks myself - behind glass - foolish, even - but for what, my desire? Yes, I felt foolish for that.

Time to go, I packed my rag-tag entourage and headed for the Honda in the final taxi night, driving off in anti-climax.

As mentioned, Steve Silberman had told me that I was going to be included in the article he was writing about Ginsberg. He hurriedly brought it over to me when he picked up an early edition of the Sunday paper. I was dumbfounded - he referred to me once by name and then for the remainder of the article as Mr. Biceps - my sleeveless shirt had made an impression obviously. But the article had a strange bite to it, a jealousy it seemed - since I was getting preferential treatment from Ginsberg. I felt with a creeping horror that I was coming off as some sort of poetry bimbo - a hanger-on like a gangster's moll. Steve seemed oblivious. I was even on the cover of the Sunday supplement - ON TOUR WITH ALLEN GINSBERG. There was the photo with Ginsberg's hand on my thigh, though not particularly obvious - just an unconscious hint - a further damnation that I was not really a colleague but a kind of whore - or so I thought. I thanked Silberman in a kind of numb horror. I was doing what I had done all the way back to childhood - I didn't say what I felt. I'd go away and figure it out later.

> "...and the entourage splits into two for the trip to a KHTE-TV interview: Ginsberg and Mr. Biceps in the front car, the press crew trailing behind" -
> ON TOUR WITH ALLEN GINSBERG By Steve Silberman.

I was pretty upset. Here I'd just returned from Hollywood where my only artistic recognition had been receiving a copy of the Allen Ginsberg tribute to which I'd been invited to write something. (I opened the contents and nearly everyone was famous but me.) At the same time, I was getting rejection upon rejection except for being able to scribble story analyses on scripts for studios. All these frustrated writers turn into script readers with poison pens - much like critics - so here at last in S.F. some recognition...? And then it turns sour with my worst fear - maybe I'd unconsciously summoned my own back-stabbing publicity with a kicked heart that felt it was no good (I fell for that "manifesting" nonsense then) - so I shared about it in an 12-Step meeting - not mentioning Ginsberg in particular - but enough that people knew it was in the paper and I actually got a call from Silberman a day later - "I heard you felt like a poetry bimbo when you read my article," he said. Someone had heard me at the meeting and knew Steve and went and told him! Definitely not anonymity, my dears, but in this case it actually worked to clear the air - he himself genuinely sorry - he'd meant no conscious harm - very distraught - you could almost see him yanking his hair on the other side of the phone line.

We agreed to have dinner.

Over Chinese food it came gushing out - he'd apprenticed for Ginsberg at Naropa College - always wanting to sleep with him - but he was fat and felt unattractive. He finally got up the nerve to ask Allen: "I get the feeling you don't like me." Allen said simply, "I am not a guru, or a psychiatrist." And left it at that. The portrait that developed was one of unconscious jealousy - not even totally acknowledged here in our greasy spoon Chinese restaurant on the Haight - but there was something different in me since I'd sobered. I knew he'd meant no conscious harm and I also knew such jealousy in myself - it was possible to forget the whole thing - especially since no one else reading it even gave a shit. Only William Burroughs's secretary later told me he thought it was "pissy" - having had his own travails with the press. But I did admonish Steve that Allen most certainly wouldn't like his portrait of me. A letter from Allen came later congratulating him on the article and on my "amusing" appearance in it.

Allen came into town and visited me at the Meditation Center. It caused a stir among those who recognized him as I took him through the house - I couldn't help but enjoy it. Finally we returned to the shrine room and did Chenrezig practice with everyone, including the household and the visitors.

Libby, Lama Lodu's consort, said "There are obviously things I don't know about you." I kissed her cheek. "I have many secrets."

Lama Lodu came home from lecturing elsewhere and Allen hoped to meet him. Libby followed after Lama and quickly reported back that he was too tired. She then disappeared behind the curtain to Lama's quarters, where she told me later he said, "But I'm not too tired for *you*."

Two rejection
 letters for my novel
 coming on the
 same day -
 important agent
and publishing
house I'd hoped
 to be sympathetic -
The famous old
 poet visits and
  is a comfort -
  he advises giving
up fame -
 "They're published
  in heaven - prepare
  your manuscripts
  for death"
      A weight
  on my shoulders
perhaps finally
discarded?
 "Don't worry,

Don't Hesitate

secret vanity
remains" the
poet reassures -
we kissed and
hugged as his
taxi cab glowed
impatiently

'89 letter lost

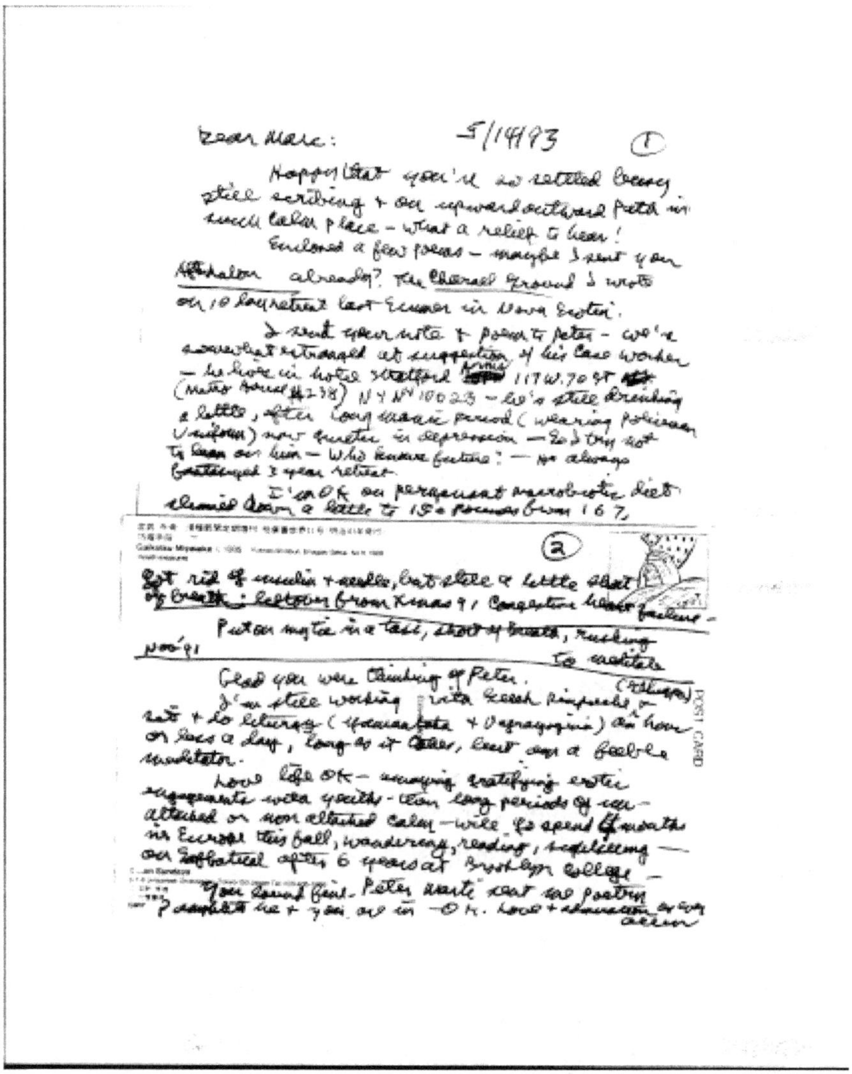

Dear Marc: 5/14/93 ①

Happy that you're so settled being still scribing + on upward outward path in such calm place – what a relief to hear!

Enclosed a few poems – maybe I sent you Athalon already? The Charnel Ground I wrote on 10 day retreat last summer in Nova Scotia.

I sent your note + poem to Peter – we're somewhat estranged at suggestion of his case worker – he lives in hotel Stratford Arms 117 W. 70 St (Metro Apt #238) NY NY 10023 – he's still drinking a little, after long manic period (wearing policeman uniform) now quieter in depression – so I try not to lean on him – who knows future? – he always [illegible] 3 year retreat.

I'm OK on permanent macrobiotic diet slimmed down a little to 150 pounds from 167,

②

Got rid of insulin + needles, but still a little short of breath: leftover from Xmas 91 congestive heart failure –

Put on my tie in a taxi, short of breath, rushing to meditate

Nov '91

Glad you were thinking of Peter.

I'm still working with Gelek Rinpoche (Tibetan) + do liturgy (Yamantaka + Vajrayogini) an hour or less a day, long as it takes, least days a feeble meditator.

Love life OK – enjoying gratifying erotic engagements with youths – then long periods of un-attached or non attached calm – will go spend 4 months in Europe this fall, wandering, reading, sightseeing – on sabbatical after 6 years at Brooklyn College –

You sound fine. Peter wants that [illegible] poetry pamphlet he + you are in – OK. Love + admiration as ever Allen

POST CARD

It was the middle of November '89 and I was home on the weekend. The doorbell rang. It was also the middle of the afternoon on Saturday and I wasn't happy about having to answer the door, because it meant somebody probably wanted something that I couldn't give them – if they knew their way around the Center they would have come in around the side if visiting a friend. No, ringing the doorbell during "off-hours" was rarely a good sign. It meant that somebody wanted a tour, information, something from the bookstore. And I, great bodhisattva example, was just not into it.

But I go down the stairs and Jeezus Christ, it's Bill Voigt – out of retreat!

"Hello, Billy," he says, calm and cool like a jazz musician hipster. I welcome him in, overjoyed, make him tea, close him off in my own room, ask if he's moving back in. The answer was no. After 3 years of a claustrophobic group activity, Bill was quite ready to be on his own. In fact, he was vague about his plans, other than expressing an interest in writing – he had after all been a student of Allen's out at Naropa. And, as one might imagine, he had much to write about. Finally, other matters called for his attention and he had to go. An extremely low key meeting that left me with one certainty. This is what I wanted to be. His manner was humble, open, grounded, spacious. He remained the inspiration he had always been for me, and had now crossed over to some unspoken, undelineated shore.

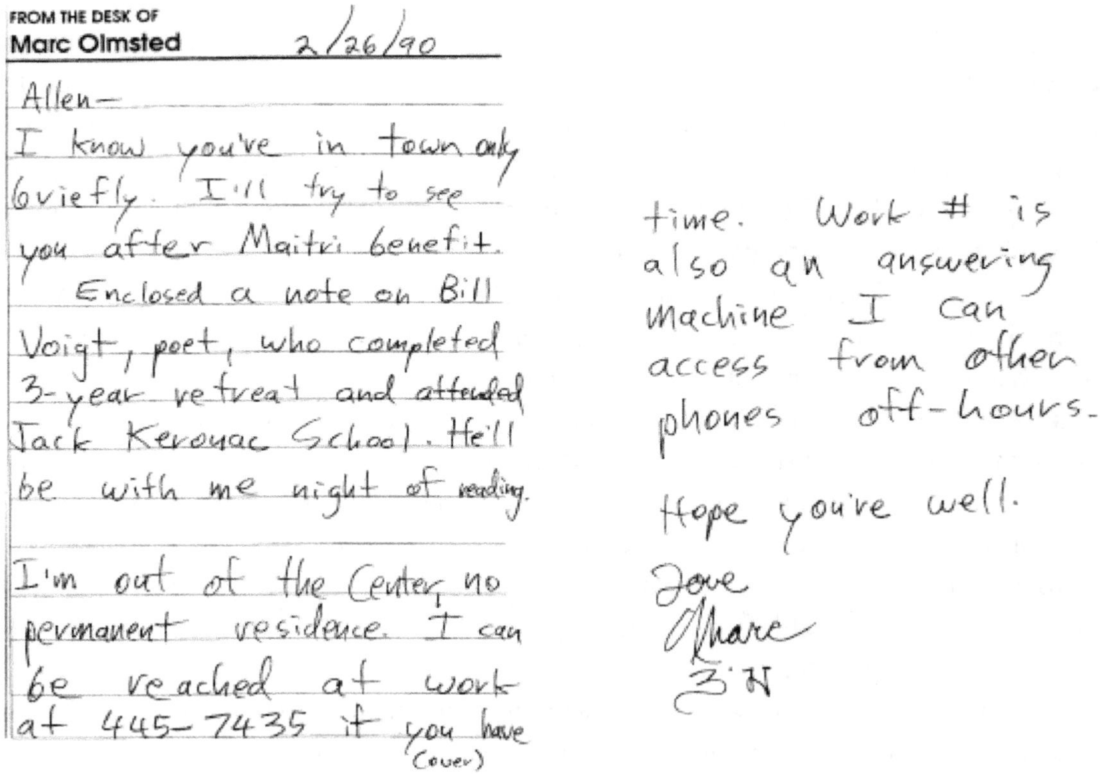
FROM THE DESK OF
Marc Olmsted 2/26/90

Allen—
I know you've in town only briefly. I'll try to see you after Maitri benefit.
Enclosed a note on Bill Voigt, poet, who completed 3-year retreat and attended Jack Kerouac School. He'll be with me night of reading.

I'm out of the Center, no permanent residence. I can be reached at work at 445-7435 if you have (over)

time. Work # is also an answering machine I can access from other phones off-hours.

Hope you're well.

Love
Marc
3:N

The Maitri Benefit was for the San Francisco Zen Center's new hospice (*maitri* is Sanskrit for compassion), and included Philip Whalen, Michael McClure, Ginsberg, trumpeter Don Cherry, and others. Bill Voigt was hoping for a letter of recommendation from Allen for some writing program, but unfortunately Allen didn't remember him. Libby came, too. Most hilariously, Don Cherry kept noodling on his horn as if warming up with a seeming acid casualty glee during some of the other lesser poets. It was clear that Don knew pretty well what he was doing, but he acted like he didn't so there was no calling him on it and certainly no controlling it. It had a Corso-esque prankster element that really showed the true selves of the various posturing poets who attempted to read with his merciless punctuations of blat and bleep. Cherry was mainly there to read with Ginsberg, and he behaved himself then. Afterward, McClure asked Philip, Allen, and me to sign his poster, which I appreciated. I saw a young man preparing to squire Allen away, and he had that self-important look that I knew was difficult to avoid.

A series of personality conflicts with other students (to put it mildly) led to my departure from KDK.

Things came to a head when Trangu Rinpoche was giving a weekend retreat Friday and Saturday on *The Ways of the Bodhisattva*, Shantideva's famous text of Mahayana conduct, a situation soon to have an ironic twist. Don, house manager and right hand man to Lama, began pressuring me to take up a portable sampler of the bookstore to this event. Thing was, I was also on shrine duty – you know, the shrine bowls. I was supposed to find a replacement for the shrine duty, which no one definitely wanted to do on the weekend. Plus the retreat cost $80 dollars unless you had been a member for two years. I had been a member for about a year and half. I had to pay the $80, and money was tight. I would also have to take Friday off from work. I just didn't think I could do any of this but Don kept at me – "You are responsible for the bookstore!" It was pretty clear I never intended to take on the responsibilities I was now being subtly and not so subtly manipulated, shamed and guilt-tripped into it. As I saw it, my involvement in the bookstore was my generosity and not my obligation, so this kind of pressure was really pissing me off. Foolish mortal, it was all a setup by my Lama, a forced surrender, but I didn't get that at all. I had long gotten away with doing what I wanted – if I was going to make the transition to serious student, this would apparently have to end. I mean, this is the lineage where Marpa made Milarepa build and tear down a building 3 times, hauling around stones on his back until his bloody bones showed. This is the lineage where Tilopa had Naropa jumping off a cliff. 3-year-retreat? Some serious boot camp was required before that, my dear. But you see, I just didn't get it. Maybe you would run for the hills, too, but we American fuckers really have it soft, baby.

So Don was just hammering me – he was Lama's hit man. I was totally exhausted as the weekend approached – I'd been doing the shrine bowls, dig, so I'm really crabby now and it's the day before the retreat and Don is on me again. "So have you found your replacement for the shrine duty? You'll need to have the Center book store packed by tomorrow morning."

"Fuck the bookstore, fuck KDK, and fuck you!"

Libby left with me. Lama Lodu had encouraged a romance between us. I was literally staying at the San Remo Hotel across the alley from Peter Marti's North Beach apartment. Peter was also now sober, his wife had left him, and we'd patched things up between us. Just as there had been no trace of Peter the hippie, there now was no trace of Peter the cokehead. Both our rock bands forgotten, we'd get together and read our poetry to each other. Good memories.

Libby and I had a tumultuous affair that eventually resolved into a lasting friendship. She'd heard about this interesting teacher, Lama Tharchin Rinpoche, and took me to an empowerment (dimly recalled as padmasambhava) that he was giving in Berkeley. I came into the small apartment where it was being given, and Lama Tharchin looked up from his preparations and directly into my eyes. His expression seemed to say, "Oh, it's you." For me it was an immediate connection that remains to this day. And Libby wound up his consort after our affair had burned out, which was her slumming between lamas.

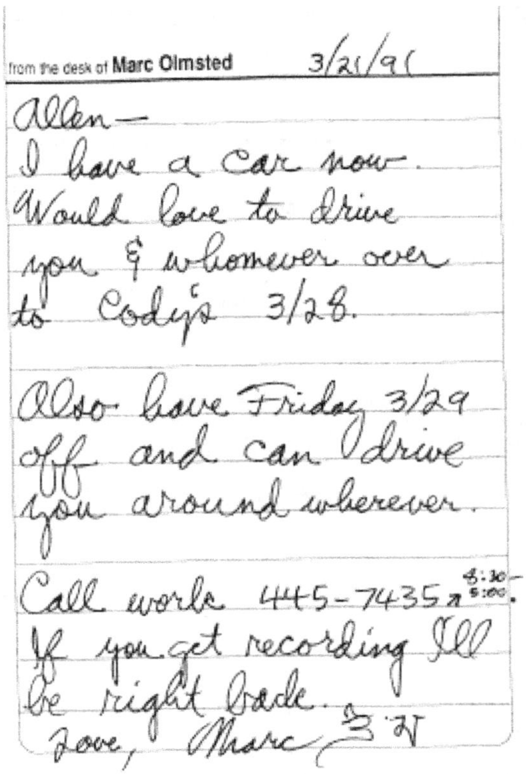
from the desk of Marc Olmsted 3/21/91

Allen—
I have a car now.
Would love to drive
you & whomever over
to Cody's 3/28.

Also have Friday 3/29
off and can drive
you around wherever.

Call work 445-7435 8:30–5:00.
If you get recording I'll
be right back.
Love, Marc 3.21

When Allen read with Andy Clausen at Cody's in Berkeley, the place was absolutely packed. Allen saved me a seat, thankfully – the scene extended far beyond the ability to view him. As per usual, he was gracious and mentioned to the audience how nice it was to be in the company of old poet friends, and I was listed. I have always loved Clausen's work, an enormously underappreciated poet and great reader of his own stuff – a real American voice, gravely, bear-like, voice of the blue collar with strange baroque Whitmanic expansiveness, the poetic equivalent of Orson Welles but with a downhome intelligence, like the wisdom of a hobo. We wound up over at Clausen's in Oakland afterward, and I sat next to Wavy Gravy, charming old doper who remembered everyone from the Merry Prankster Electric Kool-Aid '60s – mentioning that a lot of people had died trying to imitate Neal Cassady.

The next day we walked around the Haight, looking into the used bookstores. With Allen was a new boyfriend that must've been my age when we first met. I've forgotten his name, but Allen showed good taste. Sweet, gentle bespectacled intellectual kid – I had one of those amazing moments where one readjusts one's own sense of age, for this boy's face was completely without lines, as if newborn, or even still of the womb. It was similar to the way college freshmen just look younger and younger as time progresses and the carcass grows tired. We chatted a little – he knew I was an old boyfriend, he was a little shy, perhaps thought I'd try to make him like I had been hounded at his age. Allen bought me a couple of finds, including a copy of Antler's poetry that had been signed by Antler as well to some ingrate who'd sold it. We ate in a place called Hell's Kitchen that didn't last long – the service was so terrible everyone had to be on drugs.

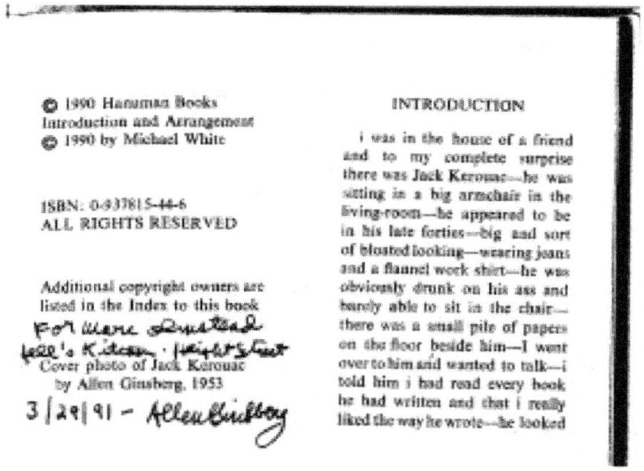

© 1990 Hanuman Books
Introduction and Arrangement
© 1990 by Michael White

ISBN: 0-937815-44-6
ALL RIGHTS RESERVED

Additional copyright owners are listed in the Index to this book

For Marc Olmsted
Hell's Kitchen · Haight Street

Cover photo of Jack Kerouac
by Allen Ginsberg, 1953

3/29/91 – Allen Ginsberg

INTRODUCTION

i was in the house of a friend and to my complete surprise there was Jack Kerouac—he was sitting in a big armchair in the living-room—he appeared to be in his late forties—big and sort of bloated looking—wearing jeans and a flannel work shirt—he was obviously drunk on his ass and barely able to sit in the chair—there was a small pile of papers on the floor beside him—I went over to him and wanted to talk—i told him i had read every book he had written and that i really liked the way he wrote—he looked

Safe in Heaven Dead by Jack Kerouac

Photographer Chris Felver was along for the ride. I remember driving up Market Street past the Cinema Theater, and somehow getting into an extended explanation as to how it mainly pitched out-of-town porn stars with gigantic tits – and I mean behemoth – they're main act was that they'd altered their tits to near-beach ball size. Allen asked me if I'd ever gone and I said no. I only knew about it from ads. Funny, I actually wound up in 3-year-retreat with a woman who danced there, but the local strippers were not of this mutated variety.

Walking Castro Street, Allen announced that he'd joined NAMBLA. "What's that?" "North American Man-Boy Love Association." So I figured, oh teenagers, big deal. I also figured any teenager who'd slept with Allen hadn't been seduced like one of those predator chickenhawks giving a kid a hard-on with porn and then offering a blowjob. I'd certainly heard enough queer coming-of-age stories from my gay friends who knew what they felt at an early age. Frankly, I'd never seen anyone around Allen who didn't go to college.

But after all, he said in his 1965 poem "Kraj Majales" (King Of May): "And I am the King of May that sleeps with teenagers laughing." Allen was quite amused that the photo of him in front of a blackboard used in the release of his 1990 CD *The Lion For Real* had snuk in "that sleeps with teenagers" in chalk above his head.

Once I asked the age of the youngest kid he ever slept with. "14," he said. Later, in print I saw he said "18." For once, he played it safe, though it was the only time I recalled him not telling the truth about his sex life.

Years later, Allen had already passed when I learned that NAMBLA included boy children. Around this same time, his posthumous *Deliberate Prose* came out and his one essay "Thoughts on NAMBLA" said he wasn't interested in children and didn't advocate sex with children. He advocated free speech, and felt that was what NAMBLA was about. The ACLU, at least in specific instance, had also felt the same.

On the other hand, there was that *Law & Order: SVU* TV portrait of NAMBLA as a ring of pedophiles scheming together on how to elude capture, trade porn or go to Thailand for a sex romp. One had to consider this was the *Dragnet* view of things. Still, it seemed naive not to imagine such discussions, even in private after the meetings. I never got to ask Allen about this.

Allen also appeared in a hour-long NAMBLA film called "Chicken Hawk" that I saw on YouTube. Teen lust only. I remember three other men in it - one a painter of high school football players who seemed sane and harmless, one guy who was lightly sleazy, and one guy who seemed delusional and creepy. Unfortunately this last guy got the most screen time. _

This delusional element seemed the most disturbing and demarcating line in the whole discussion. It is of course, the demarcation in any consideration of consent - even with hetero adults. "She wanted it." "She seduced me."

At any rate, by the time I investigated NAMBLA, it had already been pretty thoroughly destroyed by the FBI.

Finally, I talked to Peter Hale, who is now in charge of Ginsberg's estate, and had been Allen's friend and assistant for more than 15 years. Peter said that Allen finally regretted joining NAMBLA, realized it was a mistake, and didn't quite know how to clean it up.

I figure there were enough things to jail me for in future America, but NAMBLA advocate would not be one of them.

But back to 1991, Chris Felver in tow.

We visited a venerable queer hippie commune in the Mission that had been around since the '60s. It was Irving Rosenthal's place, known as the "Kaliflower" commune. Allen somehow managed to get Felver to wait in the car (at least for a while) just to get a break from the camera and not agitate the soft-spoken Rosenthal. Felver eventually grew restless and knocked on the door, video camera under his t-shirt like a strange bionic growth. Needless to say, Rosenthal wasn't fooled. We talked about the Gulf War, how everyone he knew was against it except for Burroughs, who said, "Those Arabs, give 'em an inch, they'll take a mile." Ginsberg laughed, repeating it. Of course, Allen knew all the political history that had led up to it, the incredible meddling we'd done in the mid-East that kept backfiring, even the father of the then-current General Schwarzkopf helping the newly enthroned Shah of Iran develop his dreaded secret police.

Felver caught the new boyfriend with me in the Booksmith on Haight St.

Allen signed books at the Booksmith, so I stepped outside for some air. I ran into McClure who was very nice to me, also waiting for Allen. Diamond Dave, an acid fry of the good old days, came up and began holding forth on Allen like I had no idea who Allen was. McClure smiled and said, "You may not know who you're talking to." Dave looked at McClure and said, "After 40 you get your real face." It was a compliment for McClure, of course. Less so for Diamond Dave, who looked like a cheery derelict, only shorted out with electricity rather than alcohol.

I went to a week of Lama Tharchin Rinpoche's summer retreat in the Santa Cruz mountains - his new property that he'd christened *Pema Osel Ling*, Land of Lotus Light. The practice was Vajrakilaya, a wrathful blue-black Buddha clutching his consort in ritual union. Given that Vajrakilaya had 3 heads, wings, 6 arms and 4 legs, there was little that obviously identified him as a Buddha. Add the cosmic flames, visualized ritual intercourse and my continuing the practice to this day, it remains likely I will be put in a camp if Christian dominion is ever completely established in this country – and that's if I'm not burned.

The experience of Vajrakilaya was like an internal explosion of a subconscious A-bomb – I was completely roto-rootered. I'd never practiced anything so wrathful before – and the wrath meant no prisoners were taken in the pathetic kingdom of my obscurations. By the end of the retreat, I stood in line for the coup de grace, Lama Tharchin touching of the ritual three-sided dagger to my forehead, throat and heart. I was overcome by a whirlpool of agitating emotions as I looked up at the image of Lama Tharchin's master, Dudjom Rinpoche. In my head, beyond my own control, a tape loop of my own crude English mantra spontaneously revolved: "I surrender to the guru – fuck you – I surrender to the guru – fuck you – I surrender to the guru – fuck you…"

The dagger touched me and I sat down and began to convulsively sob. When this subsided, I stumbled up to Lama Tharchin and said "Will you formerly accept me as your student." "Absolutely," he said, and then, eyeing my obvious terror that I had just married him in a psychic shotgun wedding, he softened it with "I will help however I can."

7/30/91

Dear Allen,

Because you're on retreat with Khenpo Tsultrim, I thought you'd be amused by a section from my novel **WILD KINGDOM** when I went to Disneyland with him and Ken McLeod. In it, Tsultrim is called Khambu, Ken is called Mel, and Trungpa is mentioned as Dabsig.

I look forward to your visit to S.F. end of August.

My retreat with Lama Tarchen Rinpoche doing the Vajrakilaya practice was devastating, I'll tell you more in person. Wrenching! Lama Tarchen has just acquired some retreat land in Santa Cruz and is now trying to pay for it. This was where the retreat was held, and it was quite beautiful. A 3 year retreat is planned (Tarchen is Nyingmapa). Don't think I'm up to that.

I'm looking into putting on a poetry benefit for the land, thought I'd get Clausen (who has already agreed) maybe with Chris Funkhouser's back-up band Thelemonaid, Steve Silberman, Peter Marti, myself and musician partner Gary Schwantes. Not sure if we'll do it up here or in Santa Cruz. I'd love to include you if you're so inclined, perhaps around your November visit. Will talk to you in S.F. about it.

Love,

Marc Olmsted

I misspelled my lama's name, which was actually Tharchin. This misspelling would find its way into Allen's poem, "Death and Fame." Lama Tharchin Rinpoche remembered meeting Allen in Spokane, Washington some years back. "A nice guy."

In 2012, this late eighties photo of Ginsberg and Tharchin was located:

Allen, like meeting Trungpa in India, had no memory of it. Still, Allen agreed to the benefit. Everything went very well in the planning stages, including booking local club DNA Lounge, until he called me the day before the event, short of breath. He had mild congestive heart failure, he said, not life-threatening, but he had fluid around the lungs and had checked himself into a hospital.

Of course, relatively speaking, all Hell broke loose, including Steve Silberman deciding to tell the club on his own that we'd carry on anyway. I opted out of that one. A reporter called me, and I had my first experience of how an extremely low-key conversation, "off the record," literally became national news. I was quoted again and again across the country.

News clipping of Allen's heart problems…

1-3-92 BAY AREA REPORTER

Out There

Gay & Funny Tidbits From Around the World

by Daniel Mangin and Kevin Davis

ALLEN GINSBERG ILL: Poet Allen Ginsberg suffered mild congestive heart failure early last week and had to cancel a benefit reading at DNA Lounge for the Pema Osel Ling Tibetan Retreat. Ginsberg had tried to get Michael McClure to fill in, but couldn't. One of the event organizers, Marc Olmsted (who was also to have read), says Ginsberg "should be back on his feet in a week" and will attend a future benefit for the retreat.

Illness sidelines Allen Ginsberg.

A-12/CAPE COD TIMES **TUESDAY, DECEMBER 31, 1991**

PEOPLE

Poet **Allen Ginsberg** canceled an appearance in San Francisco because he was recuperating from a mild heart problem that kept him hospitalized for a week, an associate said.

Ginsberg, 65, was discharged Saturday from Mary Imogene Bassett Hospital in Cooperstown, N.Y., a hospital spokesman said.

Marc Olmsted, an associate of Ginsberg's in San Francisco, said Ginsberg suffered "mild congestive heart failure" on Dec. 21.

"The situation is not life-threatening," Olmsted said. "He was not feeling well and checked himself into the hospital. He had felt shortness of breath and had fluid around the lungs."

The author of "Howl" and other "beat" poetry had been scheduled to do a reading Sunday in San Francisco at the national convention of the Modern Language Association of America.

Ginsberg was recuperating yesterday at a cousin's cottage near Cooperstown, a housekeeper answering the telephone there said.

■ ■ ■

Bob Rosenthal, Ginsberg's longtime secretary, gave me a lot of shit about leaking this to the press without Allen's direct authorization (a statement for Lucien Carr to release had been in the works), saying, "You won't get famous that way, Marc." But Allen later said that it was a "tasteful and accurate" response.

Still, I hadn't renounced Hollywood. My 4th script was actually optioned (the 3rd, *Chemical Man*, a drug-update of *The Lost Weekend*, met with complete indifference before my leaving L.A.). This new one, which I finished in San Francisco, was a sci fi called *The Hive*, written with old friend and Hollywood gaffer (a.k.a. hanger of lights on the set), Kevin Brennan. My L.A. 12-Step sponsor Sean had established a Canadian film company, made one movie already, and expressed interest. But the deal fell through with his partner.

Then my sister Lynn calls in the night: "Dad's had a stroke!

The airport shuttle drivers argue over who will take me to my father's death.

All day Tibetan prayers by the hospital of my father the agnostic.

His head titled back mouth open my first sight he looked like a corpse.

Instructions from my lama I remove the iron ritual dagger from its tied silk wrapper – touch to father's head – place it under his pillow.

Prayers to the Buddha as guru – prayers to the wrathful loving One with adamantine wings terrifying protection.

High school Buddhist friend Richard M. now gray-haired sits by the hospital bed chanting with me.

Father – your eyes know me – I think you speak in my mind – when I reply you look relieved.

Excerpted from "Poe's Voice"

I returned from L.A., my father still in some half-alive state, maybe lingering for months. Jeffra, a Buddhist student and brief affair who was all of 21, was apparently already over me, certainly if I was going to be a big drag about my dad. She said she'd meet me at a lecture of

Lama Tharchin's over in Oakland. I sat there, feeling the full weight of expectation, the deep yearning for her, anyone, to comfort me, morose over my father, and there in front of my new teacher I knew she wasn't coming, and the hammer blow that was samsara hit me on the head with a konk, almost like that stoned shower wake-up of 1985 when I realized I was a drunk.

I thought, you know, if there's an inheritance, I should use it to do 3-year retreat. When the lecture was over, I went out to his car and asked him if it was possible. "It's definitely possible," he said. "But we need to talk."

Part 9 - Drubdra

Driving the black Plymouth Valiant '64 through the wooden gate onto the retreat site, my lama ahead of me in the dark with a flashlight, my ex-girlfriend behind me, she: "give me a hug" I love you I said starting the engine and pulling inside, leaving her behind. What movie is this?

My father passed after six weeks. I used the money for retreat. Whatever ambiguities of feeling I had, he gave me art. His death was devastating.

3 years, 3 months, 3 days is a classical length of Tibetan Buddhist retreat. Supervised by Lama Tharchin Rinpoche, the first two years for me were preliminary purification (Ngöndro) and *long* devotional "guru yoga." Third year, mostly "deity" practice - visualized manifestations of enlightened mind. It was not uncommon for me to do 4 meditation sessions a day, each at least 2 hours in length. This was no Buddha valium health spa. Like an Arctic research station, we remained an isolated community. By the end, as students joined at various times, there were 11 of us in the Santa Cruz mountains.

When I entered retreat, my older sister asked me what I expected to get out of it. "To deepen my experience and understanding." "Well, then you won't be disappointed."

I wasn't.

And Allen's shamatha meditation instructions lead directly to this 3-year retreat.

MARLON BRANDO, ON THE SET OF APOCALYPSE NOW.
PHOTOGRAPH BY MARY ELLEN MARK

Allen –
Another birthday,
huh?

Love
Marc Olmsted
3'N

Allen Ginsberg
P.O.B. 582
Stuyvesant Station
New York, NY
10009

Dear Marc: 5/14/93 (1)

Happy that you're so settled being still scribing & on upward outward path in such calm place – what a relief to hear!

Enclosed a few poems – maybe I sent you [illegible] already? The Charnel Ground I wrote on 10 day retreat last summer in Nova Scotia.

I sent your note & poem to Peter – we're somewhat estranged at suggestion of his case worker – he lives in hotel Stratford Arms 117 W. 70 St (Metro Hotel #238) NY NY 10023 – he's still drinking a little, after long manic period (wearing policeman uniform) now quieter in depression – so I try not to lean on him – who knows future? – he always [illegible] 3 year retreat.

I'm OK on permanent macrobiotic diet slimmed down a little to 150 pounds from 167,

(2)

Got rid of insulin & needles, but still a little short of breath: leftover from Xmas 91 congestive heart failure – Peter maybe in a taxi, short of breath, rushing to hospital Nov '91

Glad you were thinking of Peter.

I'm still working with Gelek Rinpoche (Tibetan) on sits & do liturgy (Yamantaka & Vajrayogini) an hour or less a day, long as it takes, but am a feeble meditator.

Love life OK – occasionally gratifying erotic engagements with youths – then long periods of un-attached or non attached calm – will go spend 4 months in Europe this fall, wandering, reading, sightseeing – on sabbatical after 6 years at Brooklyn College –

You sound fine. Peter wants to see the poetry pamphlets he & you are in – OK. Love & admiration as ever
Allen

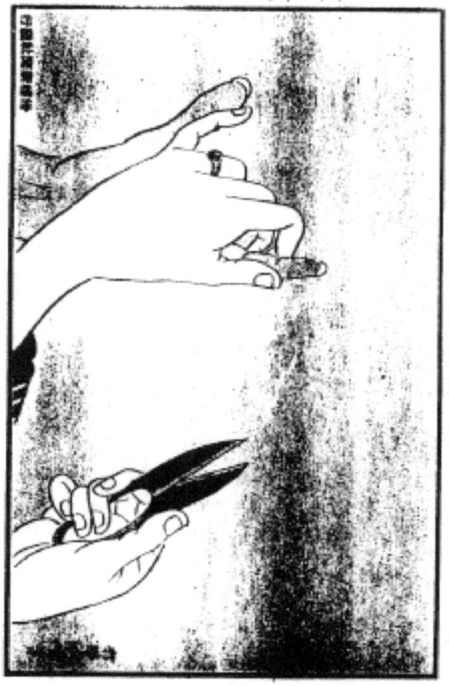

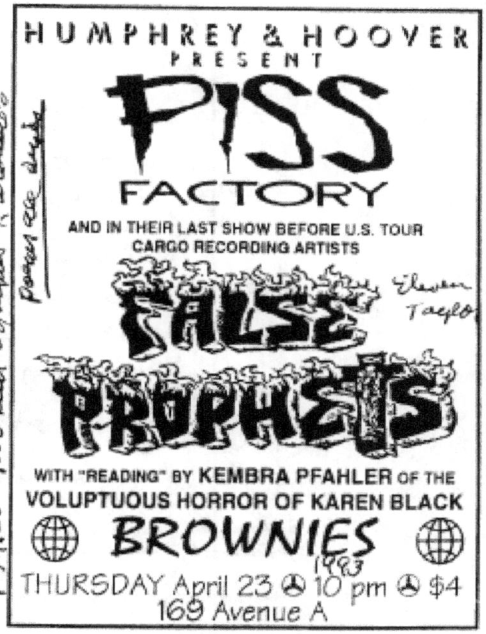

To my amazement in editing this book, I realized this particular poem had, to my knowledge, never been published, not even in Allen's posthumous revised *Collected Poems*:

Thoughts in Fort Lee

Diana & Roger Napoleon's real estate empire
extended up to the Napoleon Castle Hotel's penthouse
stainless steel & gold doorknobs bathtubs bars & windowsills
But Roger got Alzheimers & couldn't keep his money books
    straight
Diana went to jail for back taxes & cheating at cards
Lost control of her castle, lawyers ate her Empire
She got sick & spent years maintaining her body,
skin growths, liver failure, kidney disturbances, upset sto-
    mach
But the castle of flesh ceased to function
She was left inside with her soul.
What is that? Where will it go? Who am I?
asked Napoleon in bed, eyes closing for the last time on
    Elba.

9/7/92   3 PM

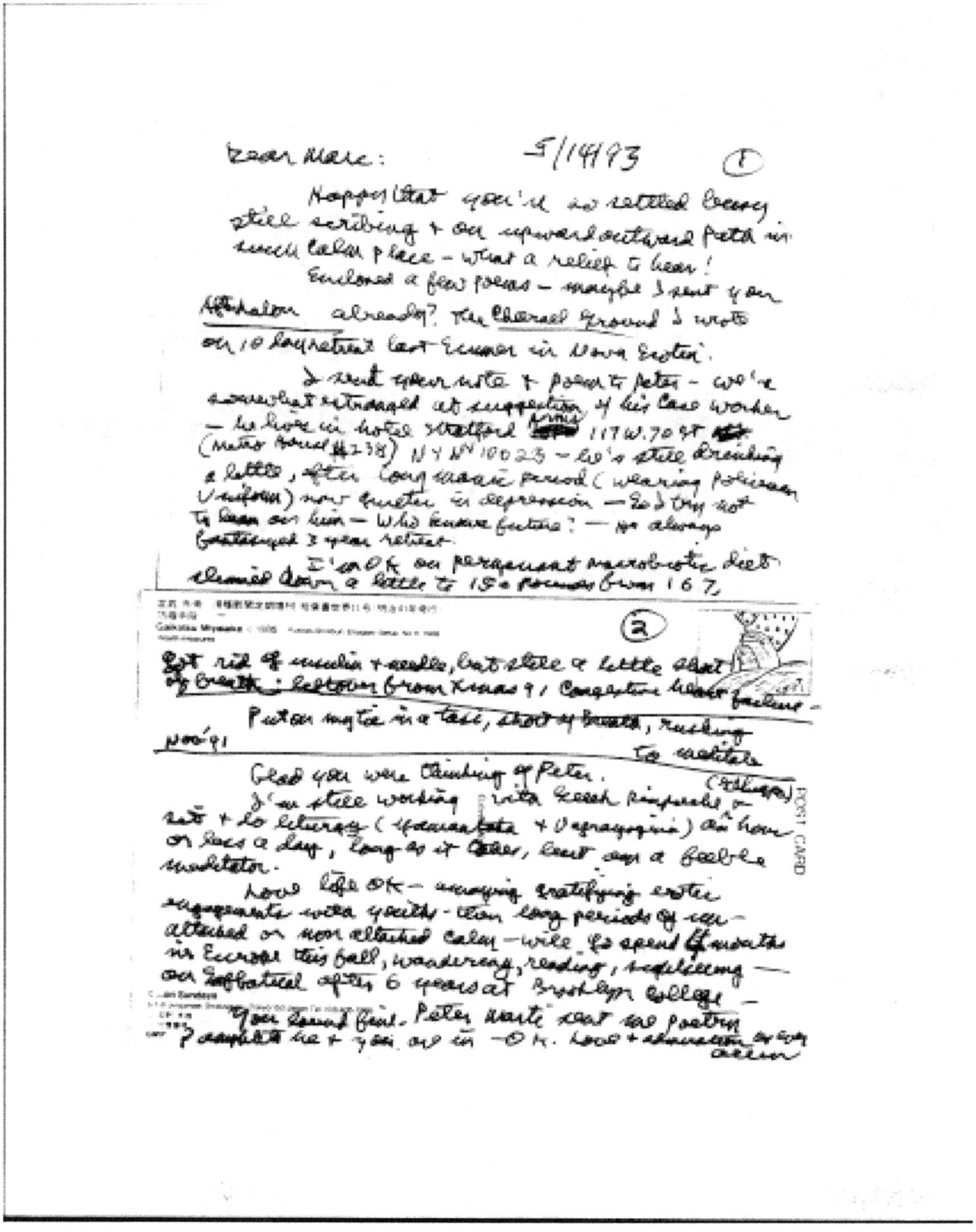

Dear Marc: 5/19/93 (1)

Happy that you're so settled being still scribing + on upward outward path in such calm place — what a relief to hear!

Enclosed a few poems — maybe I sent you Athalon already? The Charnel Ground I wrote on 10 day retreat last Summer in Nova Scotia.

I sent your note + poem to Peter — we're somewhat estranged at suggestion of his case worker — he lives in hotel Stratford Arms 117 W. 70 St (Metro House #238) NY NY 10023 — he's still drinking a little, after long manic period (wearing policeman uniform) now quieter in depression — so I try not to lean on him — Who knows future? — He always [illegible] 3 year retreat.

I'm OK on permanent macrobiotic diet slimmed down a little to 150 pounds from 167,

(2)

got rid of insulin + needles, but still a little short of breath: leftover from Xmas 91 Congestive heart failure —

Put on my tie in a taxi, short of breath, rushing to meditate Nov '91

Glad you were thinking of Peter.

I'm still working with Gelek Rinpoche on sits + do liturgy (Yamantaka + Vajrayogini) an hour or less a day, long as it takes, tho I'm a feeble meditator.

Love life OK — occasionally gratifying erotic engagements with youths — then long periods of un-attached or non attached calm — will go spend 4 months in Europe this fall, wandering, reading, sightseeing — on sabbatical after 6 years at Brooklyn College —

Your sound fine. Peter wrote that the poetry pamphlet he + you are in — OK. Love + admiration as ever Allen

POST CARD

Marc Olmsted

Allen — ✓ 9/2

Wanted you to know my teacher, Lama Tharchin Rinpoche, will be at John Giorno's Sept. 24 eve. Hope you can meet him. He knows who you are already.

I trust you are well.

I am deeply immersed in ritual music, language. Still scribbling and of course practicing. Charming correspondence with Diane Di Prima & her lover Sheppard — both have studied with Lama Tharchin — Sheppard has decided to be his student formally. Forgive sloppy card executed in tiny free moment. I'll send poems early '94.

Love
Marc

"BEGINNER'S MIND"
Green Gulch Farm
Muir Beach, California

From the original watercolor by
Catherine Anderson
Sausalito, California

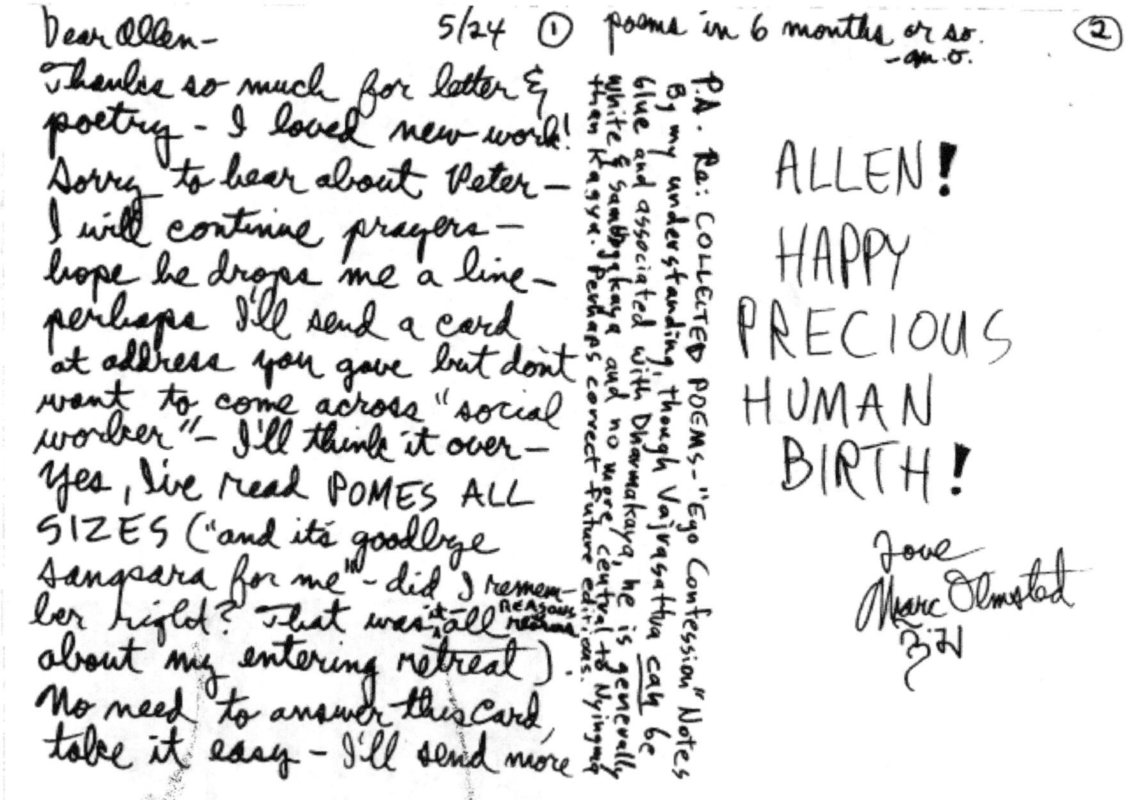

Dear Allen- 5/24 ①

Thanks so much for letter & poetry - I loved new work! Sorry to hear about Peter - I will continue prayers - hope he drops me a line - perhaps I'll send a card at address you gave but don't want to come across "social worker" - I'll think it over - Yes, I've read POMES ALL SIZES ("and it's goodbye Sangsara for me" - did I remember right? That was, it, all REASONS about my entering retreat). No need to answer this card, take it easy - I'll send more poems in 6 months or so. -M.O. ②

P.S. Re: COLLECTED POEMS - "Ego Confession" Notes
By my understanding, though Vajrasattva can be blue and associated with Dharmakaya, he is generally white & Sambhogakaya and no more, central to Nyingma then Kagyu. Perhaps correct future editions.

ALLEN! HAPPY PRECIOUS HUMAN BIRTH!

Love
Marc Olmsted

Marc Olmsted

May 26, 93
20139 Eureka Canyon Rd
Watsonville Cal.

ADDENDUM
PLEASE READ CARD FIRST

Final thoughts before sending off card –

Since theme of "Better Prepare for Death" is evident in recent work sent, I feel there is some Tibetan Death Insurance that would really benefit you: Phowa.

Phowa can usually be learned in a week retreat and can be practiced only once a month at full moon or not at all.

What is important is the transmission and who it's received from. *Highly* respected is Ayang Rinpoche, Drikung Kagyu, but respected beyond his school even by my own Nyingma teacher. Ayang Rinpoche travels nationally on a regular basis just giving Phowa. There must be a Drikung Kagyu Center in New York that knows his travel. If not, try Lama Norlha's Karma Kagyu Center for info.

Phowa is *not* too advanced etc. etc. It is a technique for consciously exiting at death that primarily needs a teacher to "plug in" connection. I feel it is *very* important for you. Please ask Gelek Rinpoche his opinion.

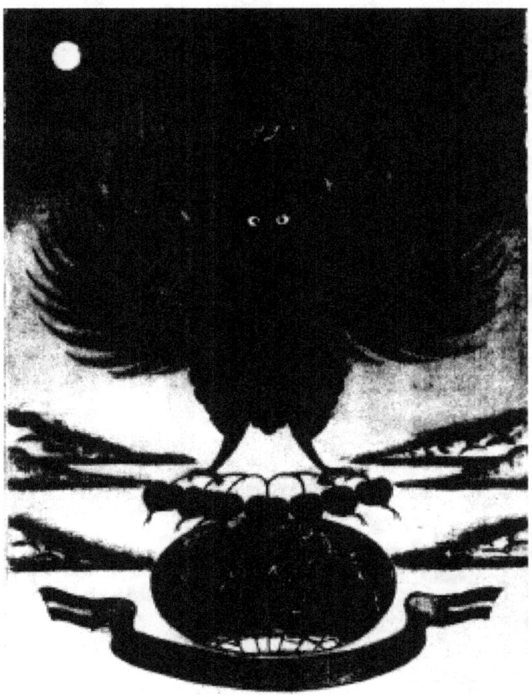

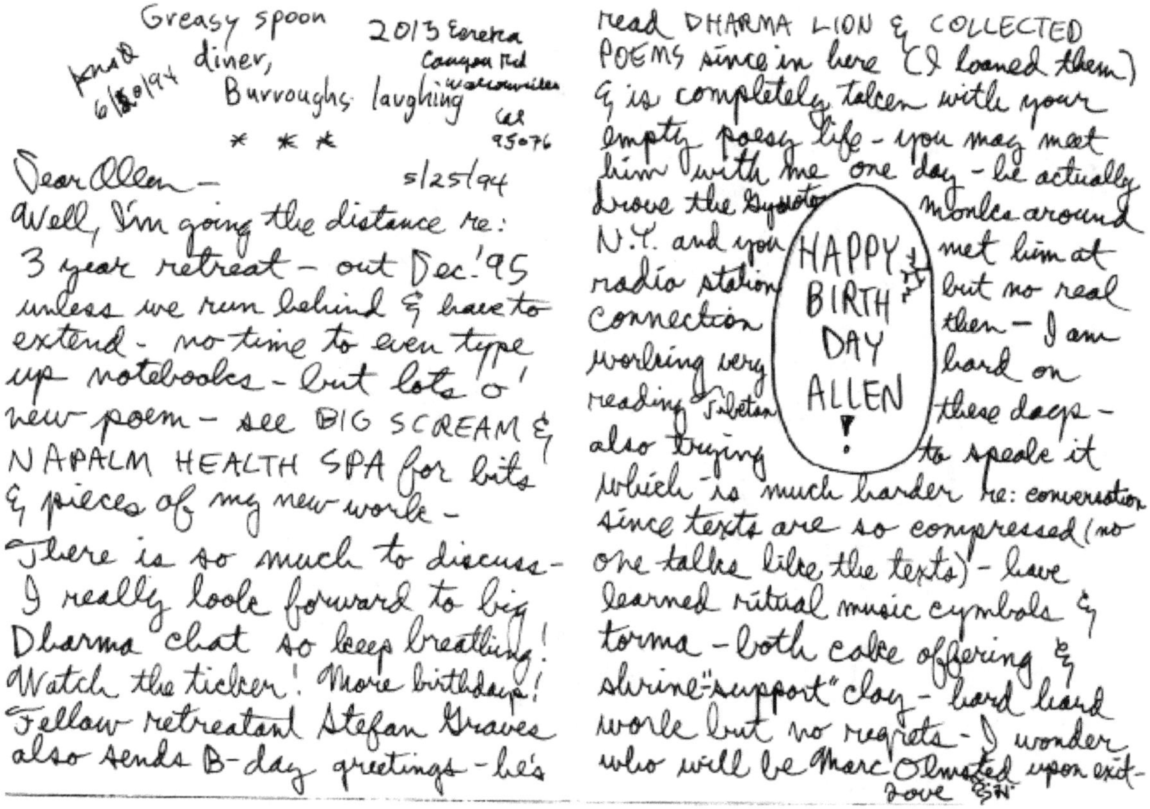
Greasy spoon
diner,
Burroughs laughing
* * *

June 6/10/94

2013 Eureka
Canyon Rd
Watsonville
Cal
95076

Dear Allen — 5/25/94
Well, I'm going the distance re:
3 year retreat — out Dec.'95
unless we run behind & have to
extend - no time to even type
up notebooks - but lots o'
new poem - see BIG SCREAM &
NAPALM HEALTH SPA for bits
& pieces of my new work -
There is so much to discuss -
I really look forward to big
Dharma chat so keep breathing!
Watch the ticker! More birthdays!
Fellow retreatant Stefan Graves
also sends B-day greetings - he's
read DHARMA LION & COLLECTED
POEMS since in here (I loaned them)
& is completely taken with your
empty poesy life - you may meet
him with me one day - he actually
drove the Gyuto monks around
N.Y. and you met him at
radio station but no real
connection then - I am
working very hard on
reading Tibetan these days -
also trying to speak it
which is much harder re: conversation
since texts are so compressed (no
one talks like the texts) - have
learned ritual music cymbals &
torma - both cake offering &
shrine "support" clay - hard hard
work but no regrets - I wonder
who will be Marc Olmsted upon exit -
Love
S.N.

HAPPY
BIRTH
DAY
ALLEN
!

June 22, '94:

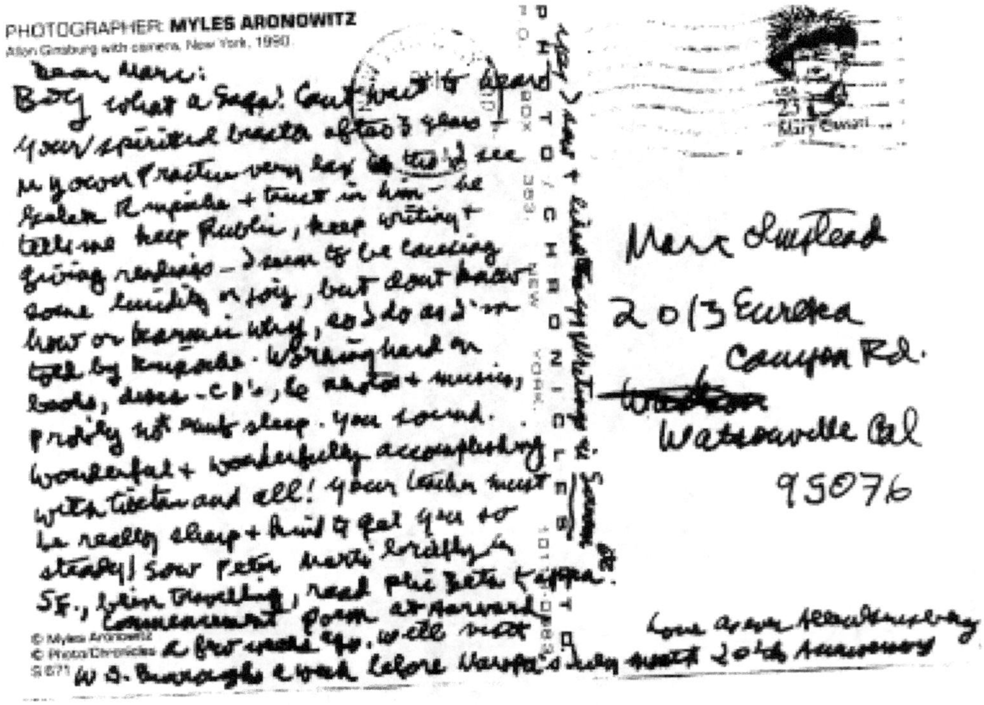
PHOTOGRAPHER: MYLES ARONOWITZ
Allen Ginsberg with camera, New York, 1990

Dear Marc:
Boy what a Saga! Can't wait to hear
your spiritual tracks after 3 years —
[illegible] very [illegible] see
[illegible] Rinpoche + trust in him — he
[illegible] keep writing +
tell me [illegible]
giving readings — I seem to be [illegible]
some lucidity or joy, but dont know
how or karmic why, as I do as I'm
told by Rinpoche. Working hard on
books, [illegible] - CD's, [illegible] + music,
[illegible] sleep. You sound
wonderful + wonderfully accomplished
with Tibetan and all! Your teacher must
be really sharp + kind to get you so
steady! Saw Peter [illegible] in
S.F., [illegible], read Phi Beta Kappa
Commencement poem at Harvard
a few weeks ago, will visit
W. S. Burroughs a week before Naropa's [illegible] 20th Anniversary
Love as ever [illegible]

Marc Olmsted
2013 Eureka
Canyon Rd.
~~Watson~~
Watsonville Cal
95076

© Myles Aronowitz
© PhotoChronicles
S.671

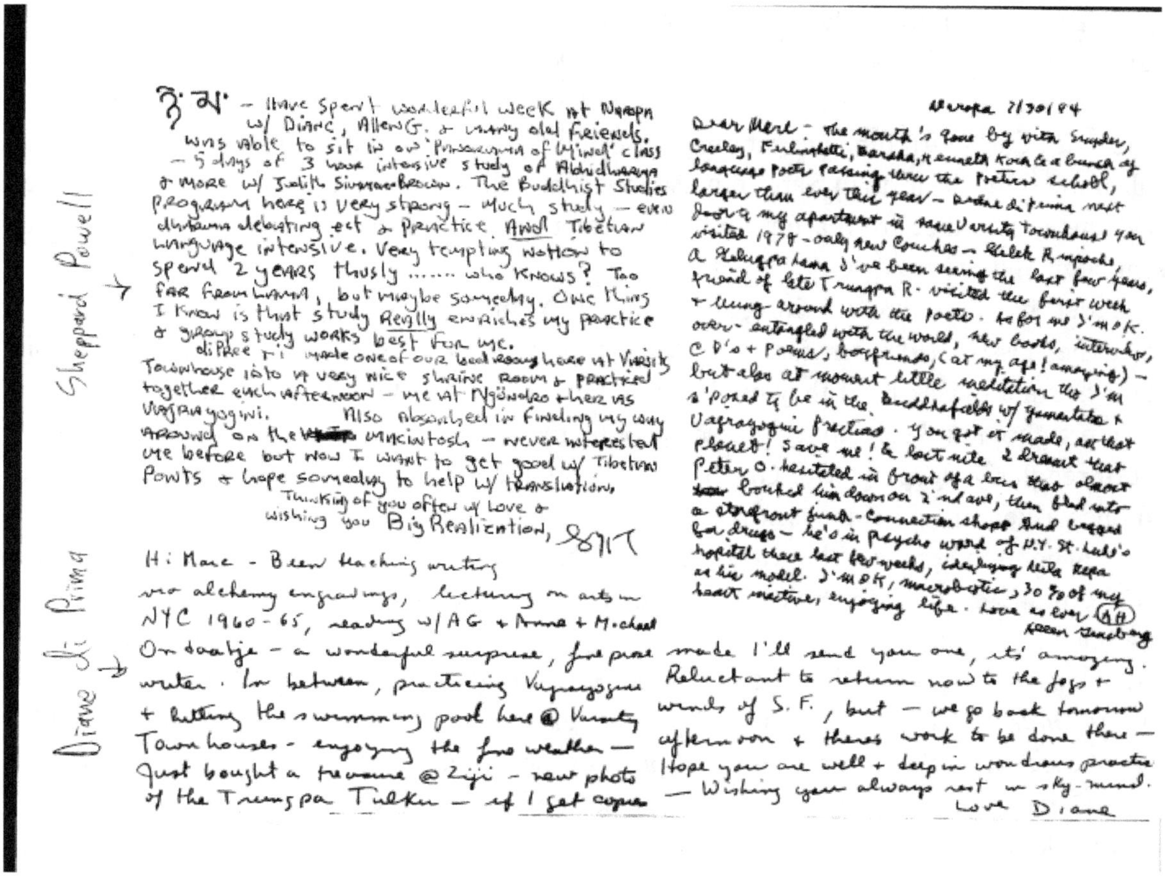

Sheppard Powell →

[illegible] – Have spent wonderful week at Naropa w/ Diane, Allen G. & many old friends. Was able to sit in on 'Phenomena of Mind' class – 5 days of 3 hour intensive study of Abhidharma & more w/ Judith Simmer-Brown. The Buddhist Studies program here is very strong – much study – even dharma debating etc & practice. And Tibetan language intensive. Very tempting notion to spend 2 years thusly ...... who knows? Too far from home, but maybe someday. One thing I know is that study really enriches my practice & group study works best for me.

Diane & I made one of our bedrooms here at Varsity Townhouse into a very nice shrine room & practiced together each afternoon – me at Ngöndro & her as Vajrayogini. Also absorbed in finding my way around on the [illegible] Macintosh – never interested me before but now I want to get good w/ Tibetan fonts & hope someday to help w/ translation.

Thinking of you often w/ love & wishing you Big Realization, [illegible]

Naropa 7/30/94

Dear Marc – The month's gone by with Snyder, Creeley, Ferlinghetti, Baraka, Kenneth Koch & a bunch of language poets passing thru the poetics school, larger than ever this year – Diane di Prima next door & my apartment in same Varsity Townhouse you visited 1978 – only new couches – Gelek Rinpoche, a Gelugpa lama I've been seeing the last few years, friend of late Trungpa R. visited the first week & hung around with the poets. As for me I'm OK. over-entangled with the world, new books, interviews, CD's & poems, boyfriends, (at my age! amazing) – but also at moment little meditation tho I'm s'posed to be in the Buddhafields w/ Yamantaka & Vajrayogini practices. You got it made, all that peace! Save me! & last nite I dreamt that Peter O. hesitated in front of a bus that almost knocked him down on 2nd ave, then fled into a storefront junk-connection shop and begged for drugs – he's in psycho ward of N.Y. St. Luke's hospital there last few weeks, idealizing Milarepa as his model. I'm OK, macrobiotic, 30% of my heart inactive, enjoying life. Love as ever (AH) Allen Ginsberg

Diane di Prima →

Hi Marc – Been teaching writing via alchemy engravings, lecturing on arts in NYC 1960–65, reading w/ AG & Anne & Michael Ondaatje – a wonderful surprise, fine prose writer. In between, practicing Vajrayogini & hitting the swimming pool here @ Varsity Townhouses – enjoying the fine weather – Just bought a [illegible] @ Ziji – new photo of the Trungpa Tulku – if I get copies made I'll send you one, it's amazing. Reluctant to return now to the fogs & winds of S.F., but – we go back tomorrow afternoon & theres work to be done there – Hope you are well & deep in wondrous practice – Wishing you always rest in sky-mind. Love Diane

I was finally out. I spent 10 days on the land before I even crossed the street in big country Santa Cruz mountains. Thought I would stay in tender bliss forever. My brother Ross actually came down to see me because he wanted a gander at my virgin unsullied mind. He brought his malamute dog, most beloved, whom he named Tashi, not knowing that it meant "Auspicious" in Tibetan, not even knowing the word. He gave a white scarf to my lama, as is tradition, and said, "Thanks for what you did for my brother." Tharchin Rinpoche remarked that Tashi was a common name for dogs in Tibet, which definitely got my brother. Ross already had a funny interview with Chagdud Tulku Rinpoche at my recommendation, but still wasn't hooked. That reticence didn't last. He wound up completing his ngondro practice, prostrations and all, under Lama Drimed, an amazingly charismatic Westerner who became Chagdud Tulku's dharma heir after his death.

Going down into Santa Cruz to get my car's brakes fixed was another matter. It was not unlike an acid trip, and not a particularly pleasant one.

This kind of sensitivity lasted about 2 months. I put off getting a job for a long as possible and wandered around without a permanent address.

I regularly visited my mom in L.A as well as Richard, who now lived there again. I found myself connecting with the L.A. poetry scene, which turned out to be quite developed. It was as if a spaceship of misfits had crashed in Hollywood, and were reading to each other until the engines got fixed. Richard first met Amelie Frank, which led to the group known as the Valley Contemporary Poets. In particular, Rick Lupert and Brendan Constantine also illuminated the scene, with Carlye Archibeque hanging out from over the hill. I was welcomed in with a great deal more enthusiasm than San Francisco ever had, though it may in part have been due to my status as a prince from a foreign land. Later I would meet neo-Beats S.A. Griffin, Scott Wannberg, and Steve Abee.

Allen was teaching a writing seminar in L.A. in Santa Monica, and invited me to meet him at the class. I had been visiting my mother and stepfather in L.A. and my mom absolutely astonished me by asking if they could come meet Ginsberg, too. For a woman who read me with a praeternatural sensitivity ("Didja give up the cocaine, too, Marc?"), it appeared that my past of regularly sleeping with Ginsberg was not on her radar, and this is from someone who had once asked me if I was bisexual. Maybe she *did* know. What she told me was that Allen had been good to her kid. She was right about that. A far cry from "Ginsberg and his ringlets" that she muttered in 1968, gakked on vodka while watching him on Merv Griffin. Ed, her Republican husband who had been astoundingly softened by his 12-Step work (where they'd met, natch) actually framed the poster of the benefit I *almost* did with Allen in 1991. And he'd sent me *Dharma Lion* while I was in 3-year retreat. My mom also seemed to think I could get them to meet the Dalai Lama. Very cool old lady, now gone. But I declined to take them along this time, now with some regret. There still seemed like there would be many times ahead.

I walked into a giant auditorium, which was filled to the brim. We were in the middle of various exercises, and I participated in one where you wrote down your worst secret. Although I cannot recall exactly what my confession was, such a exercise prepared me for writing this memoir, as a good deal of what I've said here was at the very least seriously compartmentalized at that time.

Allen asked me to go pick up Peter Orlovsky at Oscar Janinger's in Santa Monica, where they were staying. He drew out a little map for me. Dr. Janinger was a cousin of Allen's, a psychiatrist who had advocated and experimented with LSD. They actually never had a relationship until late in life, though as I saw later, Oscar had on his shelves many rare *Big Table* issues, that initial magazine of Beat authors . However, I could not find Peter anywhere in the house or guest house, despite calling out many times. The only place I didn't go was the master bedroom, which was dumb (I guess I assumed that was Janinger's room), because Peter was deep asleep there, though it was now noon. I drove back and told Allen Peter wasn't there. Poor Allen, he obviously thought Peter was wandering around like a lost benevolent Frankenstein. We rushed back and there was Peter. Oops. Peter still wanted to stay, though, and he did.

Allen was quite forgiving, though I'd seen him be tough on others. I think I'd always let him know if he hurt my feelings so he was pretty gentle with me. We returned to an interview where the woman asked Allen about his various medications. He candidly admitted that the heart medicine kept him from getting hard but he could still come. She actually asked quite a bit about the details. She seemed to have some sort of geriatric nursing interest. I began laughing at the sheer surrealism of her precise investigations.

Then we went down and had an early supper. I met Natalie Goldberg for the first time, whom Allen privately explained has absorbed her Naropa school lessons well and created a little cottage industry for herself as a popular writing instructor. Allen also showed me his initial sketched out efforts of frame the process of writing in terms of the Ground, Path, and Fruit of Tibetan Buddhist meditation. It was basically the Inspiration, Process, and Result of the writing experience. I was fascinated and wound up developing it further in some of my own later teaching of creative writing. There was a brief hubbub when a flashy mysterious elder woman came to the table and magnetized many of the Santa Monica matrons into going off with her. They were apparently dashing to a private audience with Carlos Castaneda, the famous author and sorcerer's apprentice of the Don Juan books. I was struck by their hunger, since they all seemed pretty wealthy with their various gold accessories. But they still wanted SOMETHING and it was **Power!** Like running to phone your broker with a hot stock tip, they furtively left with a smugness that read: By Invitation Only. Those of us left behind were unmoved.

When it was done, Allen and I walked across the parking lot and a young man called out "*Howl* was great." Allen answered, "*Kaddish* was better."

Oct. 1, 1996, the De Young Museum presented the Whitney's traveling Beat show. At the reception I sat with Allen and Dennis Hopper on the inside steps. Allen introduced me, told Hopper about my 3-year-retreat, who found that pretty interesting, it seemed. Cameras flashed. There again was Bruce Conner, who had returned to his pre-Devo brunette look.

Finally, on October 3rd of 1996, we got to do the benefit we didn't do before retreat. I went back to the DNA Lounge and pitched the benefit again, without realizing the club had changed hands and I owed the new owners nothing. The booker had a crush on Beth Lisick, and suggested she be part of the line-up. She actually was a good choice, her energy just right – but it would be the only good thing the guy could give. He promised print ads that never came about, literally anywhere. Not the local Bay Guardian, S.F. Weekly, or the Chronicle. It would cost us heavily in turnout.

Also on the bill were Diane di Prima, Gary Schwantes (my old sax player friend from the Job), and Peter Marti, now a devoted student of Lama Tharchin himself. Steven Taylor accompanied Allen on guitar.

Allen's secretary Bob Rosenthal sent a description of Ginsey's dietary needs. I glanced at them and thought I understood. Jill , Peter Marti's girlfriend, went to great trouble to prepare a macrobiotic meal. Allen opened it and knew instantly that it was too salty for his current health. I had misread the information and interpreted it from old intel. Allen was very nice about it as we arranged another simple steamed vegetable meal immediately. As for Steven Taylor, he went next door and got a pizza slice.

Allen had me get on the stage with Anam Thubten Rinpoche, whom I'd invited in some vague capacity – more just as an official Tibetan representative. Allen actually asked Anam Thubten Rinpoche what he did with sexual desire in retreat.

Thubten Rinpoche demurred. "Ask Nyima. [My dharma name – MO] He has a PhD in sexual education." Tibetan humor.

So Allen asked me.

"We weren't allowed to have sex in retreat."

"Not even with yourself?" Allen pursued.

"W-e-e-e-l-l-l-l-l, at certain points in retreat it was discouraged. At other points, it was neither encouraged nor discouraged."

"Good answer."

I was glad to get out of it so easily.

Allen also read a poem that has yet to be published. My arrangement of lines is strictly intuitive:

Dream of Carl Solomon

I meet Carl Solomon.

"What's it like in the afterworld?"

"It's just like in the mental hospital.
You get along if you follow the rules."

"What are the rules?"

"The first rule is: Remember you're dead.
The second rule is: Act like you're dead."

Next day, Allen read at the De Young. Richard had flown into town with a Chinese paramour he was courting, and we sat up close. Hopper made a last minute appearance and sat directly in front of me, turning and asking at the break, "What'd I miss?" I said he'd basically made it just in time. We chatted briefly again, and I mentioned that he seemed to literally work without a break – he was in countless films all the time. "You're working yourself to death, it seems." "Yeah, but what a way to go," he smiled.

Allen gave a spectacular reading, including the chant *gate gate paragate parasamgate bodhi svaha* from the Prajnaparmita Heart Sutra, repeating the discourse that leads to this mantra in English translation, but performed in a Japanese Zen style (a monotone with each syllable shooting out like boxcars in a freight train). He ended by singing a standard Blake song he'd tuned - "Nurse's Song," which had the enchanting refrain, "And all the hills ecchoed" (which Allen chose to pronounce "echo-ed" – which made sense as Blake also had the word "laugh'd" in the poem, suggesting that it should be spoken as we do today, as a contraction). The audience would sing along with this refrain. It was like a mantra, we'd always get buzzed. Richard and I compared notes later and we both had the flash that we'd never hear this again. It was true. The next time we'd be singing it was at his L.A. Memorial.

As he passed me as he went up the aisle, I fell into step with Allen. "What'd ya think of the Prajnaparmita Sutra?" he asked. "I liked it, but you left off the *Om* that begins *gate gate paragate parasamgate bodhi svaha.*" Allen actually looked a little crestfallen and said he'd look into that. Richard overheard this and took me to task. "*Om* isn't in the earliest translations," he admonished me. My knowledge came from the Tibetan. As usual, Richard was right.

Allen was putting on a photo exhibition at The Robert Koch Gallery and had managed to include Robert LaVigne as a favor. LaVigne was an astonishing painter who'd done a particularly famous portrait of Peter Orlovsky back in the 1950s. I called LaVigne up, who was now in Seattle. I also hooked him back up with Latif Harris, a poet and student of Lama Tharchin who talked of running around with LaVigne "back in the day." LaVigne spoke with Latif on the phone and was a little shook. Latif's health was failing and he was on scads of medication, making him weepy and a bit delirious. LaVigne had me go to Philip Whalen's and Michael McClure's to scoop up some drawings that LaVigne had left behind in the Bay Area. Whalen had some very cool portrait sketches, as well as some more curious and less successful abstracts. McClure couldn't find his LaVigne archive, try as he might. Michael was suffering from severe clinical depression, and the medication was just kicking in. Allen had remarked he thought that McClure may be "confronting his own vanity." I brought the work to the Gallery and helped Koch figure out who everyone was in LaVigne's portraits. When it came to opening night and the official pre-dinner, the cat "neglected" to invite me. I showed up at the reception later like everyone else. There was an amusing moment when Lisa Andreini, photographer friend, somehow innocently brought up my being left out of the dinner right in front of Robert Koch. Like it really mattered, but I couldn't help but enjoy his embarrassment.

On November 17, 1996, again back in town, I went to Allen's hotel. I thought I could smell sperm on his breath at the door - I wondered whose it might be. Allen and I walked around Chinatown above North Beach, looking in windows at the gadgets. There was a dream-like quality being with him and looking at glistening displays of video cameras and other white metal toys of the future. He seemed very calm and spacious, even as the conversation turned to his health, which was full of problems, including not being able to get an erection anymore. He described it all with the same detachment as examining the techno-junk in the windows.

We went back to his hotel. .

Allen Ginsberg then dictated an introduction to my book *What Use Am I a Hungry Ghost?* He died before he saw the final transcription, but he had suggested that we include some of our dialog about certain poems and the revisions to them he suggested. Frankly, although he was right that the actual feedback he gave contained a great deal of useful instruction, I found these virtually impossible to incorporate – probably because of my own small mind and vanity as to what an introduction was supposed to be. However when it came to this lecture, I realized that I could at last make use of these previously unpublished transcripts as well as carry out his literal last wishes in making them available. (For those of you with a copy of my *Hungry Ghost*, this section would be inserted right after Allen's published *Introduction* says: **"Haikuesque poems…")**

AG: The haikuesque poems are sometimes interesting, but I think they're a little too spare. (*Then quoting from Olmsted's typewritten manuscript*):

The fat sparrow
battles his reflection
in a hubcap

…The fat sparrow where?

MO: Where did it occur?

AG: Yeah.

MO: By my car out by my cabin…

AG: So the fat sparrow outside my cabin battles his reflection in my hubcap. The fat sparrow by my car…

The fat sparrow by the car
battles his reflection
in my hubcap

The car, *my* hubcap.

MO: It's certainly more interesting now.

AG: I mean the hubcap means the car but you know, what car, whose car, where is it? But the isolate observation here is genuine "no idea ideas but in things" experienced perception.

AG: (*again reading aloud from Olmsted's typewritten manuscript*):

jet streaks
at dawn light
red hot needle

That's a little difficult…You need to put the sun in there, I dunno, a little more contextual. I would say, go back to the locale and like Kerouac says, see the picture better, wait and it'll come to you. Close your eyes now. Are there trees? Do they move? …[Anything] emotional?

MO: Could we say "jet streaks in dawn light red hot needle rocket? Would that make it clearer? Red hot rocket needle?

AG: We need something, I dunno…it needs some more information.

MO: Red hot rocket needle trailing white gas?

AG: Well, was it white gas or red?

MO: The metal of the plane is red in the dawn light.

AG: Ohhhh! I didn't get that. I thought that the streak was the red…

MO: No. It's the metal.

AG: No, then you've not got that, because the streak's here syntactically the red hot needle, not the jet.

MO: Yeah, it's supposed to be the jet that's the red hot needle.

AG: I didn't get it at all. Because the red hot needle is first. So syntactically the streak is the red hot needle, not the jet. Well ok. "Red hot needle jet plane streaks in dawn light"

MO: Trailing white gas.

AG: How long?

MO: How many syllables?

AG: No, how long is the white gas?

MO: Long, comet-tail like.

AG: Hmmm.

MO: Red hot needle jet plane streaks in dawn light?

AG: Red hot needle jet plane steaks in dawn light. Ok. But the streaks here is the verb rather than noun so then you need something like "red hot needle jet plane streaks in dawn light dissolve white gas." You need object, the jet plane streaks dissolve or the jet plane streaks disperse or something.

MO: Jet plane streaks in… Red hot needle jet plane streaks in dawn light vapor trail.

AG: Well, you have, "streaks" is "vapor trail." Ok, jet plane, I would say, I would say "red hot needle jet plane vapor trail in dawn light mist." Above what?

MO: Above the water tank?

AG: Oh. Oh yeah. "The red hot needle jet plane streaks about the water tank." Gives it context. You didn't relate it to the ground. You related to the sky but you didn't ground it. You know, the Trungpa thing, Heaven, Earth, Man. {See Chogyam Trungpa, *The Art of Calligraphy – Joining Heaven & Earth* – MO}

MO: Right.

AG: Sky. Ground.

MO: Doesn't really the classic haiku end with some kind of surprise?

AG: Well, the water tank's a surprise.

MO: Is it?

AG: Yeah, cuz you see you'd never expect that you got up in heaven and all of a sudden above the water tank. And you can have "a", that would be good, then you could take out the plane and some other information. A red hot needle jet's white vapor trail streaks above the water tank. Put white in there.

MO: White vapor trail streaks above the water tank.

AG: "The red hot needle jet's white vapor trail streaks above the water tank". You can…[play with it]. It's just a question of adding more information to get the full picture in somebody else's mind, so what are the Sherlock Holmes details that would compound, complete the symbols to make it into sensation? We could reverse it like "above the water tank white vapor trail red hot needle jet streaks by." I mean you could arrange it 4 or 5 different ways, putting all the blocks, you've got three, …jet, the white vapor trail, and the streaks above the water tank, you could realign in any direction you want.

So the final published poem in *What Use Am I a Hungry Ghost?:*

WATSONVILLE DAWN LIGHT

White vapor trail
above the water tank –
hot red needle jet

From the same book, Ginsberg began critiquing an early draft of 3RD DAY OUT which, when originally describing watching a kung fu video with some kids and Buddhist monks, said they were:

also having
fun just
like me rushing
on the action
dream

AG: (*quoting from Olmsted's manuscript*) also having fun just like me rushing on the action dream – What does that mean? Getting a "rush"? That's not clear. Rushing sounds like you're rushing to.

MO: Getting a rush on the action dream.

AG: Action dream?

MO: Action dream. We're watching this movie and, of course, it's the first poem about being out in the world, so that's also the action dream.

AG: I think "dream" is too Buddhist a word there, too overt. In fact, like a dream is the image on the TV screen, so it's not reality, but virtual reality, so I would take out the word dream and use something more technical. Like… more like the screen shadow action, the action screen, the shadow screen or something. You see dream is too vast a word for the specifics, the natural object is always the adequate symbol, so you want a symbol of dream?

MO: Getting a rush on the action screen I think is good.

AG: Well, you need a little more than screen, shadow or dots… If you can nail it down… getting a rush on the electric screen shadow action…

like me
 getting a rush
 on the shadow action
  electric screen –

Allen then continued with an anecdote that's in the published *Introduction*: **One thing I'll never forget was Swami Muktananda…**

Now I was in my 40s and I realized I was no longer even of sexual interest to him, strange wistfulness that he didn't try to make it with me. It would be the last time I ever saw him.

We did talk on the phone twice after that. The first time, Allen had the idea to give a reading in Santa Cruz, a big venue, and donate all his salary to Lama Tharchin Rinpoche. It was quite a gesture for a lama he didn't remember meeting, but I know that Diane di Prima's involvement with Lama Tharchin helped legitimize his obvious authenticity. The usual amount Allen received was $7,500.00, so it became clearer why he didn't think the DNA Lounge event had been a success.

By this time, Peter Marti and I both had both become involved with our future wives at Lama Tharchin's retreat center, Pema Osel Ling. Peter would take over the cooking from Suzi Kaplan, writer and therapist soon to complete her intern hours. She joined me in San Francisco and we moved in together. Peter took the kitchen job to be close to Nancy Menzies, who became the Head of POL's office. They remain there to this day.

I began the hunt for sponsorship through UCSC and actually received a relatively cold shoulder. Eventually this led to Beat Studies teacher William Craddock, who figured we could pull it at an outside venue. It was not to be.

I dedicated the book to all my fathers. Mind father: Rinpoches Lama Tharchin and Dungse Thinley Norbu inseparable. Speech father: Allen Ginsberg. Body father: Nelson Olmsted.

As Allen had me say at his imagined funeral in "Death & Fame": "He taught me to meditate, now I'm an old veteran of the thousand day retreat --"

Part 10 - Last Days

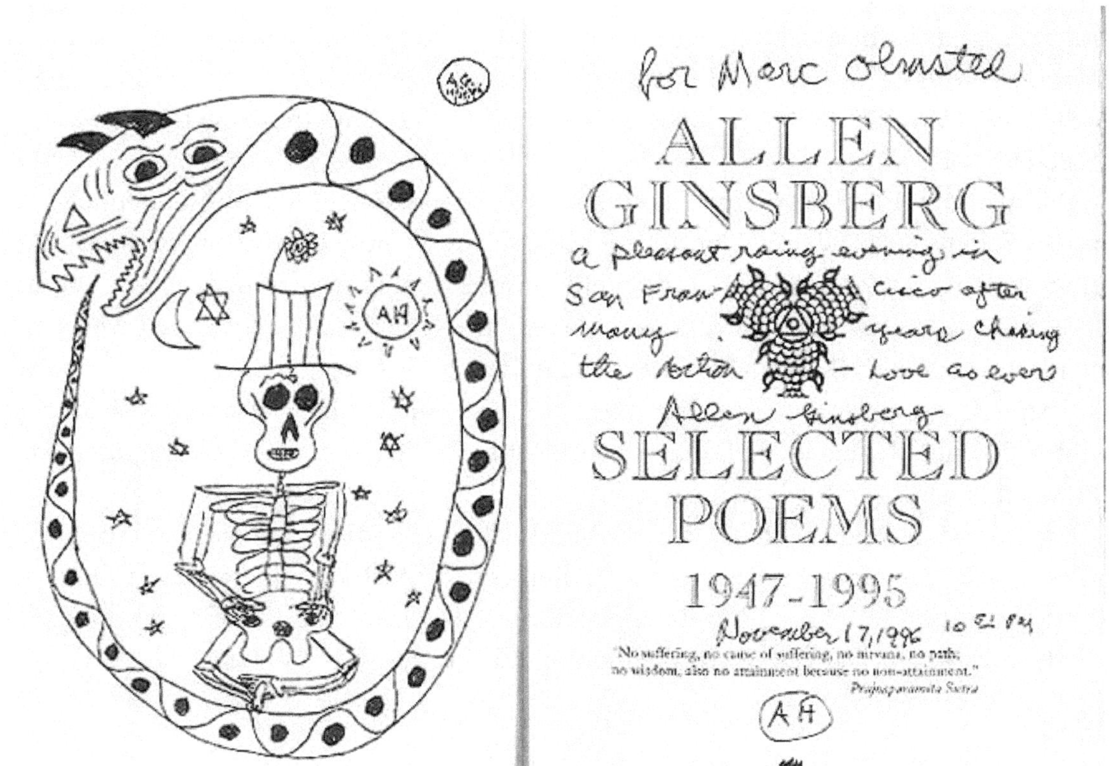

BONES

Prop plane into
 Rochester
Upstate New York
 Pilgrimage
40's movie
 - waking in
 the small
 cottage of my
old friend 3 year
 retreat partner
Carol snow out
 the window
beyond the prayer
 flags
- here I'll do
one month
wrathful blue-black
 female wisdom deity
T'hroma

*

Phonecall 2 AM -
 the famous old
poet, friend for
 23 years,
 calls to
 tell me he may
 be dead in
 a month - terminal
 liver cancer -
 result of Hepatitis
C -
 "You've been so good
to me over all
 these years" he says
I'm startled
 "You've been so
good to <u>me</u>."
 "Then it's been
a good thing."
 Will this be
our last conversation?
 he got this
 phone # off my
 Berkeley answering
machine - for
 emergency only -
 I plan to
finish retreat
& visit him in
 Manhattan for
a day - stay
 in the new loft -
 must call my
lama for instructions
 - what to do
if
 sudden dying
bedside before
 then?

*

My lama tells
 me not to
 break retreat
 - gives me
prayers to
 say if the
 poet dies -
 up goes the
plaque of mantras
 nailed to the
back door porch -
 retreat is
 closed
on female wisdom
moon day

*

5th day
the answering
machine clicks
on - volume down -
Frank from
the Dharma Center -
Allen Ginsberg
is dead
the man who
taught me to
sit watching
my breath like
Buddha
& how to write
a poem
is gone

10 minutes before
next session
weepy I go
to make a
cup of tea

time to start
praying

before I make
it I'm sobbing

*

7th day
Dad died
5 years ago today
snow out the
window
black & white movie
I still think
to tell him
things

*

8th day -
the womb
of the cottage
mad
wisdom energy
cooking
- photo of Allen
from the newspaper
Carol brought on
my
liturgy
table w/ bell
& scepter

Thinking on him
mind
wandering in
mantra practice
I picture Allen G.
sitting
in
Dharmadhatu group
shrine room -
- sudden
open space -
Allen's mind
right now!

*

10th day
burnt offerings
charcoal prayers
putting Tibetan holy
medicine &
crumbs from
my portion of
ritual feast after
finishing T'hroma
for the night
- out on the

front porch
over the
one bright
red coal
w/ a flashlight
on my text
- smoke offerings
for all buddhas
& sentient
beings - and
I'm doing it
for
Allen - my
lama says
he'll receive
it -
rich smells
in the crisp
night, sick
w/ a cold

*

One week after
Ginsberg's death
get up with
the alarm to
say a special
prayer exactly
at the time
he died 2:39 AM
- tradition says
he'll wake every
7 days
(for 49 days)
at that same time
and realize
he's dead
instead of dream-like
confusion -
at this moment
he can be
told quite
directly how
to liberate
his mind into
clear empty
space
- burning
candles in the
shrine room
reading in
the dim
flickering glow

- he'll be
fine, is fine

all these
prayers -
my way of
grieving

*

Day 19
3 years ago
high school friend
Peter S. died
of AIDS today
- now April is
the month of
death
or I'm
just getting old

but Peter did
the transference
of consciousness
technique
he knew
and went
to Amitabha
Buddha's heart

- at least that's
what I think

same practice my
Lama Tharchin
Rinpoche did for
Allen Ginsberg

- we're in Amitabha's
heart already
but we don't
know it
- I got tears
again before
I practice

*

This practice
T'hroma
was done in
charnel grounds,
cemeteries
- knee deep
in bones I
go to the
kitchen

*

Full moon keeps
wakin'
me up - 3 days
through the
venetian blinds
4 A.M. -
is that a demon
standing in
the afternoon
shade outside
the house?
Carol going to
the bathroom
10:30 PM
blue shadow?
Nope, no one
there -
on the porch,
feeding the
smoke offering,
what traffic
of spirits
swirls in the
darkness?

*

Reading Kunzang
Monlam
prayer to Allen
every day per
my lama's
instructions -
I only have
the English text -
the prayer
is long and
I experiment
w/ different
ways to keep
it fresh -
monotone chant,
dramatic voice-over
- Finally I start
reading it
like Ginsberg
himself
"I am the Primordial
Buddha/ Here to
train the six kinds of
beings through all
my manifestations"
not trying to
make fun

just be playful,
  Allen'll get
  it for sure -
  even as he picked
up his speech
   from Kerouac
- then thinking -
   who
         is reading
    to who?

APPENDIX

Part 1

Dear Marc Olmsted-
13 April '72
Lovely meaty letter short & very sweet-I sit an hour a day with mantra silent in heart area; been doing that more or less steady 1 ½ years; but mostly sing aloud,learning blues with Dylan in N.Y. last November improvising songs, as directed (suggested) by Lama Trungpa Tulku. Next time I'm around, S.F. please look me up,
c/o City Lights-yours, ever --- Allen Ginsberg
Om Ah Hum Vajra Guru Padma Siddhi Hum

28 Dec 1974
Dear Marc-

Ah what a doll you are! Merry Xmas Happy new year see you some time Spring I guess whenever I get to S.F. or you ever get here or half'way if you're passing through Boulder next summer.[*] Too much to write letters: - Still I do love you, & love your poetry as much as you &All ways we're both OK knowing death -- So I'll be sitting a month January meditating simultaneous with teethbonegum blood operation fix my mouf.

Supper Xmas eve last nite with Burroughs&: New Years with Gregory Corso & Bill B. old nostalgias purified last nite by looking in each other's eyes for half an hour's time trying to see each other -- empty headed both of us.

The soul world is open totally for us (whether there is a soul or not) because we're not afraid of loving each other forever--so love me forever and I'll love you & the soul won't worry (even if the body knits its brows)--When love wears out, there's free restful open empty space (not bitter claustrophobia)

I think of you often & your letter was heart thrill as your frankness & extra energy & generosity taking the Chance writing like a 'lover' like you did always is—it's all your own beauty & your poetry's in your case anyway —- But if you was a dwarf cripple your language would be prettier than Pope, or almost --
Love & Play --- As ever,

Allen,

Write me more! Send poems too!

[*] I'll teach poetics, Corso Burroughs and others' pass thru. Sanders Waldman Di Prima

Show yr. poems to Whalen & McClure.
Zen Center 264 Downey St.

Part 2

Dear Marc -- April 15, 1975
POB 582 Stuyvesant Sta.
N.Y. 10009

Forgive long delay replying-inundation of paper on my desk I'm that far behind mail - and my own poems untyped. Yes would love to hear your puja practice. I've begun some more extensive Buddhist daily practice including 100-300 prostrations (1 to 3 malas a day depending on time)

Amazing adventures you had on acid- I would have thought yr. meditation clarity would leave you immune to messianic delusions & sloppiness of conduct- but maybe that's just atheist Buddhist idea -- Still you seem to have center strong enough to experience, cosmic-social adventures & land on your feet like good cat you are.

Don't worry about our love life, it's alright, I don't want to <u>own</u> you (I'm not around anyway) all I wanna be baby is friends with you. We'll make it. I'll be in S.F only briefly in May toward the last half of the month, I don't know when, I'll try to phone you in advance when -- I'll be in Seattle mid-May doing Buddhist benefits. Give my love to Brad, glad you see each other. Show yr. poetry mss. to Ferlinghetti if it's ready. He <u>also</u> interested in prose last few years ---

The tone of your writing (the poems clearest) is always strong & natural & poignantly you & your mouth & heart so don't worry just have faith in your own genius and allow your self to write all the poetry you want or get inspired to. I really <u>like</u> reading your broken-line writing!-- to see what your adventures & inventions are-completely natural almost always.
I read thru the prose when I first got it months ago & enjoyed reading it. Carrying on an <u>attitude</u> (slightly macho hip-wise & mind wise is harder in prose than poetry -- because humorous exaggeration in poetry is a mind-jump, in prose it gets more tedious unless you have a solid

youniverse to present- well it's semisolid the prose I'd say -- still like stuff of yr. genius mind but younger sounding than the formal poesy--aw-- we'll talk.

Love as ever always- Allen

-Should I send you back the mss. or leave them in my files? gather dust, or rare occasion show them to anybody accidental of that special interest- Anne Waldman or someone--

Here's what I'll be doing tomorrow- see reverse page Columbian reading w/ friends – I love you really do from distance & thru time, I guess it's your cherry poet's soul- so enjoy that- confidence- Work hard I mean, write a lot freely about real things with straight eyes – Sorry long wait silence- just the fate of my desk, a mess-

Allen Ginsberg

May 1 1975

Dear Marc

Yeh amazing I didn't know you were going thru that much --- Maybe it's the hindu approach with a god or Self at Center as' a permanent entity?

It would seem to be more peaceful if there were a Budh-enlightenment of empty space awakened but no god, like, no self, just an empty center with no voice or self or thought-- and around that a mandala of illusions, experiences, etc. which we live with'& call a Self, Allen Ginsberg. But to get not-attached to the idea of A.G. or Marc and Marc's "Center which I still don't have yet" would mean giving up search because there is no center, (neither macho nor non macho tender body heart)-- There ain't no Center, no reason to be "searching for 'the' voice"--ain't no real you-voice.

Instead there's this constellation of experiences, habits & appearances to observe, welcome & swing with, sport with, dig & describe and use as vehicles to circle around no-one within you-- Maybe the idea that there is a self, pushed to limit to test it out, led to trying out Messiah role?

Humbler self role might be equally silly.

Maybe you aint no-one at all. Just a lot of voices.

Which leaves you free to be perfect poet observer & transmitter of phenomenon, with good humor & unobstructed energy, and lots of clear voices with no self illusion.

That's a Ginsberg Buddhist interpretation of your "problem" as posed in last letter.

Your poetry lovely & unfailing & selfless as ever—i.e. playful with notion of self & not stuck assertively. I'll be in S.F. some time late May –

May 20-22 & then at Padma Jong Poetry Seminar May 23-25--- Padma Jong is part of Trungpa's organization and art colony --- I've never given a seminar before like that- Up in Mendocino

country, get info. from them Padma Jong Dos Rios Calif 95429 or call 415-841-3242.
Would you like to come up there with me for the 3 or four days while I'm teaching? You could. help me, be my secretary, maybe even set an example by yr own poetry practice--and it would give us a rare chance to stay together for that week end close & intimate – same time in an active poetry situation-- I don't know what it be like -- It be some security for me, having you with me & relying on your love---at least I won't be mind-wandering trying to seduce handsome students- if any- God knows if anyone will sign up for it anyway.
In any case a free weekend for you food & countryside & some meditation scheduled I think --- we could be together there---
Then I go back to S.F. 26-27, then to Colorado the 29th. Somewhere there I'll go up visit Snyder in Nevada City and spend a little time with Brad in the city too if things work out--

OK -I'11 leave here .the 11th of May for Utah. & Seattle & call you in S.F. -- leave message where you are with Nancy Phillip at City Lites or Shig at store-- I'll get there around May 20 Tues –
Love as ever
Allen
Ginsberg

Aug 25, 75

Naropa Inst 1441 Bway
Boulder Colo

Dear Marc ---
Stop worrying! I doan' wanna lay no trip on you & hypnotize you in wierd world --The poems you sent were Great- I mean, <u>fine</u>!! I read them to Class I was teaching, relating them to W. C. Williams whom I was teaching - practice of "minute particulars"---"The natural object is always the adequate symbol" – Pound = WCW "No ideas but the facts"'-- your poetic practice is the best! you're solid, & you're mind's open --- just too worried. But your heart & poetry are <u>SOLID!</u>

I'd 'choose Trungpa's open space I were you -- I have – Peter Orlovsky & I go to R.M.D.C. Seminar "Crazy Wisdom" for a week tomorrow there til Sept 13 I sit alone there, then go to N.Y.
See you sooner or later - much & all love-Allen Ginsberg

Over Utah Sal Lake
Nov 19, 1975

Dear Marc
Taking a few days off from Rolling Thunder Review Dylan tour of New England – on way to Logan Utah Poetry Reading –
My poetry is too pessimistic –
- How're you –
When we ever see each other again!? – Soon –
Dylan's pronunciation of consonants vowels syllable by syllable is a work of genius – he keeps time with his mouth as well as bootstomp – all well Love to you – Allen

PS shaved my bear in movie scene – I look like Meher Baba for next few days.

Dear Marc – Poems are fine, all of a piece one season – fewer vague referential weak spots & scenes than before.
You ought maybe go on & allow yrself a little longer straightforward narrative, & get out of the impressionistic confusion the style or mode Kerowacky whops up.
Have you tried recently writing airy classic rhymes? – Campion, Wyatt, Dylan, songs? I've finished reading thru Wm Blake as I think I told you? & writing long poem.
Don't worry about sex, I've kind of loosed hold of that obsession or thru meditation it's become more transparent & nothing to "Cling to" as stereotype goes.
I shd be in S.F. May, in and out working reading preparing book for City Lights – I'll send sheaf of poems to New Directions see if they want some for Annual.
OK – Love as ever & clearer Easy Allen

Dear Marc – Just a note to say merry X-mas too
Love as ever, Allen
I got a secty. Working up a list of magazines for you & others.

[April ? 1976]

Marc,
I read thru all these poems --- all have some taste of body & actual mind throbs --- really dimensional &funny, like Kerouac blues – often the raw surprises are the best, shouldn't be too much revised or cleaned up --- it's enough for a book because there's a whole life situation there --- Whenever I see a man of yr. work I think, "Don't hesitate" just set it all up on page & move on go on ahead writing --- but this is a solid pile of reality ---

Love Allen
Call me

Dec 7, 1976
Dear Marc – I may be in Boulder Colo c/o Naropa the final week in Jan but I should be back at 437 E 12 St. Apt. 23 NYC 10029 phone 212-777-6786 after 5th or so. In any case if you're by yourself, you're welcome to stay here if I'm here or not, you need a place in N.Y. Hope I'm there to see you. I've been with Peter Orlovsky since Oct. 10 at Vajradhatu Seminary in Wisconsin with Trungpa & a hundred others, sitting & practicing or studying all day. Just got home to N.Y. yesterday. How's yr. poesy? Love as ever Allen Ginsberg

Part 3

April 1, 1977
c/o Naropa till April 12
traveling thru May

Dear Marc – Poems are fine, all of a piece one season – fewer vague referential weak spots & scenes than before.
You ought maybe go on & allow yrself a little longer straightforward narrative, & get out of the impressionistic confusion the style or mode Kerowacky whops up.
Have you tried recently writing airy classic rhymes? – Campion, Wyatt, Dylan, songs? I've finished reading thru Wm Blake as I think I told you? & writing long poem.
Don't worry about sex, I've kind of loosed hold of that obsession or thru meditation it's become more transparent & nothing to "Cling to" as stereotype goes.
I shd be in S.F. May, in and out working reading preparing book for City Lights – I'll send sheaf of poems to New Directions see if they want some for Annual.
OK – Love as ever & clearer Easy Allen

Tim L. lost in space line is striking ending – more definite than usual.

July 12, 78

Dear Marc –
Trungpa & Burroughs are both around then – end of July begin Aug. Burroughs can be visited across street. Spare floor in my apartment probably if need be. Or space ro share bed, whatever.
Bring film, we can show it to Bill or somewhere. There are no regular public screenings. Have to be arranged on the sport.
Peter's here –
School Ends Aug 20 –

Don't Hesitate

Love
Allen
Get 2 day visitors pass from Naropa office when you're settled in – so can see Trungpa lecture <u>Monday nites</u>. Regent Thurs. nites.

Part 4/ Part 5

No letters

Part 6

May 2, '80
Dear Marc –

Interior[?]
I'll be in SF Fri June 27 till Monday June 30 – - can film[^] then. I read at Keystone Corner w/ Antler Sunday. Perhaps some time Sat be OK. – Love Allen

May 23, 1980
Dear Marc - Sorry I'm so slovenly retuning the wrong page last time – enclosed find your letter.
I'll be at Jack Tarr Hotel nite of June 27, then read with Gregory C. at Keystone Corner June 28, then leave June 30 back to Naropa. See you one time or other. I'll be at Shig's then subsequent nites I guess.
regards to Peter Marti
You can probably use my apartment in N.Y. while I'm out here in Boulder if you need a place to crash while looking for work. Barnes & Noble Books c/o Billy MacFay often has jobs - ask Bob Rosenthal
See you in S.F.
Allen
Studying Sappho <u>and Sapphic verse</u> form I just got around to pile of mail.

STRAIGHT HEART'S DELIGHT (inscription)

Good luck with ♪♪

F _

D _

B _

G _

Every Good Boy Deserves Fun A _

Face E _

C _

A _

F _

For Marc Olmsted preparing to retire for the night at Shig's apartment overlooking Grant Street Gaté Gaté Paragaté Parasamgaté Bodhi Svaha coming over phonograph, after evening at Winston Leyland's with Mike McClure & Gregory Corso & Lisa Corso, later supper in the Chinese restaurant Stockton & Broadway –

Allen Ginsberg

c/o Naropa 1111 Pearl St. Boulder Colo 80302
June 18, 1981
Dear Marc – Thanks for Job Poster. Glad you're persevering music. I went into studio March & did another album self-produced, with Steven Taylor, Jozi Shalle David Amram & Arthur Russell & Peter – John Hammond Sr. will issue a 2 record album of song works this fall – couple 1970 cuts with Dylan & Traum, Plus the Hammond-produced album 1976 plus the new work. I wrote one Danceable New Wave lyric "Capitol Air" & have been playing it with improvised rock bands here. So I'm drifting into electric after all these years! You shoulda told me! – Never too late! Finishing book poems 77-80 for City Lights. Trimmest summer yet here, beautiful students, Peter Gregory, David Henderson, Joanne Kyger, Ann Charters so far. Be in S.F. Sept 24-27 – Love Allen
Don't know if I'll have time for Dinner Sept but hope to see you.

Friday
Dear Marc –
Here's a Birdbrain tape, dim, and a new song (also on tape home work) if you want to try it – modeled on the Jagger "went down to the station" or something similar, slow blues.

See you next week
Allen

Off to Naropa May 1 – Nov. 20
April 29, /83/
Dear Marc –
Exhausted under deadweight guilt of old unanswered mail – Yrs. Of 10/11/82 – The Single was awright – the tape – but still couldn't clearly hear all the words.
O Poe Text is like an apostrophe, "O"…and a description of who you address, but the syntactic sentence incomplete doesn't conclude with your question or declaration to him, just concludes with description of the Poe yr addressing – a "rhetorical" incompletion, so to speak. Nitpicking re style.
I'm still working music, latest as per John Lennon's (1972) advice, Jessore Road, 11 minutes with Mondrian String Quartet, recorded 2 Jan '83 Amsterdam Holland – Can't write letters no more Still Love as ever Allen

Part 7

No letters

Part 8

3/22/89
Dear Marc –
I always liked the basic tone & scatter of your poems but thought maybe it was too scattered but these seem more solidly focused & clear as to subject or main motif of each piece of writing – a pleasure to read.
City Lights (Nancy Peters ed.) Journal is still collecting for desultory issues, and also publishing small fold-out several page chapbooks I hear – maybe try them again – also interesting mimeo mag. run by David Cope called Big Scream 2783 Dixie S.W. Grandville, Mich. 49418 I think you know Cope – rather than just filing your poems I'll send them on to him. Also Have you ever tried Amer. Poetry Review? Steve Berg Ed. Also there's New York Quarterly still going – c/o William Packard 232W.14 St. N.Y. 10011 – N.Y. If you don't want them published then let me know I'm sending these poems on I missed Selby, McCleod etc. And Austrailia is now canceled. OK – Allen Ginsberg
Enclosed Bklyn Coll Course + Poetry Series Poster F + I[?] I'm learning a lot!

I'll be in S.F./LA/Vancouver – beginning with Dalai Lama's Harmonium Avendi[?] Newport Beach Oct 3 S.F. Jewish Community Center Oct. 11 National Poetry Week Oct.14 Vancouver inbetween

Part 9

Send him
Thoughts in Fort Lee
After Lalon
Charnel Ground
Autumn Leaves
with these cards
- Allen
5/14/93
Dear Marc:
Happy that you're so settled busy still scribing & on upward outward path in such calm place – what a relief to hear!
Enclosed a few poems – may I sent you After Lalon already? The Charnel Ground I wrote on 10 day retreat last summer in Nova Scotia.
I sent your note & poem to Peter – we're somewhat estranged at suggestion of his case worker – he lives in hotel Stratford Arms 117 W. 70th St. (Mailing Address #238) NY NY 10023 – he's still drinking a little, after long manic period (wearing policeman uniform) now quieter in depression – So I try not to lean on him – Who knows future ? – He always fantasized 3 year retreat.
I'm ok on permanent Macrobiotic diet slimmed down a little to 150 pounds from 167, got rid of insulin & needle, but still a little short of breath, left over from Xmas 91 congestive heart failure
Put on my tie in a taxi, short of breathing, rushing to meditate
Nov' 91
Glad you're thinking of Peter.
I'm still working with Gelek Rinpoche (Gelugpa) & sit & do liturgy (Yamantaka & Vajrapani) an hour or less as day, long as it takes, best only a feeble meditator.
Love life OK – amazing satisfying erotic engagements with youths – then long periods of un-attached or non-attached calm – will go spend 4 months in Europe this summer, wandering, reading, sight seeing. On sabbatical after 6 years Brooklyn college -

You sound fine. Peter Marti sent me poetry pamphlet he & you are in. OK – Love and admiration as ever Allen

June 22(?), '94:

Dear Marc:
Boy what a saga! Can't wait to hear your spiritual breath after 3 years – my own practice very lax tho I see Gelek Rinpoche & trust in him – he tells me keep public, keep writing & giving readings – I seem to be causing some lucidity or joy, but don't know how or karmic why, so I do as I'm told by Rinpoche. Working hard on books, discs – CD's, & photos & musings, prob'ly not enuf sleep. You sound wonderful & wonderfully accomplishing with Tibetan and all! Your teacher must be really sharp & kind to get you so steady! Saw Peter Marti briefly, been traveling, read Phi Beta Kappa commencement poem at Harvard a few weeks ago. Will visit W.S. Burroughs a week before Naropa's busy month 20th Anniversary Love as ever Allen Ginsberg
Yes I saw & liked yr writings in <u>Scream</u> etc.

ཉི་མ་ ["Nyima" i.e. "Sun" – my Tibetan Buddhist refuge name – mo] – Have spent wonderful week at Naropa w/Diane, Allen G. & visiting old friends, was able to sit in on 'Panorama of Mind' class – 5 days of 3 hour intensive study of Abhidharma & more w/ Judith Simmer-Brown. The Buddhist Studies program here is very strong – much study even dharma debating etc. & Practice <u>And</u> Tibetan language intensive. Very tempting notion how to spend 2 years thusly.......who knows? Too far from Lama, but maybe someday. One thing I know is that study <u>really</u> enriches my practice and group study works best for me.
di Pree [sic] & I make one of bedrooms here at Varsity Townhouse into a very nice shrine room & practiced together each afternoon – me at Ngöndro & her as Vajrayogini. Also absorbed in finding my way around on the Macintosh – never interested me before but now I want to get good w/ Tibetan fonts & hope someday to help w/ translations.
Thinking of you often w/ Love and wishing you Big Realization, Shep

Hi Marc – Been teaching writing via alchemy engravings, lecturing on arts in NYC 1960-65, reading w/ AG & Anne & Michal Ondaatje – a wonderful surprise, fine pure writer. In between, practicing Vajrayogini and hitting the swimming pool here @ Varsity Townhouses – amazing the fine weather, just bought a treasure @ Ziji – new photos of the Trungpa Tulku – if I get copies made I'll send you one, it's amazing. Reluctuant to return now to the fogs & winds of S.F., but – we go back tomorrow afternoon & there's work to be done there – Hope you are well & deep in wondrous practice – Wishing you always rest in sky-mind. Love, Diane

Naropa 7/30/94
Dear Marc – The month's gone by with Snyder, Creely, Ferlinghetti, Baraka, Kenneth Koch & a bunch of language poets passing through the Poetics School, larger than ever this year – Diane di Prima next door to my apartment in same Varsity Townhouse you visited 1978 – only new couches – Gelek Rinpoche, a Gelugpa Lama I've been seeing the last few years, friend of late Trungpa R. visited the first week and hung around with the poets. As for me I'm o.k. over-entangled with the world, new books, interviews, CD's & poems, boyfriends, (at my age! Amazing) but alas at moment little meditation tho I'm s'posed to be in the Buddhafields w/ Yamantaka & Vajrayogini Practices. You got it made, all that planet! Save me! & last nite I dreamt that Peter O. hesitated in front of a bus that almost bonked him down on 2nd ave, then fled into a storefront junk-connection shop and begged for drugs – he's in psycho ward of N.Y. St. Luke's hospital there last few weeks, idealizing Art Kleps as his model. I'm OK, macrobiotic, 50% of my heart inactive, enjoying life. Love as ever AH Allen Ginsberg

Part 10

For Marc Olmsted
a pleasant rainy evening in San Fran-cisco after many years chasing the Action – Love as ever
Allen Ginsberg
November 17, 1996 10<u>51</u> PM
AH
Grant & Pine corner
Grant Playa Hotel -

www.ingramcontent.com/pod-product-compliance
Lightning Source LLC
Chambersburg PA
CBHW060512300426
44112CB00017B/2643
* 9 7 8 0 9 5 6 9 5 2 5 7 8 *